NEW ARABIAN STUDIES

5

مجلة
الدراسات العربية الجديدة

NEW ARABIAN STUDIES

5

EDITED BY
G. REX SMITH
J.R. SMART
AND
B.R. PRIDHAM

UNIVERSITY
of
EXETER
PRESS

First published 2000 by
University of Exeter Press
Reed Hall, Streatham Drive
Exeter, Devon EX4 4QR
UK

British Library Cataloguing in Publication Data
A catalogue record of this book
is available from the British Library

ISSN 1351–4709
ISBN 0 85989 645 5

Typeset in Times New Roman
by Colin Bakké Typesetting, Exeter

Printed and bound in Great Britain
by Short Run Press Limited, Exeter

Contents

Editorial Foreword

Again the editors would like to express their extreme gratitude to H.H. Dr Shaikh Sultan bin Muhammad al-Qasimi, Ruler of Sharjah, whose generous financial support has made the publication of this volume possible. The editors are also greatly appreciative of the secretarial help rendered by Jennifer Davies, Centre for Arab Gulf Studies, University of Exeter.

Readers are reminded that *NAS* is designed to cater for all academic fields in the humanities, in so far as they relate to the Arabian Peninsula, and that we continue to seek articles and reviews for future issues. Potential contributors are reminded that, with Volume 3 published in 1996, the transliteration and house rules changed radically and they are asked to follow to the letter the guidlines published in Volumes 3, 4 and in this volume immediately after this foreword. Failure to do so in future will by necessity result in the return of the articles to the author without assessment. Contributors should send *two* copies of their articles *with double line spacing* and, if possible, computer disks, stating exactly which word processing programme was used, to the following address:

J.R. Smart
c/o The Secretary
Institute of Arab and Islamic Studies
Old Library
University of Exeter
Prince of Wales Road
Exeter EX4 4JZ, U.K.

Originals of photographs, diagrams and other art work should *not* be sent to the editors. Please ensure that you retain these and send a copy, as *NAS* cannot be held responsible. Photographs, slides, etc. should also be *clearly labelled*, and precise indication given of where they should be included in the text. Brief biographical details should also be supplied for the 'Notes on Contributors' section.

Finally, the editors apologize to all contributors and readers of *NAS* for the long delay in publishing this volume.

GUIDELINES AND TRANSLITERATION SCHEME FOR CONTRIBUTORS

Transliteration

ا When used as a ‘seat’ for *hamzah* transliterate with the original vowel of the *hamzah*, even if this is technically elided, e.g. *wa-ismuhu*. The definite article should always be *al-*, even with sun letters, e.g. *wa-al-salām*.

Vowels: a, ā, i, ī, u, ū
Dipthongs: aw, ay

ء Transliterate as ’ when medial or final; do not transliterate inital *hamzah*, e.g. *su’āl*, *nisā’*, but *islām*.

ة Normallly h (*raḥmah*), but t in *iḍāfah* constructions (*raḥmat allāh*).

Case and mood endings: Except in quotations from the Qur’ān, and classical poetry those case endings which consist only of short vowels should generally be omitted unless they are essential to the meaning, or some special point is to be made, e.g. *fī al-qarn al-sādis*.

One-letter words: These should be separated by a hyphen from the word to which they are joined in Arabic, e.g. *wa-al-natīǧah*, *bi-al-raḡm*.

Other letters:

ب	b	ز	z	ف	f
ت	t	س	s	ق	q
ث	ṯ	ش	š	ك	k
ج	ǧ	ص	ṣ	ل	l
ح	ḥ	ض	ḍ	م	m
خ	ẖ	ط	ṭ	ن	n
د	d	ظ	ẓ	ه	h
ذ	ḏ	ع	‘	و	w
ر	r	غ	ḡ	ي	y

Alif maqṣūrah should be transliterated by *-ā*. If there is a sound linguistic need to distinguish between final *alif* and *alif maqṣūrah*, then *-à* may be used for the latter.

Personal and place names: Where these are well known and have accepted English spellings, they should not be transliterated (Riyadh, Muscat, Khartoum, Mecca, Medina, Dhofar, Nasser, Saladin). There are grey areas here and, where in doubt, the name should be fully transliterated. Contributors using primarily European archive sources may employ the spelling of names as they find them in the original. However, an *early* footnote should explain precisely the method followed.

Vernacular Arabic: Contributors dealing with dialect pronunciation (e.g. proverbs, folklore) may deviate from the above system, but should list in an *early* footnote the symbols they intend to use and their phonetic descriptions.

Bibliography

The bibliography should follow the Harvard system using the author-date form. References should be listed at the end of the article in alphabetical order of author. Works by the same author should be listed chronologically, with those published the same year labelled 1990a, 1990b, etc. Works by a single author should precede those written by the same author with collaborators. If there are three or more authors, the first name should be followed by '*et al.*'. Please follow the following examples exactly:

1) Article in a journal:

Beeston, A.F.L. 1975a. Epigraphic South Arabian auxiliaries. *JSS* 20: 191–2.
Beeston, A.F.L. 1975b. The Realm of King Uusuf (Dhu Nuwas). *BSOAS* 38: 124–6.
Gingrich, A. and Heiss, J. 1986. A Note on traditional agricultural tools in Ṣa'da province. *PSAS* 16: 51–63.

NB: Common journals may be abbreviated as above. Other titles should be given in full. NB also where capital letters should be used in titles and where not. No inverted commas are needed.

2) Book:

Serjeant, R.B. 1974. *The South Arabian Hunt*. London.

NB: Capitals on all words in the title with the exception of prepositions and articles with the exception of an initial article.

3) Contribution:

Müller, W.W. 1988. Outline of the history of ancient Southern Arabia. In Daum, W. (ed.), *Yemen: 3000 Years of Art and Civilization in Arabia Felix*. Innsbruck and Frankfurt/Main, 49–54.

4) Book published in series:

Potts, D. 1991. *The Pre-Islamic Coinage of Eastern Arabia*. Copenhagen: Carsten Niebuhr Institute Publications no. 14.

5) Multi-volume books:

Löfgren, Oscar. 1936–50. *Arabische Texte zur Kenntnis der Stadt Aden im Mittelalter.* Uppsala. 2 vols.

6) Unpublished dissertation:

Hakeim, Abd al-Aziz. 1977. A Critical and comparative study of early Arabian coins on the basis of Arabic textual evidence and actual finds. PhD thesis. University of Leeds.

Citations

Where possible and appropriate, simple citations should be given in the text in brackets and should give the author, year of publication and page reference as follows:

(Beeston 1975a: 192)
(Potts 1991: 33)

Apart from these, all notes should be given as end notes. It is appreciated that short citations in brackets in the text are not always appropriate and contributors working for example from manuscript sources, or from medieval edited texts, or from archives may certainly use end notes rather than the simple citation method outlined above. If the author's name forms part of the text, it should not be repeated in the brackets.

E.g. The domestic architecture had significantly changed since the beginning of the occupation (Jones 1992: 137–9).

Several researchers have addressed this issue, most notably Assaf (1937) and Strauss (1951: 255–7).

In multi-volume works, the volume number should be given as in the work (1, i, I), if it is possible to decide. If this is not clear, please use lower case Roman as follows: Löfgren 1936–50 i: 48.

Dates

Contributors mentioning Islamic dates should ALWAYS provide the corresponding Christian date or century and vice versa. The former should stand first followed by an oblique stroke followed by the Christian date/century. AD and AH are not necessary. E.g. 386/996; 7th/13th century (always using Arabic numerals, not, in these circumstances, writing out the numerals in full.

Review Notice

Arabian Diversions: Studies on the Dialects of Arabia

by Bruce Ingham, Ithaca Press: Reading
1997, xv, 193 pp. £35.

The present volume is a collection of eight articles which have appeared in journals over a period of twenty years. They are presented here as chapters. The earliest, 'Urban and Rural Arabic in Khūzistān', which was published in the *Bulletin of the School of Oriental and African Studies* (*BSOAS*), is perhaps one of the first articles with which the author, Dr Bruce Ingham, made his entry into Arabic dialectology. Since then he has become a well known and respected specialist in the field, as he himself quite rightly points out in the introduction (xii). Not all the chapters in this volume are linguistic investigations. The last two describe some of the oral literature of Arabia. Chapter 7 deals with the historical narrative, the *sālfah*, detailing its subject matter, and analysing its literary style and language. Chapter 8, entitled 'Camel terminology among the Āl Murra Bedouins' is a short but highly interesting study. Published originally in the German review *Zeitschrift für arabische Linguistik* (*ZAL*), it enumerates and discussed the different terms used to describe camels. The chapter ends with samples of oral poetry, usually the opening verses of odes, in which camels figure.

The rest of the chapters deal with the dialects the author has studied over the years. They are the spoken Arabic varieties of Central, Eastern and Northern Arabia which he classifies as 'Najdi', and those of Southern Iraq and Khūzistān which he calls 'Mesopotamian' . The chapters on language concentrate on phonology, and to a lesser extent on morphology, with the exception of chapter 6 which is a detailed syntactic analysis of conditional and time clauses, a grammatical feature that is rarely encountered in studies of Arabic dialects. Four of the chapters end in texts transcribed from spontaneous speech which the author himself has recorded and translated into English. Texts are generally considered to be an important part of dialect study as they provide authentic examples of sentence structure and lexical usage. In this work the texts are not only linguistic documents, but are also evocative descriptions of the way of life and customs of Arabia, southern Iraq and Iran. Apart from traditional stories, there are accounts of palm cultivation and animal husbandry. The author seems to have a wide range of vocabulary at his disposal which shows his intimate knowledge of the dialects of the region. He rarely repeats a word more than once when illustrating a point, but keeps citing different terms, some of which are little known in other parts of the Arabic speaking world.

In the first two chapters the transliterated examples and texts appear in Roman script, whereas they are produced in italics elsewhere. There is no standardization either in the way the texts and their translations are presented. In the chapters originally published in *BSOAS* all the transcribed texts appear first, followed by their translations. In chapter 3, originally published in *ZAL*, on the other hand, each text and its translation appear on facing pages so that the reader does not have the irksome task of having to move backwards and forwards when trying to follow the Arabic. Despite their interesting and diverse topics, the texts are marred by misprints which include the wrong addition or omission of diacritics or letters, the splitting up of a word, or the incorrect joining of two words. The following are a few random examples: the fourth line of the poem on p. 19 is *mā ṃiḍatni mā ṃiḏatni mā ṃ iḍatni* 'she did not pass away from me', where the word *ṃiḏatni* is repeated three times, but printed differently each time; in *hiya 'ariīd* 'it (fem. sing.) is wide' the feminine marker is omitted and there is a redundant medial vowel *i* (18); in *nišdat* 'she asked' *š* is printed as *s* without a diacritic (37); *irrimiḥ* 'the lance' appears as *irri miḥ* (18), where *'alē gāl* … 'for him', (he) said …' occurs as *'alēgāl* (18). A subscript dot appears sometimes under the -h- of the third person pronominal suffix, as, for example, *waddīḥim* 'send (masc. sing.) them!' (38); both *mniygiṣṣūnḥa* 'when they cut it', with a subscript dot, and *wiyḥiṭtha* 'he puts it', without, occur in the same text (17). The same symbol /'/ is used to represent the voiced pharyngeal continuant /ع/ and the inverted commas denoting direct speech, which causes some confusion. Apart from a few guidelines on the realization of phonemes in the first chapter (3–4) and cursory remarks in the introduction (xii) and footnotes, the author would have done well to provide a table explaining all the symbols.

In the translation of a text (106) the form *'arabs* occurs several times. As this is a transcription of the Arabic plural form, the use of the English plural marker *-s* is redundant. In the examples classified as 'Baghdadi' (17), there are some forms which are clearly not typical of the speech of Baghdad. For example, *'alēš* 'what', which Ingham cites, is realized either as two words: *'ala 'ēš*, or as a compound *'alawēš*, in Baghdadi Arabic. The first person singular of the verb *'axaḏ* 'to take, to marry' is *āxuḏ* in Baghdadi. The term used by Ingham, *āxiḏ*, is of non-urban provenance.

No attempt has been made to fill the gaps left in the earlier chapters where the author has not supplied certain terms. On p. 13, for example, the urban terms for 'he improved' and 'he fainted', which he has left untranslated, are *ṣilaḥ* and *ġima ʿalē* respectively. On p. 32 the author has not given the Šaṭṭ al-ʿArab equivalent of the ʿAmarah Arabic form *čīf* 'how?, what?' In a footnote (47) he adds that there is a form *kēf* which means 'state, condition'. *kēf*, however, should not be confused with *čēf* 'because'. Both forms, which are derived from classical Arabic *kayfa* 'how?', occur frequently throughout central and southern Iraq. On p. 35, the author cites the deictic particle *hiwwēn-* 'there is' for the Šaṭṭ al-ʿArab and southern Khūzistān dialects, and says, in a footnote, that 'there do not seem to be parallel elements in the rest of the area considered' (48). An equivalent *hawwēn-* occurs in Baghdad and Basrah, usually in the spoken Arabic of the Christian communities. On p. 38, Ingham has not given the sedentary equivalent of rural *ytibāha* 'he looks after', adding in a footnote (49) that the sedentary varieties are *ywāḍib* or *ydīr bāla*. The form *yitbaha* exists and is widely used throughout central Iraq where it has acquired the additional meaning 'to show off'.

In chapter 1 referred to above, on the varieties of spoken Arabic in southern Iraq and Iran, the author states that in the towns of the region Iranian cultural influence is dominant where there is a tendency 'to adopt Western styles of dress and behaviour' (2). This might sound baffling to present-day readers until one realizes that the author is talking about Iran in the days of the shah, seeing that the research work for this chapter/article was carried out in 1969 and 1971. Ingham still refers to Iran as 'Persia' (xii). All the articles in this volume seem to have been reproduced without any noticeable amendments or a coherent link between one chapter and the next. Although the author says in the introduction that 'there are some details in the earlier chapters which are corrected in later ones in this volume' (xii), a good part of the work could have been profitably revised.

In the past twenty years or so there has been a considerable increase in the number of works on Arabic dialectology. In some of these works the authors' inability to grasp the nuances and grammatical intricacies of the dialects they describe is often camouflaged by their excessive use of technical language. Ingham's works, on the other hand, have always been written in a lucid, accessible style where technical terms are used sparingly. This volume is no exception. One can safely say that Bruce Ingham is one of the very few present-day Arabic dialectologists who display an intuitive and almost native knowledge of Arabic. It is all the more reason why he should have taken greater care in revising and updating the studies which comprise this volume, so that, as he himself hopes, it would prove of use 'to future and present Arabists' (xiv).

Farida Abu-Haidar

Some Notes on Two Yemeni Contemporary Documents

Hussein Abdullah al-Amri

This brief article provides some observations on two documents which are of some importance in modern, even contemporary, Yemenite history: the Sacred National Charter (1947–1948) (*al-Mīṯāq al-Waṭanī al-Muqaddas*) and the National Charter of 1982.

1. The Sacred National Charter (1947–1948)

The Sacred National Charter (hereafter the SNC) represents the theoretical guidance and first provisional constitution of the Patriotic Movement and the forces of opposition to Imām Yaḥyā Ḥamīd al-Dīn (1905–1948) and his autocratic and backward system of government. It also reflects the advanced thinking within the outlook of the existing forms of Arab liberalism represented at that time by the constitutional monarchical systems in Iraq and Egypt, though mirroring Yemen's own particular circumstances.

The text of the SNC with its 39 articles and appendices was crystallized in late 1947 and the beginning of 1948[1] under the guidance and effective contribution of one of the leading lights of the Muslim Brotherhood Movement in Egypt, the Algerian activist al-Wartalānī al-Fuḍayl (d. 1959), as well as that of the leadership of the Movement. Also involved were some of the great thinkers of the Yemen Patriotic Movement, such as Ḥusayn al-Kibsī,[2] Aḥmad al-Muṭā'[2] and others. A copy of the SNC, hand-written by the young nationalist and ambitious Sayyid Aḥmad M. al-Shāmī, was dispatched from Ṣan'ā' to al-Zubayrī (d. 1965) and al-Nu'mān (d. 1996) in Aden, so that large numbers of copies could be printed and kept there in secret until such time as the revolution was to be declared.[3] The revolution had been expected to take place on the demise of the elderly and sick Imām Yaḥyā. It was planned to capture his wily Crown Prince Aḥmad who was in Ta'izz at that time and to declare Sayyid 'Abdallāh b. Aḥmad al-Wazīr[2] the new imām at the helm of a constitutional government. The details and appendices of the SNC include a list of names of members of the government and other bodies and institutions.

The SNC comprises 39 articles preceded by a brief, but extremely important introduction (*dibājah*). This latter defines the reasons for the deterioration of the situation in the Yemen due to 'the repressive autocracy and egotism that characterized Imām Yaḥyā b. Ḥamīd al-Dīn—hence the grounds of legitimacy for opposing him and the duty to change the existing state of affairs—discharging that duty towards God and the Muslims.'

The introduction concludes by issuing a call unprecedented in the modern and contemporary history of the Yemen to 'the representatives of the Yemeni people to convene a conference dedicated to the task of examining the components of a legally sound system and the designation of a leader whose charge would be to implement it as well as to control law and order and to safeguard the interests of the nation. He was also to dispense with both the religious and earthly duties towards the Yemen on the death of the present Imām.'

The first article stipulates that 'the investiture of His Highness al-Sayyid … as a legal *šūrawī* and constitutional imām in accordance with the path chosen by the most advanced nations in today's civilized world, provided that it does not in any way contradict the tolerant and correct teaching of Islam.'

The second article specifies the conditions attached by the people's representatives to the nominated imām, as well as defining the limits of his constitutional powers. The third article defines the system of government as *šūrawī*, constitutional and one which should not breach the Sharī'ah. The subsequent articles deal with the draft of a constitution for the country to be presented to a constituent assembly for its endorsement. This was to be followed by the formation of a provisional Consultative Council (*Šūrā*) consisting of 70 members, including members of the Council of Ministers and others. 'This was because it was not possible to recall the constituent assembly which was assigned the task of formulating a constitution and setting out permanent responsibilities.' The SNC determines the responsibilities of the Government and *Šūrā* for the interim period until the election of a Council of Deputies or *Šūrā*.

The SNC touches on the issues of civil liberties, stressing 'the sanctity of human life, equality, private property, dignity of the individual, freedom of speech and assembly.' It dwells on the need to modernize public administration, the army, the police, and setting up assemblies for the prefectures and municipalities, with special emphasis placed on education, public health, transportation, agriculture and combating poverty, ignorance and disease as well as action 'to revive agriculture as the foundation of economic life in Yemen.'

Finally the SNC highlights the importance of bolstering ties with the Arab League and the Arab States as well as opening up to the outside world through 'the appointment of political representatives (ambassadors) in the sister Arab States ..., initiating contacts with the civilized world by means of diplomatic and consular relations, so as to serve the high national interests of the Yemen and to cooperate in the lofty task of bringing happiness to all mankind.'

As for the appendices of the SNC, they comprise four, the first of which provided for the appointment of al-Wartalānī al-Fuḍayl as general advisor to the State. The second opens the door for 'any member of Imām Yaḥyā's family who demonstrates his willingness to accept the wish of the nation embodied in this Charter, and shows commitment to its contents, to be treated in the same way as any other citizen.' The third provides for the appointment of Qāḍī 'Abdallāh Ḥusayn al-'Amrī as Minister of State. The final appendix directs that 'full care should be given to all patriots and freedom fighters for the sacrifice they have made in the service of the people.'

The appendices are followed by four lists containing members of the Council of Ministers headed by al-Sayyid 'Alī b. 'Abdallāh al-Wazīr[2] as well as names of the directors of government departments, followed by members of the Consultative *Šūrā* under the chairmanship of Amīr Ibrāhīm b. Yaḥyā Ḥamīd al-Dīn (Sayf al-Ḥaqq). Finally comes the list of the senior officials including the governors and princes of the prefectures, and at the top of this list is the name of Qāḍī 'Abdallāh al-'Amrī, the Minister of State.

The SNC and its appendices could not be kept secret as the liberals and the leadership of the Patriotic Movement had hoped, as news and documents were leaked to Crown Prince Aḥmad who was in Ta'izz and thence to his father. Therefore, rather than waiting for the death of Imām Yaḥyā, they felt it necessary to hasten his elimination despite the immense risks involved. Indeed 'the assassination of the Imām was about to be postponed when it was found that 'Abdallāh al-'Amrī had been travelling with the Imām, as it was felt the Revolution had to seek the assistance of al-'Amrī for his abilities and experience.' The assassination took place on 18th February, 1948, opening the way for the revolution of the constitutionalists and their SNC.

The revolution was destined to last three weeks, when the Crown Prince was able to abort it and execute its leaders, as well as throwing many of them into the ghastly Ḥajjah prison. However, the SNC remained a landmark guiding the Patriotic Movement and one of its historical documents which cannot be properly studied and appraised outside the context of the objective conditions prevalent in the Yemen at a time of her appalling isolation from the rest of the world. Under those dreadful conditions the SNC represented a qualitative leap towards rescuing the Yemen from those conditions, so as to take its rightful place in the community of civilized nations.

2. The National Charter of 1982

The inception and circumstances of the NC were as follows. Since the 1962 revolution in the North and the independence of the South in 1967 the Yemen passed through difficult periods of strife and instability. Since we speak of the NC, I shall confine myself to dealing briefly with two aspects of it as follows:

1) The necessity and circumstances that called for the formulation of this document;
2) It took about four years to prepare the NC which was later put to a national referendum. Having obtained popular consent it became a national covenant in 1982.

The latter part of the 1970s was marked by upheavals in the North, where two presidents had been assassinated within a period of less than eight months in 1977–1978. Similar events were taking place in the South where the head of state Sālim Rubayyi‘ ‘Alī was executed. The North found itself facing a tidal wave of extremism and it became an arena for the infiltration of revolutionary Marxist ideas from the South. These troubles led to a brief armed conflict between the North and the South in the spring of 1979 which ended with a summit meeting in Kuwait in April, where a renewed call was issued for the unification of the two parts of the country as the only way out of wars and conflicts in the future.

The climate of the Yemen, however, was conducive to the spread of extremism, and the various views of the Islamic right and the Marxist-Leninist left. Since the permanent constitution of the North, which was a rather liberal document formulated in 1970, banned political parties, it was necessary to find a compromise between various tendencies within a framework of a national document based on consensus. Thus a committee was established to promote national dialogue. It was composed of more than 50 politicians and intellectuals representing varying trends and opinions. The committee carried out its work from late 1979 until August 1982.

What then, is the NC? The answer to that question is as follows: ‘The National covenant is not the creation of a group or party, nor the will of an individual or a single authority, but it is the thought of our people and their aspiration. Thus, it was directly formulated by them. This is what induces all to rally around it because it is the theory for a national course of action binding upon all our people and upon the state and its officials so that its values may materialize both as objectives and in actual conduct.’

After the introduction, the NC is divided into five parts:

1) Islam and the Faith and the Sharī‘ah;
2) Man and the Homeland;

3) Administration, Social Justice, Economic Development, Education and Culture;
4) National Defence;
5) Foreign Policy.

In conclusion the NC explains itself as follows.

> The ... includes the most important principles and fundamentals which unite all factions of the people and which bind the popular base with the leadership under the auspices of a democratic republican system based on:
>
> – unrestricted belief in the faith of Islam as a way of life, a system and a code of conduct.
> – democracy in government, represented by constitutional institutions and by the guarantee of total freedom for the people and for the homeland.
> – social justice which guarantees the organization of social relations, equal opportunity and social security for every citizen.
> – national loyalty, which is associated with loyalty to God, and by which we can preserve the sovereignty and independence of the homeland and prepare the way for the achievement of Yemeni unity, land, people and government.
> – enabling the state and the people to implement development plans and to develop life in all fields.
> – the completion of the formation and organization of the armed forces and the security forces for defence of the homeland and for the protection, security and safety of the citizen and of society.
> – the consolidation of bases of political stability, internally and externally.
>
> If understanding and conviction on our part of what this covenant has provided is of importance, then defending its objectives and following its directives is even more important and more necessary to be upheld by all factions of the people with the aim of the success of the progress of social and economic prosperity and political stability under the auspices of true national unity which is considered the basis of insuring every honest patriotic activity and for the success of any plan which is drawn up. Without that, we shall not achieve any of our legitimate aspirations in this life.
>
> If this covenant forms the intellectual framework for our course, then the work programmes must not depart from this framework, no matter how different their methods of application are. For the movement of popular and governmental activities within this intellectual framework makes the movement constructive, which shall rid us of divisiveness and the consequences of unpatriotic affiliation and the ills of individual interpretation and profiting groupings, and makes creative, peaceful competition under democratic practices an alternative to destructive conflicts.
>
> Let us then move forward, united and co-operating towards a prosperous and honest future, relying—after God—on ourselves and on our unity and our own capabilities so that we may achieve all our aspirations and ambitions.

The NC has become the intellectual and political framework which guides the General Peoples Congress Party in its political action and policy formulation.

Notes and References

1. *al-Mawsū'ah al-Yamaniyyah* (Ṣan'ā', 1992), II, 941–43.
2. Executed after the failure of the revolution.
3. 'Abdallāh al-Shamāḥī, *al-Yaman al-insān wa-al-ḥaḍārah*, 270, 257, 209; Aḥmad al-Shāmī, *Riyāḥ al-tāgyīr fī al-Yaman*.

Erythraean Ichthyophagi: Arabian Fish-eaters Observed*

William J. Donaldson

Introduction

The subject of this paper is the fisheries of Arabia as recorded by visitors from outside the region from the Greeks through to the present century. To attempt to cover 2500 years is of course a very tall order for a short article such as this. Nevertheless, such a survey is possible by virtue of one prominent feature: that the fisheries of this region, as will be shown, underwent no substantial change in their technology from the earliest historical times right up until recent decades when the effects of oil exports made themselves felt.

Three introductory points must be made as background.

1) The extent of the region to be covered will be the coastal areas of the Arabian Peninsula bordering the Red Sea, the Arabian Sea, the Gulf of Oman and the Arabian Gulf, and in addition the Makrān and Lāristān coasts of Iran because of their long-standing contacts with the Arabian shores.
2) The physical nature of these coasts much be considered. They are predominantly hot desert or semi-desert and generally sparsely populated. With the exception of the Bāṭinah coast of northern Oman, parts of the Yemeni and Saudi Tihāmah, and a few smaller stretches, such as the north of Bahrain Island and the Ṣalālah area, opportunities for coastal agriculture are confined to small and sparsely distributed locations. Consequently, not

* I am very grateful to Dr Carole Hillenbrand for her kind comments on an early draft of this paper, and to Professor G. Rex Smith and Dr Dionisius Agius for their helpful suggestions on the penultimate version.

only are the means of livelihood from agricultural and livestock production generally limited on these coasts, but there is a dearth of the types of natural materials needed for making fishing craft and tackle. In particular, locally produced good timber is generally lacking.

3) The nature of the marine environment of the region and its relationship to the distribution of population are also important considerations. Generally speaking, by far the richest fishing areas are those off the southeastern coasts of the Peninsula by reason of what oceanographers call the Arabian Sea Upwelling which brings cold nutrient-rich water from the depths to the surface[1]. By comparison, both the Red Sea and the Arabian Gulf are far less prolific in their fish resources. Most of the population of the Peninsula on the other hand have always tended to reside nearer the Red Sea and Arabian Gulf coasts. We have it from several historical travellers to the area that the southeastern coasts were very sparsely populated, as indeed they are today. It is however these relatively unpopulated coasts which have the richest stocks of fish.

The references quoted may well seem after a while to be repetitive in the information they give. There is a reason for this which, it is hoped, will become apparent eventually.

The article will first indicate the primary sources selected. Then the earliest (archaeological) information available will be briefly overviewed, after which will follow a review, in chronological order, of records of observers from the earliest literary sources (from ancient Greece), through some medieval descriptions, to arrive finally at some more modern accounts.

Sources

The earliest literary information available comes from Arrian's *Indica*, the account of the voyage of Nearchus along the Arabian Gulf and Makrān coasts in the 4th century BC, the English translation of which employed here is that of P.A. Brunt.[2] Then there is the famous trader's guide to the Red Sea and Indian Ocean of around AD 100 called *The Periplus of the Erythraean Sea*, for which the translations of W.H. Schoff and G.W.B. Huntingford have been consulted.[3]

For the medieval period, Ibn Ḥawqal's *Ṣūrat al-arḍ*[4] has been chosen from the late 4th/10th century, Ibn al-Muǧāwir's *Ta'rīḫ al-Mustabṣir*[5] from the early 7th/13th century, Marco Polo's *Travels*[6] from the late 13th century, and Ibn Baṭṭūṭah's *Riḥlah*[7] from the second quarter of the 8th/14th century. So we have one traveller from Venice (Marco Polo), one from the Maghrib (Ibn Baṭṭūṭah), one from the Iraqi Jazīrah in the central Islamic lands (Ibn Ḥawqal), and one from the east (Ibn al-Muǧāwir).[8]

In such studies as this, a distinction must be made between travellers who witnessed for themselves on the one hand, and geographers who were reliant only on secondary sources on the other. It would appear that Marco Polo, Ibn Baṭṭūṭah and Ibn al-Muǧāwir, as travellers, did record what they had personally seen, but there is some doubt as to whether Ibn Ḥawqal's descriptions of at least the southern and southeastern coasts of the Peninsula are from his own personal observations. Even Ibn Baṭṭūṭah's account may have been embellished by the Maghribī scholar Ibn Ǧuzayy when it was written down some four years after Ibn Baṭṭūṭah returned to his native Morocco.[9]

From the 18th century onwards, beginning with Carsten Niebuhr,[10] descriptions by travellers to the region become much more frequent, and the information they give on the fisheries is generally more detailed. The sources for this modern period will be cited as they become relevant.

Prehistoric Evidence

In the last two or three decades much archaeological work has been carried out in several parts of the Peninsula which indicate the importance of fish to not only its coastal inhabitants but also by way of trade to the peoples of the interior. The archaeological evidence is now too large to be reviewed comprehensively here, but a few findings may be taken from Oman by way of example.

Since the accession of the reforming and modernizing Sultan Qābūs b. Sa'īd Āl Bū Sa'īd in 1970, Oman has been the subject of intense archaeological fieldwork. Beatrice de Cardi, Paolo Costa and Karen Frifelt were among the first in the field. The findings of these archaeologists and others indicate that fishing communities existed in Oman as early as the third millennium BC when the area was the centre of a distinctive culture in touch with the civilisations of Mesopotamia and the Indus valley. Fish bones, mollusc shells and grooved stones which have been interpreted, probably correctly, as fishing net weights, have been found at several coastal sites in northern Oman and can probably be associated with types of burial cairns typical of the third millennium BC.[11] There is also archaeological evidence for a trade in at least shellfish (and therefore probably other sea fish) in many third millennium sites throughout the interior of the country.[12]

Similar archaeological information is available for other sites in the Arabian Gulf, and, no doubt, for other parts of the Arabian Peninsula.

Greek Descriptions

The earliest written references to fishing in the Arabian Peninsula and contiguous parts of the coast come from Greek sources. As has been earlier indicated, foremost among these are the account of the voyage of Nearchus in the 4th century BC as recounted in Arrian's *Indica*[13] and the anonymous *Periplus of the Erythraean Sea*[14] of around AD 100.

Both these works call certain communities of the Arabian and Makrān coasts the *Ichthyophagi*, that is, the Fish-Eaters. Since it is by no means remarkable that coastal dwellers should eat fish, the fact that communities should be referred to specifically as 'fish-eaters' suggests that fishing was an outstandingly important aspect of their livelihood.

In Arrian's account Nearchus described on the Makrān coast the catching of anchovies and sardines by castnet, fishing craft propelled by paddles rather than oars, and a 'flour' or 'meal' made from grinding dried fish,[15] and some of these characteristics are described similarly in the *Periplus* which adds that dugout canoes and fish traps were also used.[16] Castnets, paddles, dugout canoes, fishing with traps, and ground dried fish are however found in many fisheries throughout the world both in the past and in present times. More remarkable are two other features of the fisheries of the region described by these Classical sources. First, domestic livestock were fed on fish,[17] and second, craft were not constructed with iron nails but were rather sewn together with palm-fibre.[18] Both these unusual features will be remarked on again later.

Arrian remarks also that Nearchus observed fishermen on the Makrān coast fishing close to the shore with nets 'mostly about two stades in length. They plait them from the bark of the date-palm, twisting the bark like twine.'[19] The date 'bark' is probably better translated as date fibre or coir. As for the 'stade' (that is, the stadium as a measure of distance), its length is not precisely known, being calculated variously as between 75 m and 150 m. But what is obviously being described here is fishing with beach seines. This is then followed by a reference to castnets also being used.[20]

A further reference related to fish in Arrian's account concerns houses built from the bones of 'fish'.[21] In view of Arrian's following description of Nearchus' encounters with huge sea animals which blow spouts of water, the reference to whale bones is unavoidable.

Medieval Descriptions

1) Ibn Ḥawqal:

Skipping some nine centuries, during which literary evidence would seem to be sparse or even non-existent, we come to Ibn Ḥawqal, the Arab geographer and traveller from Upper Iraq.[22] Ibn Ḥawqal's main work was *Kitāb al-Masālik wa-al-mamālik*, known also as *Kitāb Ṣūrat al-arḍ*, is highly dependent in places on the work of the 4th/10th century geographer al-Iṣṭaḫrī.[23]

As well as a traveller, Ibn Ḥawqal was also a merchant, a fact which shows in his great interest in recording details of the trade of the places he passed through. In addition, it is possible that he acted during his travels as a Fatimid *dā'ī* (propagandist or missionary), though this is not certain. He was born in Naṣībīn in al-Ğazīrah and began his travels in 331/943, travels which took him to most parts of the Islamic world from Spain to Transoxiana, including the coasts of the Red Sea and the Arabian Gulf.[24]

As far as Arabia is concerned he gives much detail on certain geographical, economic, historical and other topics (the locations of places, the distances between them, their religious affiliations, their agricultural products, and much else). His references to fish and fishing in Arabia are however rather sparse. He does speak of pearl fishing at certain locations, specifically off Aden and Oman and at Ḫarak (on the Persian coast),[25] noting

ولا أعلم معدناً للؤلؤ إلا ببحر الفارس

I do not know of any place of production for pearls other than in the Baḥr Fāris [i.e., the Arabian Gulf][26]

but fishing proper seems to have little interest for him. In fact, there would seem to be only three references to fish in the whole of the two chapters of his *Ṣūrah* which deal with the Arabian Peninsula (the chapters headed *Diyār al-'Arab* and *Baḥr Fāris*). Two of them concern the northern end of Baḥr al-Qulzum (the Red Sea). In one he notes:

ففيه سمك كثير كبير مختلف الألوان والأنواع

In it [the Baḥr al-Qulzum] there are many large fish of various different kinds[27]

but he offers no details, technical or otherwise.

The second mention similarly gives no interesting detail. In the coastal area around the town of Qulzum (at the northern end of the Red Sea) he says:

فلا تكون بها مدينة سوى مواضع بها ناس مقيمون على
صَيد من هذا البحر وشيء من النخيل

There are no towns or villages here except the places where there dwell people who live from fishing in this sea and a little from date-palms.[28]

The other mention however is much more revealing. It occurs in the passage in which he is describing the Mahrah coast, a stretch of coast which he may not have personally visited. After stating that the people of Mahrah speak an unintelligible language and that it is a poor country, he says:

وليس بها نخل ولا زرع وإنما أموالهم الإبل والمَعَز ولإبل
والدواب، تعلف السمك الصغار المعروف بالورق، وهم
وسائر حيوانهم لا يعرفون الخبز ولا يأكلونه ، وأكلهم
السمك والألبان والتمور

> There are no date-palms or sown crops here, and their possessions are only camels and goats and camels and beasts of burden [probably meaning donkeys], which are fed with the small fish know as waraq. Neither the people nor their animals are acquainted with bread and they do not eat it, their food being fish, dairy products and dates.[29]

Here we have an echo of what Nearchus saw elsewhere in the region some 1200 years before: fish being used as fodder for livestock. Why precisely the fish are known as *waraq* is not given, but the fact that they are small fish undoubtedly indicates that they were sardines, and sardines in the same area today become thin and somewhat flaky when they are dried. Perhaps this is the reason for their being called *waraq*, with its connotations of leaves and paper. On the other hand, the present-day name in Dhofar (Ẓafār) for anchovies is *ğaraq* (غَرق),[30] which opens the possibility that the version of the text of Ibn Ḥawqal's *Ṣūrah* used by the present author is wrongly edited, and that 'anchovies' is meant—though, if so, then this would be the only known source stating that anchovies (as opposed to sardines) were used for fodder.[31]

2) *Ibn al-Muğāwir:*

Some 250 years after Ibn Ḥawqal, Ibn al-Muğāwir wrote his *Ta'rīẖ al-Mustabṣir*, which G. Rex Smith has called 'a businessman's guide' to the Peninsula in the early 7th/13th century.[32] The work largely concerns itineraries in the Ḥiğāz and the Yemen, interspersed with observations and stories about the places mentioned. The 'Middle Arabic' in which it is written is sometimes obscure, especially when a highly technical subject is being described, though his references to fish, fishing and fishermen are fairly straightforward. Unfortunately, however, there would seem to be only about ten substantive references to the subject in the whole work, though they do give rather more detail than those of Ibn Ḥawqal.

He describes Qalhāt (the now ruined port on the eastern coast of Oman just northwest of Ṣūr) in some detail, but of its fishermen he says merely that they live on the shore,[33] a fact which is hardly remarkable.

He records also fishermen living on the island of Qays (on the Persian side of the Arabian Gulf). Concerning what the people of Qays eat, Ibn al-Muğāwir goes on to say:

مأكولهم السمك ويعلمون منه الهرائس ويُؤكَل مع التمر وليس لأهلها مأكول سواه

> Their food is fish and they make from it *harā'is* [sing. *harīsah*, a mash usually made from cracked wheat and meat]. This is eaten with dried dates, and the people of the place have no food other than this.[34]

The last part of this statement is rather surprising, given the fact that Ibn Muğāwir has immediately before recorded that the island was well endowed with wells, streams and gardens, as well as having a flourishing *entrepôt* trade, all facts picked up also by Yāqūt in his *Mu'ğam al-buldān*.[35]

Of the people living on the Farasān Islands in the Red Sea Ibn al-Muğāwir says that they have large numbers of domestic animals and also fish and *dawābb al-baḥr*, the latter presumably meaning either turtles or cetaceans, or both.[36] Again, any detail is unfortunately lacking.

Other mentions of fish occur in the passages Ibn al Muğāwir devotes to the southern coasts of the Peninsula. On the island of Socotra (Suquṭrā) he notes that there are fish, but gives similarly no details.[37]

He does supply more information however about the province of Dhofar, and particularly about the coastal settlement of al-Manṣūrah between Raysūt and Mirbāṭ, roughly where the present day Ṣalālah, the modern capital of Dhofar, stands.[38] He says:

ويقال إنما يُعقِدون الهريسة إلا بلحم السمك لا غير

> It is said that they thicken the *harīsah* only with fish-meat, nothing else[39]

which is similar to the comment he made on the people of Qays, and equally surprising since the reference comes similarly just after his description of great fertility of the area.

Of the dependence of the people of al-Manṣūrah on fish he also says:

ومأكولهم السَمك والذُرة والكَنب ، ومطوم دوابّهم

السمك اليابس وهو العَيْد ولم يَزبلوا أراضيهم إلا بالسمك

Their food is fish, *ḏurah* [sorghum/millet], and *kanib*. The fodder of their animals is dried fish which is [called] *'ayd*, and they fertilize their land with nothing but fish.[40]

The *kanib* has been identified by R.B. Serjeant as a species of cereal, *Eleusine coracana*, of which two crops can be harvested in a year, according to the 8th/14th century Rasūlid document the *Buġyat al-fallāḥīn*.[41] Here Ibn al-Muǧāwir confirms what both the classical Greek sources and Ibn Ḥawqal had already said of fishermen in the area: that they used fish as fodder. More interestingly, he gives the fish concerned a name, *'ayd*. This term is still today the

Plate 1: Ibn al-Muǧāwir (*Ta'rīḫ al Mustabṣir*. 265_{16-17}) on the use of sardines at al-Manṣūrah, the modern Ṣalālah, Dhofar:

ومطعوم دوابّهم السمك اليابس وهو العَيْد ولم يزبلوا أراضيهم إلا بالسمك

'The fodder of their animals is dried fish which is [called] *'ayd*, and they fertilize their land with nothing but fish.'

The photograph is of sardines (*'ayd*) drying on the upper beach at Ṣalālah in the winter of 1977/78.

name for sardines in the Yemen and Dhofar (though not in the north of Oman and the Arabian Gulf: there sardines are *'ūmah/'ūm*[42]), and he adds that fish is the only fertilizer the people of the area use.

3) Marco Polo:

About half a century after Ibn al-Muǧāwir, next in chronological order from among our selected travellers comes the Venetian Marco Polo. He gives what seem to be the earliest detailed descriptions of types and uses of fish in Arabia as observed by a visitor from Medieval Europe.[43]

Polo visited both the southeastern coasts of the Peninsula and the Hormuz (Hurmūz) area at the entrance to the Arabian Gulf in the 1290s. His descriptions and comments, like those of both the Greek and Arabic sources before him, indicate that fish was a mainstay of life in the region, and some of what he reports repeats the observations of previous travellers. After describing the (to him) strange sheep of the port of al-Šiḥr on the Mahrah coast, he says in wonderment:

> And here is something else that may strike you as marvellous: their domestic animals—sheep, oxen, camels, and little ponies—are fed on fish. They are reduced to this diet because in all this country and in all the surrounding regions there is no grass; but it is the driest place in the world. The fish on which these animals feed are very small and are caught in March, April and May in quantities that are truly amazing. They are then dried and stored in the houses and given to the animals as food throughout the year. I can tell you further that the animals also eat them alive, as soon as they are drawn out of the water. There are also big fish here—and good ones too—in great profusion and very cheap.[44]

The echoes of Nearchus, some 1600 years earlier, and also of Ibn Ḥawqal and Ibn al-Muǧāwir, are clear. As for Polo's 'small fish' that are dried and fed to livestock, they are undoubtedly the *'ayd* (sardines) of Ibn al-Muǧāwir, and may include anchovies as well (if, that is, Ibn Ḥawqal's *waraq* should be read *ǧaraq*, as was discussed above). As for the 'big fish', they must include tuna species, since Polo has already remarked on the abundance of these species at al-Šiḥr.[45]

Polo does provide also some interesting details about fish, fishing and fish handling in the region in his day which are not found in the previous accounts.

First, seasonally variable catches could be utilized throughout the year by means of at least two methods of preservation, namely, by sun-drying and by salting, the method chosen depending on the species of fish. According to Polo, sun-drying was carried out in the case of the sardines, while the tuna species was cured by salting.[46] In addition, at al-Šiḥr a 'biscuit' of chopped, dried fish (of unspecified type, but possibly shark) was made for human consumption,[47] echoing the fish 'flour' noted by Nearchus.

Second, Polo also notes, at Hormuz at least, one by-product of fish was a type of oil which was used to preserve ships' timbers.[48] He does not mention the species from which the oil was extracted. Bearing in mind the Greek accounts, the source could have been derived from the blubber of beached whales; but later evidence (including the present writer's own fieldwork) suggests either sardine oil (collected in pits on the beach) or shark liver oil (extracted by boiling), or else a combination of both.[49] Also at Hormuz Polo remarks that the timbers of craft are not fastened with iron nails, but stitched together with cord made from coir (coconut fibre). He says:

> They soak the [coconut] husk till it assumes the texture of horsehair; then they make it into threads and stitch their ships. It is not spoilt by the water, but lasts remarkably well. … They have no iron for nails; so they employ wooden pegs and stitch with thread.[50]

He then adds the ominous warning:

> This makes it a risky undertaking to sail in these ships. And you can take my word that many of them sink, because the Indian Ocean is often very stormy.[51]

Plate 2.

Plates 2 & 3: Marco Polo (*Travels* transl. Latham 1958: 66), on boat-building at Hormuz:

'They soak the [coconut] husk till it assumes the texture of horsehair; then they make it into threads and stitch their ships. It is not spoilt by the water, but lasts remarkably well. … They have no iron for nails; so they employ wooden pegs and stitch with thread.'

Ibn Baṭṭūṭah (*Riḥlah*: 255_{5-6}), referring to Arabian boat-building, probably in Dhofar):

وعليها ليف شبه الشعر ، وهم يصنعون به حبالا
يخيطون بها المراكب عوضاً من مسامير الحديد

'On [the coconut] is līf (coir) which resembles hair. With it they make cord with which they sew the boats together as a substitute for iron nails.'

The photographs are of a fishing *sanbūq/sambūk* at Ṣalālah, Dhofar, which was still in use in late 1977 when the photographs were taken. The vessel is held together wholly by the means of the millennia-old technique of stitching the timbers. This stitching can be seen clearly in the detailed photograph of the prow section. That the technique of sewing boats was still alive in the late 1970s is witnessed by the fact that a third or so of the criss-cross stitching in the detailed photograph is not of the traditional coir cord, but rather a recent repair in imported green nylon cord.

Lastly, Polo, again echoing the earlier sources, and talking now of Qalhāt, remarks that fish formed a major constituent in the diet of the majority of the coastal population, but he adds significantly that 'foods of better quality' were preferred by those who could afford them. He says:

> You may take it for a fact that the people of this country live on dates and salt fish, of which they enjoy abundant supplies. But admittedly there are some among them, men of wealth and consequence, who eat foods of better quality.[52]

So dates and fish are the staples and are less highly regarded than more expensive other foods, presumably including meat. This is still a characteristic attitude of the coastal dwellers of Oman and other parts of the region.

4) Ibn Baṭṭūṭah:

Just a decade after Marco Polo's visit to Arabia, Ibn Baṭṭūṭah[53] was born at Tangiers in 703/1304 and became in due course one of the world's most famous travellers. Starting from his homeland in 725/1325, his travels lasted just over a quarter of a century and took him as far east as China. He was in Arabia at least twice, and visited the Ḥiğāz, the Yemen, Aden, Oman and the Arabian Gulf. On his journeys he made notes of his itineraries and what had captured his attention, but seems unfortunately to have lost them more than once. The present text of his journeys was written down by a Maġribī scholar Ibn Ğuzayy at Ibn Baṭṭūṭah's dictation about four years after his return, and it may be suspected that in certain passages at least Ibn Ğuzayy incorporated some embellishments and possibly even inventions.[54]

Nevertheless, as far as the fisheries of Arabia and the contiguous coasts are concerned, Ibn Baṭṭūṭah's descriptions ring true enough in the light of what previous and subsequent visitors have said.

Of Maṣīrah Island, off the coast of southeastern Oman, he says:

(جزيرة مصيرة) جزيرة كبيرة لا عيش لأهلها إلا من
السمك

> [Maṣīrah] is a large island the people of which have no subsistence other than from fish.[55]

This is the only fact he gives about Maṣīrah. The people's dependence on fish must therefore have struck him forcefully.

He says much the same of the people of Ḥāsik, the former port, now in ruins, on the Dhofar coast to the east of Ṣalālah, adding that even their houses were built using 'fish' bones roofed with camel hide.[56] Similarly, of Ğabal Lam'ān[57] (which must be the largest of the Kuria Muria Islands called nowadays al-Ḥallāniyyah), he says that it is topped with a hermitage built of stone and roofed with 'fish' bones.[58] The 'fish' bones are undoubtedly the bones of whales, probably from animals washed ashore and stranded, rather than caught deliberately by the fishermen, and there are clear parallels here with the ancient Greek accounts, written 1300 to 2000 years before, and already mentioned above. In a region where good timber is scarce, whale bones would provide a passable substitute in building construction.

Concerning Ḥāsik, Ibn Baṭṭūṭah gives some detail about curing sharks, saying:

وسمكهم يعرف باللخم ، وهو شبيه كلب البحر ، ويشرح ويقدد

> Their fish is known as *luẖ(a)m* and is similar to the *kalb al-baḥr* (shark). It is cut open (*yušrah*), and cut lengthwise into strips and dried [in the sun] (*yuqaddad*).[59]

The term *luẖam/luẖm* (root *l-ẖ-m*, to do with sluggishness) is still the name for shark in southern Arabia today (though not in northern Oman, where the generic term is *ǧarǧūr*).[60] The method Ibn Baṭṭūṭah gives for preserving the sharks (cutting lengthwise and drying in the sun) was still in extensive use in the 1970s, especially on the southeastern coasts of Oman.[61]

Ibn Baṭṭūṭah elsewhere gives three other fish names. At Muscat he remarks on the great quantities of fish caught of a kind he records as قلب الماس *qalb* (or *qulb*) *al-mās*[62] which C.F. Beckingham has clarified as being not Arabic but the Maldivian *kaḷu bili mas*, which signifies a member of the Scombridae (the tuna and kingfish family).[63] Another fish, off the southeastern coasts of the Peninsula, he says is called in Fārsī *šīr māhī*, and helpfully translates it into Arabic as *asad al-samak* ('lion of fish'), though it would seem not to correspond with any modern name, and its taxonomic identification remains elusive.[64]

The third fish name he gives is interesting. Speaking of Dhofar, and after echoing much of what previous visitors had said, he records:

وأكثر سمكهم النوع المعروف بالسردين وهو بها في النهاية من السمن ، ومن العجائب أن دوابّهم إنما علفها من هذا السردين ، وكذلك غنمهم ، ولم أرَ ذلك في سواهم

> The most abundant fish is the kind known as sardīn, in which there is a considerable amount of oil. It is an extraordinary thing that their beasts of burden

are fed only on this *sardīn*, and similarly also their goats. I have never seen the like of that.[65]

The term *sardīn* Ibn Baṭṭūṭah has clearly brought with him from the Mediterranean, where it is still the name for that fish in the Arabic of that region. As has been quoted, Ibn al-Muǧāwir has already informed us that the local name on the southeastern coasts of Arabia for sardines was *'ayd* (and indeed the same term remains current today on those coasts).[66]

Plate 4: Ibn Baṭṭūṭah (*Riḥlah*: $258_{2\text{–}3}$) on curing sharks at Ḥāsik, to the east of Ṣalālah, says:

وسمكهم يعرف باللخم ، وهو شبيه كلب البحر ، ويشرح ويقدد

'Their fish is known as *luḫ(a)m* and is similar to the *kalb al-baḥr* (shark). It is cut open (*yušraḥ*), and cut lengthwise into strips and dried [in the sun] (*yuqaddad*).'

The photograph is of the auction of a pile of small dried shark at 'Ibrī (northern Oman), in February 1975. The northern Omani term for small shark (*qaṣqūṣ*) which has been cut open lengthwise and dried in the sun is *'uwāl*. The *'uwāl* in the photograph being auctioned were caught, cured and dried on the southeastern coasts of Oman (specifically, the area of Duqm).

At Qalhāt, Ibn Baṭṭūṭah remarked on how good the fish he ate was, and describes how it is cooked, but does not give its name:

وأكلت بهذه المدينة سمكاً لم آكل مثله في إقليم من الأقاليم وكنت أفضله على جميع اللحوم ، فلا آكل سواه ، ويشوونه على ورق الشجر ، ويجعلونه على الأرز ويأكلونه

At this town I ate some fish the like of which I had never eaten in any region. I preferred it to any sort of meat, and I ate nothing else. They roast it over [a fire made from] tree leaves, and put it on rice and eat it.[67]

Ibn Baṭṭūṭah's appreciation of fish at Qalhāt was therefore considerably higher than Marco Polo's observations on the preferences of the population at the same place just a few decades earlier. Ibn Baṭṭūṭah does agree with Polo however in his observations on boat building in the region. At one point, Ibn Baṭṭūṭah says:

وعليها ليف شبه الشعر ، وهم يصنعون به حبالا يخيطون بها المراكب عوضاً من مسامير الحديد

On [the coconut] is *līf* (coir) which resembles hair. With it they make cord with which they sew the boats together as a substitute for iron nails.[68]

Here again we have an echo of Nearchus, witnessed and recorded almost two millennia before, and of the *Periplus*, of over one millennium before: sewn boats in Arabia.

Ibn Baṭṭūṭah's fascination with the coconut palm causes him to devote two pages to describing the uses of the tree and its fruit. It is not entirely clear which precise area he is referring to when he describes the sewing of boats. The passage comes in between descriptions of Dhofar, and perhaps may be taken to refer to that area since coconuts are a major crop there, though he does also mention in the same passage the Ğazīrat D̲ībat al-Maḥall, that is, the Maldive Islands, where coconuts are also important.

One further small point about craft can be mentioned from Ibn Baṭṭūṭah's account: he mentions the term *ṣunbūq* (with a *ṣād*) for a small boat.[69] The term is well attested in slightly varied forms (*sunbuq*, *sunbuk*, *sumbūq*, etc., with either *sīn* or *ṣād*, *qāf* or *kāf*, *mīm* or *nūn*, and a long or short vowel in the second syllable[70]) in the dialects of the southern and southwestern Arabian coasts including Dhofar to mean a small boat such as is used in fishing. The etymology of the word is not clear, but Löfgren in a work on medieval Aden[71] suggests its source as Sanskrit (or one of its descendent languages) via Persian, and Yule's well-known compendium of Anglo-Indian terms (*Hobson-Jobson*) does not rule this possibility out.[72] That it is not originally Arabic may possibly be supported by the fact that it appears in several spellings and would seem to be confined to a relatively limited area of the Arabic-speaking world.

Post-medieval Descriptions

Descriptions of the fisheries of Arabia by observers become more abundant from the middle of the eighteenth century, beginning with the Danish traveller and scientist Carsten Niebuhr. In the 1760s Niebuhr visited the region, including on his journey the Yemen, Oman and the Makrān coast of Iran. Concerning the fisheries of these areas he confirms much of what had already been described but he himself adds little to it.

He remarked at the similarity of the Arabs of the southern Persian and Makrān coasts with the Ichthyophagi of classical times.[73] Like others before him, he was struck by the quantities of fish caught by the fishermen of the region, remarking that fish in Oman were so abundant and so easily caught that they were used not only as fodder, echoing descriptions as far back as Nearchus, 'but even as manure to the fields',[74] echoing Ibn Ḥawqal, eight centuries before, and Ibn al-Muǧāwir, over five centuries before.

European visitors to the region began to become what might be called frequent only in the nineteenth century. At first, members of the British Indian army and navy were particularly prominent, and the reports of the journeys they made often contain references to fish, fishing and fish trading though they are rarely systematic accounts. Largely educated in the Greek and Latin classics, they too commented on the similarities of the classical descriptions of the fisheries of the region with the situation they witnessed.

Thus for example Lt G.B. Kempthorne, in following Nearchus' route along the Iranian coast,[75] noted that its inhabitants and those of the Arabian coast opposite subsisted largely on fish and that they also fed fish to their livestock.[76] He was also struck by the similarity of the canoes he saw, which he records were often sewn with palm-fibre cord and propelled by paddles rather than oars, with those described by Nearchus.[77]

Some ten years after Kempthorne, Lt F. Whitelock repeated similar observations, and added that off H̱aṣab on the Musandam Peninsula at least the main types of fish caught in particularly large quantities were mullet, kingfish and various 'rock fish'.[78] About the same time—that is, the 1830s—Lt J.R. Wellsted listed among the principal exports of the port of Muscat shark fins destined for China and salt fish.[79]

A quarter of a century later, around 1860, two accounts by British observers, one by Lt Col L. Pelly and another by W.M. Pengelley (the then British Agent at Muscat), repeat much of what had already been described by earlier visitors but also add some interesting details. Pelly stressed the importance of the export of salt fish and also of pearls to the economy of what is now the coast of the United Arab Emirates.[80] According to him, the main export markets for the fish were Zanzibar (which, until 1865, was still part of the Omani 'Empire') and the East African coast on the one hand, and the Malabar coast of India on the other.

Pengelley's account, published in 1860,[81] would seem to be the earliest which gives details specifically of the Bāṭinah coast of northern Oman, the most densely populated and most heavily cultivated continuous coastal stretch of the Arabian Peninsula. He noted that although the mass of the people on this coast subsisted solely on fish and dates, and that given the relatively dense population, the demand for fish could therefore be expected to be high, fish was nevertheless 'taken diurnally in the vicinity of the beach in such abundance as occasionally to exceed even the magnitude of the demand.'[82]

Pengelley also gave what appears to be the earliest written description by a European of a particular kind of fishing craft built of date-palm fronds called the *šāšah* (coll. *šāš*, pl. *šāšāt*) found on the Bāṭinah coast of Oman and likewise on the coasts of the Arabian Gulf.[83] Technically speaking, the *šāšah* is a raft rather than a boat, since it floats by virtue of the lightness of the materials of which it is constructed and not because it is watertight. Pengelley rightly testified to its great utility and its suitability for local conditions, particularly in that because of its considerable buoyancy and flexibility fishermen can take it to sea even in storms which are frequent in the Gulf of Oman and which deter wooden-built craft, and also because it can be beached by a single fisherman without assistance.[84]

It is from the 1880s that descriptions by Westerners of the fisheries of the region and the contiguous coasts become more systematic, detailed and scientific. Moreover, it is from then that the first attempts at estimating the size of the fish catch and the numbers of fishing boats and fishermen on various stretches of the Arabian and Persian coasts were attempted. A comprehensive survey of all the visitors who have left records, many of which are preserved among the records of the British Persian Gulf Political Residency and the Muscat Political Agency, would be tedious, largely because much of what they say is repetitious. Some however do deserve mention, and especially those who add to what had already been recorded.

Foremost among these are the Administration Report for 1880–81 written by I. MacIvor,[85] the classic *Gazetteer of the Persian Gulf, Oman and Central Arabia* of J.G. Lorimer (published between 1908 and 1915),[86] and the publications of Col S.B. Miles, especially his extensive work *The Countries and Tribes of the Persian Gulf*, published posthumously in 1919 but based on the author's personal knowledge of eastern Arabia and particularly Oman some three to four decades earlier, when he served as British Political Agent and Consul in Muscat.[87]

However, it was not until well into this present century that any surveys of Arabian fisheries were carried out by fisheries experts. The first expert studies in the whole Peninsula seem to have been by the fisheries officers of the Aden Protectorate[88] and a report commissioned in 1947/48 by the Omani Sultan Sa'īd b. Taymur from the eminent fisheries expert Dr G.C.L. Bertram.[89] But it is clear from the combined corpus of evidence over the centuries that these reports of the 1940s described a fishery that had remained substantially unchanged since early historical times, and probably even prehistoric times.

Conclusions

Combining all the information gained from the above sources it is possible, in conclusion, to compile the following description of Arabian fisheries from the earliest times right up until recent decades. Some of the features are illustrated in the accompanying photographs which were taken by the present author in the 1970s.

1) The fisheries of the region had remained unchanged for a considerable number of centuries. Different observers over many centuries tend to note the same things. Indeed, many of the observations made by the ancient Greeks or the medieval travellers could still have been observed in the 1970s in areas such as Oman where modernization brought by oil wealth came rather late.
2) Fish were caught in great numbers off especially the southeastern coasts of the Peninsula. Among the fish specified by travellers were particularly sardines, tuna and sharks.
3) Largely because of the seasonality of certain species, especially the shoaling species including sardines and tuna, fish curing was developed at an early date so that they could be used throughout the year. The curing method depended on the species in question. Tuna were wet-salted. Sharks were split open, cut lengthwise and dried in the sun. Sardines were spread out on the ground and dried in the sun, and their oil was collected in pits.
4) From the nineteenth century reports one may add that there was also a substantial export trade (with India and East Africa) in cured fish and (with China) in shark fins. It is likely that such trade had been going on for many centuries. It is curious that Ibn Ḥawqal, being a merchant himself, does not seem to refer to it, since he often gives details of the commerce of the

places he visited, and this omission may be additional evidence that he did not personally visit these southeastern coasts.

5) Sardines had a great economic importance beyond direct human nutrition. They were used as fodder for livestock and also as fertilizer. Both features are relatively rare among world fisheries, and both may be put down firstly to the huge abundance of sardines off the southeastern coasts, and secondly to the relative scarcity of land resources there.
6) Fishing craft in the region were of three basic types: the date-palm frond *šāšah*; the dugout canoe; and the plank-built larger boats which were sewn together with the fibre from coconut or date-palm.
7) As for fishing methods and fishing tackle, the historical accounts before the nineteenth century provide very little detail. Only castnets, beach seines and traps are indicated in the ancient and medieval sources; but it may be presumed that other fishing methods including various types of set nets and drift nets had been used for a long period, since they are already well established in the nineteenth century. This omission from the earlier historical sources is not really surprising. Travellers have a tendency to record features which are for them unusual for them, whereas fishing methods and technology are in fact very similar throughout the world, as fishermen over the ages have found the same or similar solutions to the same ubiquitous problems.[90]

Bibliography

Abbreviations:

AdminReptPGPR: *Administration Report of the Persian Gulf Political Residency and Muscat Political Agency*
GJ: *Geographical Journal*
JRGS: *Journal of the Royal Geographical Society*
TransBGS: *Transactions of the Bombay Geographical Society*
EI[1] and *EI*[2]: *Encyclopaedia of Islam*, Brill, Leiden, First and New

Editions

Agius 1997: Dionisius A. Agius, 'Historical-linguistic reliability of Muqaddasī's information on types of ships', *Across the Mediterranean Frontiers: Trade, Politics and Religion, 650–1450: Selected Proceedings of the International Medieval Congress, University of Leeds, July 1995 & 1996*, edited by Dionisius A. Agius and Ian Richard Netton, Turnhout, Brepols, 1997.

Arberry 1939: Arthur J. Arberry, 'A Baghdad Cookery Book, translated from the Arabic', *Islamic Culture*: XIII (1979).

Arrian transl. Brunt 1983: Arrian, *Indica* (Book VIII of *Anabasis Alexandri*: II, 306–446), transl. and ed. P.A. Brunt, London, 1983.

Bertram 1944: G.C.L. Bertram, 'Aden and its fisheries', typescript report dated 29th December, 1944, and collected as Report 19 in Bertram 1953 (*q.v.*).

Bertram 1948: G.C.L. Bertram, *The Fisheries of the Sultanate of Muscat and Oman*, Report to the Sultan of Muscat and Oman, Muscat, 1948.

Bertram 1953: G.C.L. Bertram, *The Fisheries of the Middle East: Collected Reports of Dr G.C.L. Bertram, 1943 to 1949*, circulated as UN Food and Agriculture Organisation Report No. FAO/53/2/976.

von Brandt 1971: A. von Brandt, *Fish Catching Methods of the World* (2nd ed.), London, 1971.

Currie *et al.* 1973: R.I. Currie, A.E. Fisher and P.M. Hargreaves, 'Arabian Sea Upwelling', in: Zeitzschel (ed.) 1973 (*q.v.*): 37–52.

Donaldson 1979: W.J. Donaldson, 'Fishing and Fish Marketing in Northern Oman: a Case Study of Artisanal Fisheries Development', unpublished PhD thesis, University of Durham, 1979.

Donaldson 1980: William Donaldson, 'Enterprise and innovation in an indigenous fishery: the case of the Sultanate of Oman', *Development and Change*: XI (1980), 479–95.

Dozy 1927: R. Dozy, *Supplément aux dictionnaires arabes* (2 vols), 2nd edition Leiden, 1927.

Hartley 1941: B.J. Hartley, *The Mahra Coast Fisheries*, Report for the Government of Aden (unpublished typescript), 1941.

Hastings *et al.* 1975: A. Hastings, J.H. Humphries, and R.H. Meadows, 'Oman in the third millennium BCE,' *Journal of Oman Studies*: I (1972), 9–55.

Hava 1899: J.G. Hava, *Al-Farā'id al-durriyyah: Arabic–English Dictionary*, Beirut, 1899; repr. Beirut, 1982.

Ibn Baṭṭūṭah *Riḥlah*: Ibn Baṭṭūṭah (Šams al-Dīn Abū 'Abdallāh Muḥammad b. 'Abdallāh al-Lawātī al-Tanǧī), *al-Riḥlah*, Beirut, 1388/1968.

Ibn Baṭṭūṭah *Travels* transl. Gibb and Beckingham 1958–94: Ibn Baṭṭūṭah, *The Travels of Ibn Baṭṭūṭah, AD 1325–1354*, translated with revisions and notes (from the Arabic text edited by C. Defremery and B.R. Sanguinetti) by H.A.R. Gibb (vols I (1958), II (1962) and III (1971)), and completed by C.F. Beckingham (vol. IV (1994)), Hakluyt Society, London, 1958–94.

Ibn Ḥawqal *Ṣūrah*: Ibn Ḥawqal (Abū al-Qāsim b. Ḥawqal al-Naṣībī), *Kitāb Ṣūrat al-arḍ*, Beirut [n.d.].

Ibn Manẓūr *Lisān*: Ibn Manẓūr (Ǧamāl al-Dīn Abū al-Faḍl Muḥammad b. Mukarram b. 'Alī b. Aḥmad b. Abī al-Qāsim b. Hiqbah b. Manẓūr), *Lisān al-'Arab*, Cairo [n.d.].

Ibn al-Muǧāwir *Mustabṣir*: Ibn al-Muǧāwir ([probably wrongly said to be:] Ǧamāl al-Dīn Abū al-Fatḥ Yūsuf b. Ya'qūb b. Muḥammad, *al-ma'rūf bi*-Ibn al-Muǧāwir al-Šaybānī al-Dimašqī [and more likely to be Abū Bakr b. Muḥammad b. Mas'ūd b. 'Alī b. Aḥmad Ibn al-Muǧāwir al-Baġdādī al-Nīsābūrī]), *Ṣifat Bilād al-Yaman wa-Makkah wa-ba'ḍ al-Ḥiǧāz, al-musammah Ta'rīḫ al-Mustabṣir*, ed. Oscar Löfgren (in 2 parts), Leiden, 1951–54.

Jayakar 1889: A.S.G. Jayakar, 'The O'mánee Dialect of Arabic', *JRAS*: XXI (NS) (1889), 811–80.

Kelly 1966: J.B. Kelly, Introduction to the 2nd edition (1966) of *The Countries and Tribes of the Persian Gulf* by S.B. Miles 1919 (*q.v.*).

Kempthorne 1835: G.B. Kempthorne, 'Notes made on a survey along the eastern shores of the Persian Gulf in 1828', *JRGS*: V (1835), 263–85.

Kuronuma and Abe 1972: Katsuzo Kuronuma and Yoshitaka Abe, *Fishes of Kuwait*, Kuwait Institute for Scientific Research, Kuwait, 1972.

Landberg *Gloss. daṯînois*: Le comte de Landberg, *Glossaire daṯînois* (3 vols), Leiden, 1920–42.

Lane *Lex*: E.W. Lane, *An Arabic–English Lexicon* ..., London and Edinburgh, 1863–93; repr. Islamic Texts Society, Cambridge, 1984.

Löfgren 1936–50: O. Löfgren, *Arabische Texte zur Kenntnis der Stadt Aden in Mittelalter* ..., Uppsala, 1936–50, quoted by Piamenta 1990–91: 234b (*q.v.*).

Lorimer 1908–15: J.G. Lorimer, *Gazetteer of the Persian Gulf, 'Oman and Central Arabia* (in 2 parts), Calcutta, 1908–15; repr. Farnborough and Shannon, 1970.

MacIvor 1880–81: I. MacIvor, 'Notes on sea fishing in the Persian Gulf', *AdminReptPGPR for 1880–81*, Pt III, Appendix A: 54–77, India Office Library Ref. R/15/6/480.

Miles 1876–77: S.B. Miles, 'Note on the resources and trade of Oman', *AdminReptPGPR for 1876–77*: 78–82, India Office Library Ref. V/23/29.

Miles 1885–86: S.B. Miles, 'Notes on a tour through Oman and El Dhahireh', *AdminReptPGPR for 1885–86*, Pt II, Appendix A: 22–28, India Office Library Ref. R/15/6/485.

Miles 1896: S.B. Miles. 'Journal of an excursion in Oman, in south-east Arabia', *GJ*: VII (1896), 522–37.

Miles 1910: S.B. Miles, 'On the border of the great desert: a journey in Oman', *GJ*: XXXVI (1919), 159–78 and 405–25.

Miles 1919: S.B. Miles, *The Countries and Tribes of the Persian Gulf* (2 vols), London, 1919; republ. in one vol. with introduction by J.B. Kelly, London, 1966.

Miquel *EI*²a: A. Miquel, Article 'Ibn Baṭṭūṭah', *EI*².

Miquel *EI*²b: A. Miquel, Article 'Ibn Ḥawqal', *EI*².

Niebuhr transl. and ed. Heron 1792: R. Heron (transl. and ed.), *Travels through Arabia and Other Countries in the East by M[onsieur C.] Niebuhr* (2 vols), Edinburgh, 1792; repr. Beirut [n.d.].

Pelly 1863: L. Pelly, 'Remarks on the tribes, trade and resources around the shore line of the Persian Gulf', *TransBGS*: XVII (1863), 32–112.

Pengelley 1860: W.M. Pengelley, 'Remarks on a portion of the eastern coast of Arabia between Muscat and Sohar', *TransBGS*: XVI (1860), 30–39.

Piamenta 1990–91: M. Piamenta, *Dictionary of Post-Classical Yemeni Arabic* (2 vols), Leiden, 1990–91.

Polo *Travels* transl. Latham 1958: R. Latham (transl.), *The Travels of Marco Polo*, Harmondsworth, England, 1958.

Periplus transl. Schoff 1912: W.H. Schoff (transl. and ed.), *The Periplus of the Erythraean Sea: travel and trade in the Indian Ocean by a merchant of the first century*, London, 1912.

Periplus transl. Huntingford 1980: G.W.B. Huntingford (transl. and ed.), *The Periplus of the Erythraean Sea*, The Hakluyt Society, London, 1980.

Serjeant 1974: R.B. Serjeant, 'The cultivation of cereals in medieval Yemen: a translation of the Buḡyat al-fallāḥīn of the Rasūlid Sultan, al-Malik al-Afḍal al-'Abbās b. 'Alī, composed circa 1370,' *Arabian Studies*: I, 25–74.

Smith 1985: G.R. Smith, 'Ibn al-Muǧāwir on Dhofar and Socotra,' *Proceedings of the Seminar for Arabian Studies*: XV (1985), 79–92.

Smith 1990: G.R. Smith, 'Ibn al-Muǧāwir's 7th/13th century guide to Arabia: the eastern connection', *Occasional Papers of the School of 'Abbāsid Studies*, No. 3 (1990; publ. 1991): 71–88, University of St Andrews.

Sivasubramaniam and Ibrahim 1982: K. Sivasubramaniam and Mohamed A. Ibrahim, *Common Fishes of Qatar, Scientific Atlas of Qatar*: I, Qatar, 1982.

Tosi 1975: M. Tosi, 'Distribution and exploitation of natural resources in Ancient Oman', *Journal of Oman Studies*: I (1975), 187–206.

Wehr 1971: H. Wehr, *A dictionary of Modern Written Arabic*, ed. J.M. Cowan (3rd ed.), Wiesbaden and London, 1971.

Wellsted 1837: J.R. Wellsted, 'Narrative of a journey into the interior of Oman', *JRGS*: VII (1837), 102–13.

Wellsted 1838: J.R. Wellsted, *Travels in Arabia* (2 vols), London, 1838.

White and Barwani 1971: A.W. White and M.A. Barwani, *Common Sea Fishes of the Arabian Gulf and Gulf of Oman*, Trucial States Council, Dubai, 1971.

Whitelock 1838a: F. Whitelock, 'An account of the Arabs who inhabit the coast between Ras el Kheimah and Abothubee in the Gulf of Persia, generally called the Pirate Coast', *TransBGS*: I (1836–38), 32–54.

Whitelock 1838b: F. Whitelock, 'Notes taken during a journey in Oman along the east coast of Arabia', *TransBGS*: I (1836–38), 295–8.

Whitelock 1838c: F. Whitelock, 'Descriptive sketch of the islands and coasts situated at the entrance to the Persian Gulf', *JRGS*: VIII (1838), 170–84.

Wyrtki 1971: K. Wyrtki, *Oceanographic Atlas of the International Indian Ocean Expedition*, Washington, DC, 1971.

Wyrtki 1973: K. Wyrtki, 'Physical oceanography of the Indian Ocean', in: Zeitzschel (ed.) 1973 (*q.v.*): 18–36.

Yāqūt *Mu'ǧam*: Yāqūt (Šihāb al-Dīn Abū 'Abdallāh Yāqūt b. 'Abdallāh al-Ḥamawī al-Rūmī al-Baḡdādī), *Mu'ǧam al-buldān* (5 vols), Beirut [n.d.].

Yule and Burnell 1903: H. Yule and A.C. Burnell, *Hobson-Jobson: a glossary of colloquial Anglo-Indian words and phrases, &c ...*, New edition W. Crooke, London, 1903; repr. Delhi, 1984.

Zeitzschel (ed.) 1973: B. Zeitzschel (ed), *Biology of the Indian Ocean*, London, 1973.

Notes and References

1. See e.g. Currie *et al.* 1973 and Wyrtki 1973; and also Wyrtki 1971.
2. Arrian transl. Brunt 1983.
3. *Periplus* transl. Schoff 1912; *Periplus* transl. Huntingford 1980. Huntingford discusses the difficult question of the date of the work in some detail (ibid.: 8–12), and concludes that 'the evidence would suggest some time between A.D. 95 and 130'—that is to say, rather later than the date of AD 60 suggested by Schoff (1912: 15).

4. Ibn Ḥawqal *Ṣūrah*.
5. Ibn al-Muǧāwir *Mustabṣir*.
6. Polo *Travels* transl. Latham 1958.
7. A 1388/1968 Beirut edition of the Arabic text has been used here (listed in the References under Ibn Baṭṭūṭah *Riḥlah*), though reference has also been made to H.A.R. Gibb's translation and notes completed by C.F. Beckingham. (Ibn Baṭṭūṭah *Travels* transl. Gibb & Beckingham 1958–94. Vols I (1958), II (1962) and III (1971) were the work of Gibb, and Vol. IV (1994) was completed by Beckingham. Reference here will be to Vols II and IV.)
8. According to Professor G. Rex Smith, this Ibn al-Muǧāwir was probably from Ḫurāsān, rather than the more famous Damascan writer of the same name assumed by O. Löfgren, the editor of the *Ta'rīḫ al-Mustabṣir* text (Smith 1990: 78–80 and 84–86).
9. Miquel EI^2a (article 'Ibn Baṭṭūṭah').
10. Niebuhr transl. and ed. Heron 1792.
11. Tosi 1975: 194–6.
12. Hastings *et al.* 1975: 14.
13. Arrian transl. Brunt 1983. Arrian's *Indica* constitutes Book VIII of his *Anabasis Alexandri*.
14. *Periplus* transl. Schoff 1912; *Periplus* transl. Huntingford 1980.
15. Arrian transl. Brunt 1983: 385–401.
16. *Periplus* transl. Schoff 1912: 28; *Periplus* transl. Huntingford 1980: 29–30. The stretch of coast for which the *Periplus* gives these particular details is northeast Africa, though the term *ichthyophagi* is applied to the inhabitants of certain stretches of the southern and southeastern Arabian coast (*Periplus* transl. Schoff 1912: 32 and 35; *Periplus* transl. Huntingford 1980: 35 and 39).
17. Arrian transl. Brunt 1983: 393.
18. *Periplus* transl. Schoff 1912: 28 and 36; *Periplus* transl. Huntingford 1980: 29–30 and 40.
19. Arrian transl. Brunt 1983: 393.
20. Ibid.
21. Ibid.: 395–7.
22. Abū al-Qāsim b. 'Alī al-Naṣībī, d. 371/981.
23. Abū Isḥāq Ibrāhīm al-Iṣṭaḫrī, d. 346/957.
24. Miquel EI^2b (article 'Ibn Ḥawqal').
25. Ibn Ḥawqal *Ṣūrah*: 52. According to Arrian's account, Nearchus also reported the presence of pearl fishing in the Arabian Gulf (specifically, off the island of Kekandros, which can be identified with the island now called Shaykh Shu'ayb (Arrian transl. Brunt 1983: 419 and final map)).
26. Ibid.: 52_{18-19}. The translations from the Arabic throughout this article are the present writer's own.
27. Ibid.: 51_{25}. An alternative translation for the end of the quotation might possibly be '… of different colours and kinds'.
28. Ibid.: 53_{8-9}.
29. Ibid.: 44_{14-17}.
30. For this information I am indebted to Dr Ali Omar Abdallah al-Abadi al-Rawas from

Ṣalālah, recently (1999) graduated with a PhD from the Department of Islamic and Middle Eastern Studies, University of Edinburgh.

31. In the 1970s, in northern Oman at least, anchovies (*barriyyah*, or *qāši‘* when dried) were reserved for human consumption, rather than fed to animals (Donaldson 1979: 84, 401 *et passim*).
32. Smith 1990: 78–80 and 84–6. In Professor Smith's opinion, based on close textual references, the author was Abū Bakr b. Muḥammad b. Mas‘ūd b. ‘Alī b. Aḥmad Ibn al-Muǧāwir al-Baġdādī al-Nīsābūrī who probably came from Ḫurāsān, rather than the more famous Syrian Ibn al-Muǧāwir, as has been noted already above (n. 9). See also Smith 1985 where he comments in detail on Ibn al-Muǧāwir's descriptions of Dhofar (Ẓafār) and Socotra (Suquṭrā) and which has proved of particular value in writing this section of the present article.
33. Ibn al-Muǧāwir *Mustabṣir*: 287.
34. Ibid.: 287. For *harīsah* see Lane *Lex.*: 2891b–c, entries *harīs* and *harīsah*; also Smith 1985: 89 n. 32; and Arberry 1939: 198–9. The last named reference gives two Abbasid recipes bearing the name *harīsah*, in the first of which ground [or cracked] wheat is the grain used and in the second coarsely ground rice is substituted. In both, the meat is referred to as ‘fat meat’ in Arberry's translation, and a quartered chicken is added. In neither recipe is fish mentioned as an ingredient such as Ibn al-Muǧāwir recorded at Qays.
35. Yāqūt *Mu‘ǧam*: IV, 422b, entry ‘Qays’.
36. Ibn al-Muǧāwir *Mustabṣir*, $244_{7–8}$.
37. Ibid.: 266.
38. As G.R. Smith (1985: 83 and 85) has pointed out, Ibn al-Muǧāwir records that al-Manṣūrah was built in 620/1223, immediately after the destruction of the settlement of Ẓafār (Ibn al-Muǧāwir, *Ta‘rīḫ al-Mustabṣir*: $260_{15–17}$). The settlement would therefore still be very new when Ibn al-Muǧāwir visited it.
39. Ibid.: 265_{17}–266_{1}.
40. Ibid.: $265_{16–17}$.
41. See Serjeant 1974: 55, and Smith 1985: 89 n. 30. The vowelling *kanib* is Löfgren's. Serjeant (1974: 72 n. 191) also gives this vocalization but notes that *kinib* is the Ḥaḍramī pronunciation, while Smith (1985: 85) gives a further alternative *kinab* alongside *kanib*.
42. See, for example, White and Barwani 1971: 32 (for the coasts of the former Trucial States, now the UAE); Donaldson 1979: 519–20, 532, *et passim* (for northern Oman); Sivasubramaniam and Ibrahim 1982: 123–4 (for Qatar); and Kuronuma and Abe 1972: 47 (for Kuwait): all these references give the generic name for sardines as عوم / *‘ūm* (or some variant of transliteration) on those more northerly coasts.
43. Polo *Travels* transl. Latham 1958: 68, 309ff.
44. Ibid.: 309–10.
45. Ibid.: 310.
46. Ibid.: 66, 296 and 309. Geographically, Polo is referring here respectively to the Hormuz area, Socotra, and al-Šiḥr.
47. Ibid.: 310.
48. Ibid.: 66.

49. See, for example, Bertram 1948: 28–30 and 34; also Donaldson 1979: 56–8, 60 and 84–5.
50. Polo *Travels* transl. Latham 1958: 66.
51. Ibid.: 66–7.
52. Ibid.: 311.
53. Šams al-Dīn Abū ʻAbdallāh Muḥammad b. ʻAbdallāh b. Muḥammad b. Ibrāhīm b. Muḥammad b. Ibrāhīm b. Yūsuf al-Lawātī al-Tanǧī, d. 779/1377.
54. Miquel *EI*[2]a (article ʻIbn Baṭṭūṭah').
55. Ibn Baṭṭūṭah *Riḥlah*: 2603–4.
56. Ibid.: 2583–4.
57. (Ǧabal) Lumʻān: the ḍammah on the lām is after Gibb (Ibn Baṭṭūṭah *Travels* transl. Gibb 1962: II, 391). The name is not listed in Yāqūt's *Muʻǧam al-buldān*.
58. Ibid.: 258_{6}.
59. Ibid.: 258_{2-3}.
60. *Kalb al-baḥr* (lit. ʻsea dog') is a common word for shark, widespread throughout the Arabic-speaking world. For *luḫ(a)m/luḫmah* as the common South Arabian name for shark, cf. the entries under this term in Landberg *Gloss. datînois*, Dozy *Supplément* and Piamenta 1990–91. For *ǧarǧūr* as the usual name for shark in northern Oman and the Arabian Gulf (pronounced colloquially *yaryūr* in the Gulf), see, for example, Jayakar 1889: 866; MacIvor 1880–81: 60; Lorimer 1908–15: Part II (Appendix E) 2316; Donaldson 1979: 522–3; White and Barwani 1971: 12–13; Sivasubramaniam and Ibrahim 1982: 165 and 169–72; and Kuronuma and Abe 1972: 43. In these latter areas, *luḫm* and its variants tend to signify species of ray rather than sharks proper.
61. See Donaldson 1979: esp. 343–58, *et passim*, for evidence of this, and for background and further references.
62. Ibn Baṭṭūṭah *Riḥlah*: 63615.
63. Ibn Baṭṭūṭah *Travels* transl. Beckingham 1994: IV, 823. I am grateful to Professor G. Rex Smith for directing me to this reference.
64. Gibb notes that the Persian lexicons say only that it is ʻa fish with white scales', which reduced the possible field only a little (Ibn Baṭṭūṭah *Travels* transl. Gibb 1962: II, 393 n. 92).
65. Ibn Baṭṭūṭah *Riḥlah*: 251_{10-11}.
66. H.A.R. Gibb's translation of وهو بها في النهاية السمن as ʻwhich are extremely fat here' (Ibn Baṭṭūṭah *Travels* transl. Gibb 1962: II, 383), in contrast to the present writer's version ʻin which there is a considerable amount of oil', misses the point that the major by-product of sardines in Arabia, and indeed elsewhere, has always been their oil. Further, in a note to the same passage (ibid. n. 74), Gibb somewhat curiously expresses surprise at Ibn Baṭṭūṭah's use of the term *sardīn* and feels there is a need to explain it—which he attempts to do. In the present writer's opinion, no explanation is necessary beyond the fact that Ibn Baṭṭūṭah came from the Mediterranean and is using the word by which sardines are and were known there. There need be no suggestion whatever that the term was ever in use in Southern Arabia.
67. Ibid.: 262_{1-3}.
68. Ibid.: 255_{5-6}.

69. The two places where Ibn Baṭṭūṭah uses the term *ṣunbūq* are in fact Mogadishu in East Africa (ibid.: 251_{21}) and on his trip between Basra and al-Ubullah at the head of the Arabian Gulf (ibid.: 185_{5}), though the same term is current in South Arabia and it may be considered probable that it was equally current there in Ibn Baṭṭūṭah's day.
70. Compare the entries under such roots in the lexicons of, for example, Lane, Piamenta (1990–91), Hava (1899) and Wehr (1971). Dionisius Agius has recorded also the forms *šanbūq* and *šabūq* in al-Muqaddasī's *Aḥsan al-taqāsīm fī ma'rifat al-aqālīm* (Agius 1997: 311 and 326).
71. Löfgren 1936–50, quoted by Piamenta 1990–91: 234b.
72. Yule and Burnell 1903: 788a.
73. Niebuhr *Travels* transl. Heron 1792: II, 138.
74. Ibid.: 114.
75. Kempthorne 1835: 273–4.
76. Ibid.: 270.
77. Arrian transl. Brunt 1983: 386–7; cf. *Periplus* transl. Schoff 1912: 36.
78. Whitelock 1838c: 183; also Whitelock 1838a and 1838b.
79. Wellsted 1837: 103.
80. Pelly 1863: 66–7.
81. Pengelley 1860.
82. Ibid.: 31.
83. Dionisius Agius records that the *šāšah* is called *wāriyyah* in present day Bahrain and he has tentatively identified the same craft with al-Muqaddasī's *walağiyyah* of Iraq (Agius 1997: 322 and 328).
84. For further information on the utility of the *šāšah*, see Donaldson 1980: 483–6.
85. MacIvor 1880–81. Appendix A to Part III of MacIvor's report (pp. 54–67) is devoted to fish.
86. Lorimer 1908–15. Appendix E (pp. 2308–18) to Part II is entitled 'The Fisheries of the Persian Gulf' and draws, *inter alia*, on MacIvor 1880–81.
87. Miles 1919; also Miles 1876–77; Miles 1885–86; Miles 1896; Miles 1910; see also Kelly 1966: 14–15.
88. Prominent examples among such reports are Bertram 1944 and Hartley 1948.
89. Bertram 1948.
90. See, for example, A. von Brandt (1972) who supplies numerous illustrations of almost identical fishing techniques in use in parts of the world widely separated in terms of both location and technological level.

The Ibex Hunt in the Rock Art of Oman

Ali Tigani ElMahi

Rock art is a remarkable source of information not only informative of the way of life of prehistoric people, but also of other aspects that concern anthropologists, historians and artists. It is an ancient intellectual expression that can sometimes offer valuable data on palaeoecology, palaeoeconomy, art, technology and the social and spiritual life of pre-historic communities. Study of rock art has developed greatly in the last decades. It has shifted its focus from the aesthetic and magical–religious to the classification of this art in terms of time and place and the relations between such art forms. In essence, rock art is no longer regarded as the gradual accumulation of isolated pictures each created by the need of the moment (Leroi-Gourhan 1979:37–8). Despite the large and diverse corpus of data offered by rock art, certain problems hamper our studies and appraisal of this source. Among such problems are the unattainable absolute dates of different rock arts. Though such problems are not within the scope of this paper, it remains important to mention that the rock art of Oman has not been fully documented or studied (ElMahi in preparation). At present, the work of Preston (1976), Clarke (1975), Jackli (1980) and al-Šaḥrī (1994) represents all the studies devoted to the rock art of this country.

This paper is an attempt to examine and explain certain rock scenes from southern Oman (Harrison 1977:77). They also occur in Nakhlit, al-Huqf and Wādī Sirab (Gallagher and Harrison 1988:437–42), (Map 1). From northern Oman, one individual has been reported from near Fizz (Harrison 1968: 195–381). In the light of the present data and the zoological geography of the ibex, one can possibly identify the animal depicted in the rock scenes of Dhofar

Figure 1: A drawing of a recently photographed Nubian ibex *Capra ibex nubiana* in southern Oman.

as the Nubian ibex, *Capra ibex nubiana* (Fig. 1). In comparison with other subspecies, the Nubian ibex is relatively small. Its colour is a perfect camouflage since it matches the light tones of the rock in the desert. The male ibex is also distinguished by large dark horns and a long brown-black beard. The long horns of the ibex are untwisted, scimitar-shaped and distinguished by regular anterior ridges that mark the whole length of the horn. The male has 24 to 36 ridges which clearly exhibit the annual growth rings (Grzimek 1988:525). The Nubian ibex inhabits steep mountain terrain. It differs from other desert animals in its dependency on water. For this reason ibex herds are always concentrated in areas which have surface water and rocky pools. The ibex also satisfies its needs for liquid intake by eating plants which contain water and by grazing in the early morning when the water content is highest in the plants (Grzimek 1988:526). The territory of the Nubian ibex is estimated to be *c.* 12 miles. In such a range, the leopard, caracal and eagle are the ibex's enemies, but man is the most dangerous enemy (Grzimek 1988:526). Nonetheless, the ibex is one of the most difficult animals to hunt. It lives in very difficult, steep terrain and rocky mountains. It has gone further than other animals in developing short muscular limbs and chunky rubbery hooves as an adaptation to rocky mountains and loose stony screes (Kingdom 1990:159). In addition, the ibex maintains a camouflage colour that matches the colour of its habitat. These qualities and habitat impede access to the animal and reduce the frequency of contact between the ibex and its enemies.

Man has known the ibex from very early times. The Bible makes a reference to an animal which is assumed to be the ibex when Isaac asks Esau to find him game (Genesis:23, 3). The setting of these biblical events is the steep mountains close to the Dead Sea which constitute part of the ibex's natural habitat to the present day (Grzimek 1988:525; Harrison and Bates 1991:183). It has also been suggested that the ibex was a symbol of the moon god in the days of the Queen of Sheba and that carved ibex heads decorated a capital found in the temple of the moon god in Marib (Harrison and Bates 1991:183). Furthermore,

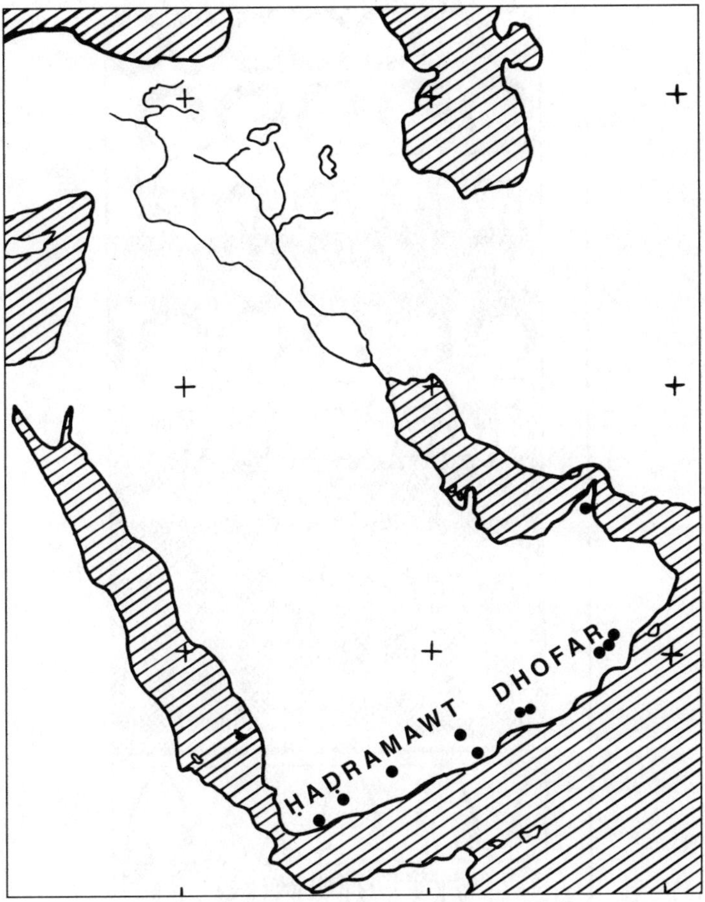

Map 1: Distribution of ibex in Southern Arabia.

rock art studies from northern Yemen report a high frequency of the ibex (Jung 1994: 149.). The ibex is indeed considered the commonest motif of decoration in southern Arabia (Serjeant 1976: 7).

The Traditional Ibex Hunt

Detailed knowledge of the methods of ibex hunting is scarce in Arabian literature. Reports generally refer to ambushes without details. Kingdom (1990: 195), for example, mentions that ibex are ambushed at water holes, but gives no details of the techniques employed in the ambush or the organization of the hunt.

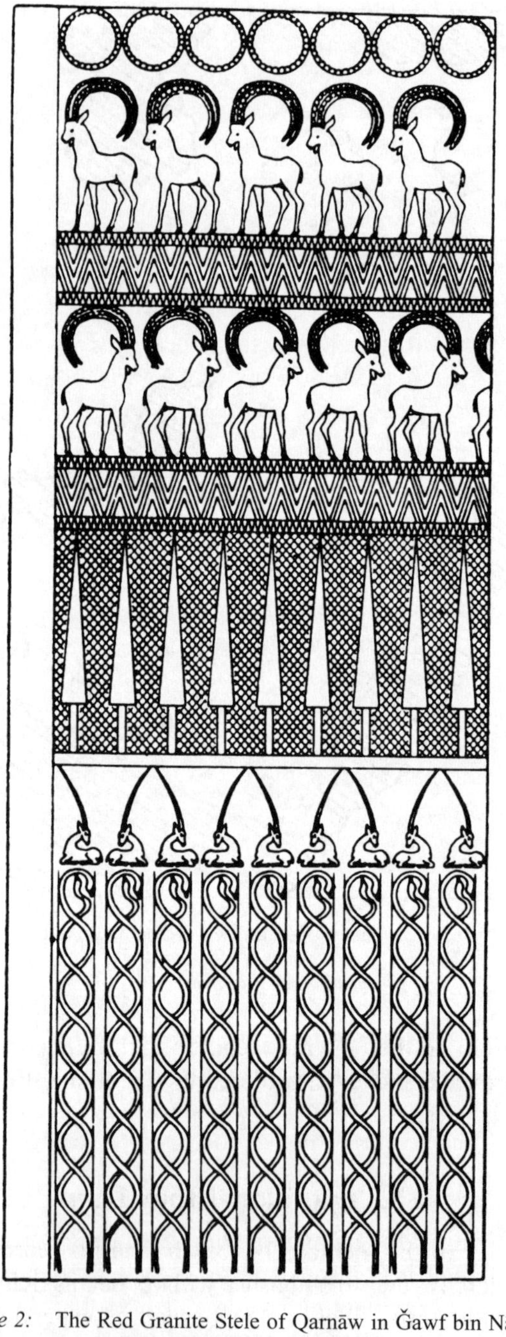

Figure 2: The Red Granite Stele of Qarnāw in Ǧawf bin Nāṣir.
(After Serjeant 1976, Figure 1)

In Oman, our efforts to trace old ways and methods of the hunt from elderly people were not successful. The records of Oman also fail to furnish us with any description of the traditional ibex hunt. Nonetheless, a considerable body of reports on the ibex hunt and its rituals comes from Ḥaḍramawt in southern Arabia. Among the first documents of the ibex hunt in Ḥaḍramawt are the works of H. Ingrams (1937: 12–13) and D. Ingrams (1947: 60) in the late thirties and forties. The two authors suggest that the origin of the organized ibex hunt in Ḥaḍramawt is pre-Islamic. Moreover, Serjeant (1976) records valuable details of the ibex hunt and its organization in Ḥaḍramawt. Again, Rodionov (1994: 123) documents ibex hunt ceremonies in Ḥaḍramawt and considers it the surviving practices of ancient religious ceremonies. As a result, a considerable part of the southern Arabian lore of the ibex hunt has been successfully documented. In addition, the geography, archaeology and history of southern Arabia assert the close connection between Dhofar and Ḥaḍramawt. Therefore, the traditional methods and techniques of the ibex hunt in Ḥaḍramawt will aid our attempt to understand and interpret the rock scenes from Dhofar.

Serjeant (1976: 27) reports from Tarīm in Wādī Ḥaḍramawt three types of ibex hunting: encountering an animal by chance on the road or elsewhere, killing an animal by shooting it from ambush using guns only, and the hunt employing both nets and guns. He also reports four classes of participant in the hunt: the beaters, the gunmen in concealment, the men in ambush with clubs and daggers, and the net-men in the hide. The headman sets up the poles and the men take up their stance behind the net with their knives, one or more at each stake or pole according to the numbers of men. Ten beaters out of a hunting party of thirty search for the ibex and drive it down towards the wadi. Once the ibex is in a wadi, it is either shot by the gunmen lying concealed behind the rocks or caught in the nets. The moment the prey is caught in net, the net-men throw the rest of it over the ibex to entangle it in the net. The beaters follow and the ibex is hemmed in on all sides. Although three to four nets are used in a one-day hunt, some ibex manage to break away to the safety of the mountains. The nets are usually woven of rope about a man's height (*qāmah*) and they vary in length between eighteen to twenty cubits. In the village of ʻInāt the nets are made of black goat wool. When the net is set, it is supported by palm stakes dug in the ground like posts. The length of the palm stakes is approximately two *qāmah*s. The poles are set at each end of the net and two or three in the middle. Usually three to four nets are used in a one-day hunt.

Serjeant (1976: 34–7) makes another reference to the ibex hunt in Wāḥidī territory where they hunt the ibex employing nets. He reports that once the ibex is entangled in the net, it is dispatched by dagger thrusts. Moreover, Serjeant (1976: 51–2) describes the hunting customs of the villagers of Madūdah in the following way. The headman of the participants in the hunt orders each man to take a pole (which represents a net) to a certain pass or wadi in the mountainous hunting ground. The net-men set their nets on the paths by inserting iron hooks in crevices of the rock. They use an iron hook for each side of the net and put the poles at certain intervals in the net. Each net is to be used by five to six men. The gunmen and the beaters are dispersed, but they are not to ascend by the paths used by the net-men. The gunmen are usually positioned on flat plateau-like mountain tops where each one sits down behind a number of stones built to conceal him from the flushed ibex. The beaters are usually fifteen persons or more. They scan the area and drive the game towards the concealed gunmen on top of the wadi or path and the nets below. The gunmen open fire as the ibex come within range. The scared ibex which are not hit by the bullets are eventually driven towards the nets. Moreover, the people of Madūdah village have a local custom known as 'the mock ibex hunt'. In such a ceremony, nets are set across a street and a man wearing ibex's horns will be chased until he is trapped in the nets (Plate 1).

As for the use of dogs in the ibex hunt, Serjeant (1976:32) informs us that the village of 'Ināt is known for its good breed of hunting dog. There, the dogs are well fed on dates, bread, meat, etc., and properly washed. They are well looked after since they are good hunters and offer great assistance to their masters in the hunt. In 'Ināt, the people claim that this breed of dogs is distinguished from both the usual 'pie-dog' of the country and the famous Saluki breed. Interestingly enough, Serjeant (ibid.) makes a reference to a pre-Islamic lamp of a hunting dog and an ibex from Eritrea (Plate 2). Moreover, Serjeant (1976:32) describes the use of dogs in the ibex hunt by the people of 'Ināt village as follows:

> On coming to the hunting area a man of 'Ināt will say to his dog,
> 'Istikbir' (pick out a big one), and along come the dogs wagging their tails. These dogs attack the game, and, seizing hold of it by the testicles so that the animal cannot move, they cling to them until the hunter arrives.

It would be more efficacious to consolidate the information provided from southern Arabia on the techniques of hunting the ibex with other areas of similar ecological conditions and reasonably equal level of technology. According to our knowledge, the Beja of eastern Sudan are the other community in the region that retains traditional methods in hunting the ibex. This community inhabits similar eco-systems in mountain ranges. The Beja follow a semi-nomadic, seasonal transhumance and are distributed into small groups in the Red Sea hills. During several trips to the Red Sea hills, the author was informed by elderly locals that hunting *'ayū*, the ibex, was hard and not always successful. In the past they hunted the ibex using two methods. The first method involved the

Plate 1: The hunting net and the mock ibex hunt in Madūdah village. (After Serjeant 1996, plate 2)

Plate 2: A bronze lamp: A hunting dog seizing an ibex. (Notice the ibex's horn is broken.) From Eritrea, a type is also found in Yemen. (After Serjeant 1976, plate 1)

building of an enclosure using rocks. It had to be well camouflaged and with one entrance. The enclosure also had be in an area where ibex frequently visited or passed through. The hunters were divided into groups. One group surveyed the area for a band of ibex and drove it in the direction of the enclosure, while the members of the second group, who were concealed in different spots, prevented the ibex from escaping and kept it on course towards the enclosure. Once some animals were inside the camouflaged enclosure, the Beja hunters closed on them using their knives and throwing sticks to end the pursuit. My informants repeatedly said that the hunt was very difficult and hard and not always successful. Moreover, when it was successful, it was not rewarding in view of the large number of men engaged in the pursuit.

The second traditional method of hunting the ibex is based on a practice similar to the first. Here, the enclosure is replaced by nets set and camouflaged in certain locations with a group of men concealed. Again, these nets are placed in water localities which are visited frequently by ibex herds. Once the animals approach the water, a group of hidden men will drive the ibex vigorously into the camouflaged nets. The ibex will try to escape through the nets but will eventually get entangled in them. The moment an ibex is caught in the nets, the pursuers descend on it. According to the informants, the hunters usually catch the males which have big horns that easily get entangled in the nets. They also explained that this hunting method requires a lot of patience and endurance.

It is obvious that the reviewed ethnographic data of the two areas bear great resemblance. The methods and techniques used for hunting the ibex in Ḥaḍramawt and in the Red Sea hills of the Sudan are not different. In fact, they are all based on the same principles. The practice of the Beja in the ibex hunt is almost identical to the methods and techniques used in southern Arabia. The only exception is that the hunters in the area of Ḥaḍramawt use fire-arms while the Beja have no access to such weapons.

The Rock Scenes of Dhofar

At this stage, it is important to realize that, like many other hunting operations, the ibex hunt consists of different phases. As described from various villages in Ḥaḍramawt, the traditional ibex hunt consists of three complementary phases. First, the search and drive of the game towards a certain locality; second, the shooting; third, the nets. Each of these hunting phases has its own activities complementary to the others. Consequently, it is possible to assume that the ibex hunt in Dhofar was equally composed of different phases to secure a successful hunt. The ibex's ability and adaptation, and the difficult environment necessitate such complementary phases of organization for any attempt to hunt it down.

Therefore, the ancient Dhofari artist could have chosen a certain moment of activity within these phases for depiction. In other words, what is portrayed on these rock scenes represents a single snapshot from a series of snapshots which constitute the whole ibex hunt.

The rock art of Dhofar has been appropriately documented where the ibex is notably depicted (al-Šaḥrī 1994). The scene in Plate 3 is painted using the single line technique. The scene presents a group of figures in action. It is one single stage of the a hunt. The painted figures in this scene number 21 ibex and four

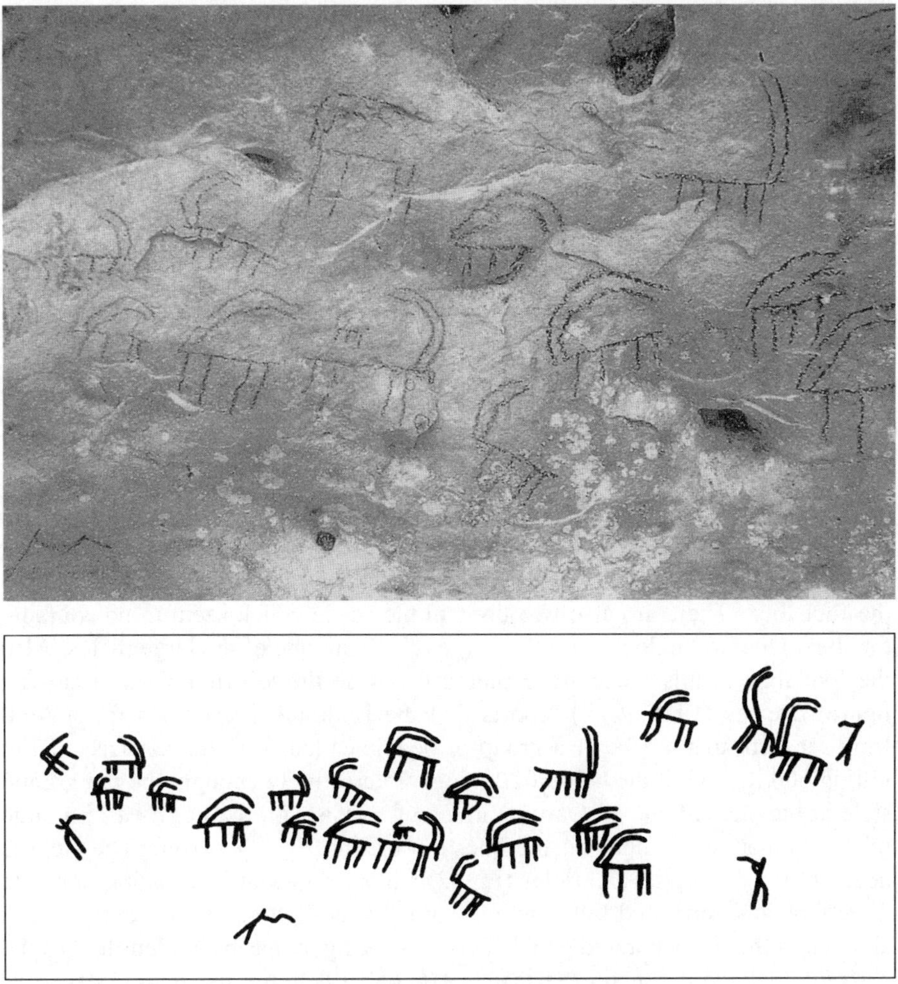

Plate 3: A rock scene from Dhofar. (After al-Šaḥrī 1994, plate 181)

men. Out of the 21 ibex, seventeen are depicted facing in one direction, to the left. The other four ibex are facing the opposite direction, to the right. The figures of the men are depicted as facing to the left. It is noticeable that the men are depicted in postures that show their arms raised. This would seem to indicate that they are either flushing and driving the animals or chasing them. It is also noticeable that the ibex are almost all in one line. Actually this indicates that they are fleeing from the men. Moreover, the men seem to be on one side of the animals and they form almost half a circle. Taking into consideration the foregoing observations, the scene can be explained in one of the following ways. It may be a group of hunters driving ibex and directing them towards a certain locality where another group of hunters is awaiting their arrival. This specific locality can be a narrow path in the mountains where the hunters have set nets similar to the contemporary traditional methods. In other words, the scene might possibly be one phase of a hunting operation which consists of two or three hunting phases. Another possibility is that it is a simple hunting scene where a group of men are chasing a herd of ibex. This can possibly mean that we are dealing with one simple, single phase of a hunting operation. This type of simple hunt does not involve any organization or planning and the pursuit does not include any phases where each individual hunter has a specific role. It is typical of the type of hunting, encountering an animal by chance, described by Serjeant (1976:27) in Ḥaḍramawt.

Plate 4 is also a hunting scene which includes a female camel with her young one. What interests us here is the ibex and the hunt scene. The scene contains four ibex, of which two can easily be identified as males and the other two as females. The long horns with prominent ridges clearly distinguish the males here, while the females are smaller and their horns do not show ridges. There are also four men with their arms raised. The men are not armed with spears or sticks. It is also noticeable that the men are in different positions in relation to the four ibex. There are also two dogs in the scene which seem to be coursing the ibex. One of the dogs is on the verge of seizing one of the large males. Also the four ibex in this scene are depicted facing to the left running in a zig-zag figure. Drewes (1954:93–4) reports that the Ḥaḍramī inscriptions from Wādī Irma set forth that a tribe or a group of people called Aḥrār have succeeded in killing 600 ibex with the help of 200 dogs. Interestingly enough, the red granite stele at the ancient city of Qarnāw in Ǧawf b. Nāṣir on the north-eastern edge of the Yemen sheds light on the question of this zig-zag design. The stele is headed by a row of seven circles (Fig. 2) and two lines of ibex facing opposite directions and separated by a zig-zag path. At the bottom are a group of oryx and below them a decorated panel. This zig-zag figure has been identified as the conventionalized mountain (Serjeant 1976:65). Likewise, the zig-zag design is also present in the door jambs from Ḫaribat Āl ʿAlī near al-Ḥazm in Ǧawf

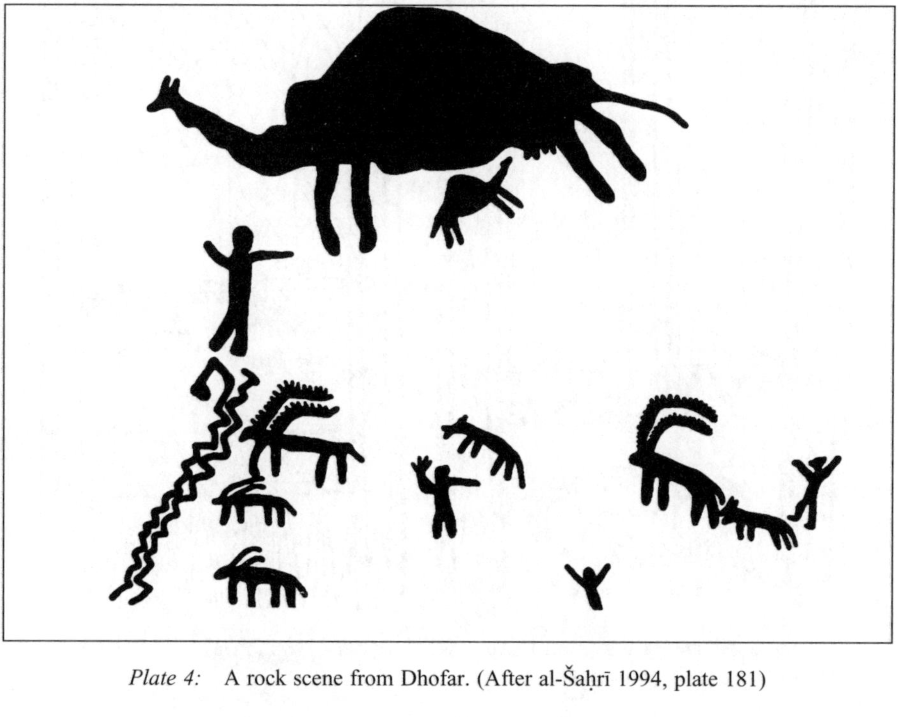

Plate 4: A rock scene from Dhofar. (After al-Šaḥrī 1994, plate 181)

b. Nāṣir (Fig. 3). Here, this design represents a net. However, some reservations are cast over this identification (Serjeant 1976:104). Hence, it seems that the zig-zag design has two possible interpretations: mountain or hunting net. The significant aspect here is that the zig-zag design is continuously associated with the ibex in Ḥaḍramawt and in Dhofar. Therefore, it must be a crucial element in both the ibex hunt and the terrain. Furthermore, it is clear that this scene

Figure 3: Door jambs from Ḥaribat Āl ʻAlī near al-Ḥazm in Ğawf bin Nāṣir. (After Serjeant 1976, figure 9)

presents one phase of the hunting operation used for hunting this mountain dweller in Oman.

Firearms deserve attention in this context of parallelism established for the ibex hunt in the Ḥaḍramawt and Dhofar areas. Firearms were introduced into southern Arabia early in the 9th/15th century. They gradually replaced the bow and arrow in combat and in the hunt. The bow and arrow were presumably crucial elements in the traditional ibex hunt before the introduction of firearms in southern Arabia. It seems that firearms are the only modern, intrusive, technical elements in addition to the methods and techniques of the traditional ibex hunt. In this context, Serjeant (1976:95) informs us that before the introduction of firearms in Ḥaḍramawt, the bowmen had the same stance as the gunmen today. Further on, among the carvings of Ḥuṣn al-'Urr, Serjeant (ibid.) reports seeing a carving of a man in a sort of kilt shooting at an ibex with a bow and arrow. Once more, rock drawings in the Ḥā'il area in northern Saudi Arabia confirm the use of the bow and arrows in the ibex hunt (Winnet and Reed 1973:80).

In conclusion, this paper has highlighted some aspects of the rock art of Oman. It has gone beyond the simple description of the graphic delineation of rock art to offer reasonable explanations of certain rock scenes. The paper has drawn attention to the fact that rock art can be viewed as a series of snapshots. A rock scene presenting certain figures can be one single snapshot in a whole series which actually forms the main theme of a particular activity that the artist had in mind when he depicted the scene. In other words, the ancient artist chose to depict a certain moment of activity from a wider temporally-extended activity. This chosen moment of activity conceptualizes the meaning of the theme depicted on the rock.

The paper has focused on the details of hunting techniques and pursued ethnographic data to establish an analogy between the past and present hunting practices. Although such details might look simple, they prove to be of significant value. They are key principles in understanding these rock hunting scenes. In reality, these details are the accumulated human experience and knowledge by which man has successfully interacted with animals. Thus, the rock art scenes under discussion reflect the relative sophistication of the hunting techniques which in turn add to the complexity of the rock art scenes. Given the concept of snapshots and the observed level of organization in the ibex hunt among traditional societies the rock scenes take on meaning. Equally, the paper has demonstrated that ethnographic information and the practices of contemporary traditional communities can be of great assistance to the understanding of rock art. Without the practices of contemporary traditional communities and ethnographic information our understanding of these rock art scenes from Oman would be incomplete.

References

The Bible: *Genesis*:23, 3.

Clarke, C. 1975. The rock art of Oman. *JOS* 1: 113–122.

Drewes, A.J. 1954. Some Hadrami inscriptions. *Bibliotheca Orientalis*. 3–4: 93–94.

ElMahi, A.T. (in preparation), Problems of faunal elements in the rock art of Oman.

Gallagher, M. and Harrison D. 1988. The small mammals of the sand. *JOS*, A Special Report 3: 437–42.

Grzimek, B. 1988. *Grzimek's Animal Life Encyclopedia*, V. New York.

Harrison, D. L. 1968. *The Mammals of Arabia: Carnivora, Hyracoidea Ardiodactyla*, II. London.

Harrison, D. L. 1977. Mammals obtained by the Expedition with a check-list of the mammals of southern Oman. *JOS*, A Special Report: Flora and Fauna.

Harrison, D.L. and Bates, P.J. 1991. *The Mammals of Arabia*. London.

Ingrams, H. 1937. A dance of the ibex hunters in the Ḥaḍramawt. *Man* 38.

Ingrams, D. 1949. *A Survey of the Social and Economic Conditions in the Aden Protectorate*. Asmara.

Jackli, R. 1980 (unpublished report). *Rock Art in Oman. An Introductory Presentation.*

Jung, M. 1994. A map of southern Yemeni rock art with notes on some of the subjects depicted. *PSAS* 24: 135–156.

Kingdom, J. 1990. *Arabian Mammals. A Natural History*. London.

Leroi-Gourhan, A. 1997. The evolution of Palaeolithic art. *Hunters, Farmers, and Civilizations: Old World Archaeology*. Scientific American, San Francisco, 37–47.

Preston, K. 1976. An introduction to the anthropomorphic content of the rock art of Jebel Akhdar. *JOS* 2: 17–38.

Rodionov, M. 1994. The ibex hunt ceremony in Ḥaḍramawt today. *NAS* 2: 123–30.

Serjeant, R.B. 1976. *Southern Arabian Hunt*. London.

al-Shaḥrī, ʿA. 1994. *Ẓufār—Kitābātu-hā wa-nuqūšu-hā al-qadīmah*. Dubai.

Winnet, F.V. and Reed, W.L. 1973. An archaeological-epigraphical survey of the the Ha'il area of northern Saudi Arabia. *Berytus* l: 27.

Smuggling and International Politics in the Red Sea in the Late Ottoman Period

Caesar E. Farah

Smuggling, or the illegal traffic in goods, and piracy have been pursued by inhabitants of the Arabian littoral from time immemorial. But it is only in the age of colonial expansion that it becomes a serious problem for the Ottoman state. When the Ottomans inherited the Red Sea region in the 1520s, they found themselves chasing Portuguese. Two centuries later they were locked in a struggle with the British, and in the late nineteenth century with the Italians in often futile attempts to prevent their interference with shipping in the Red Sea.

In the sixteenth and seventeenth centuries the Ottomans tolerated to a certain extent smuggling and the evasion of customs duty payments entailed by it, particularly when such payments did not contribute materially to the revenue of the region, nor constituted a major factor in its economy. But as the Ottoman administration found itself strapped for revenue in the nineteenth century and with the British establishing themselves in the Aden region in order to compete with Ottoman trade by promoting their own in the Yemeni highlands, the Ottomans began to entertain measures for tightening control over the commerce of the Red Sea. With smuggling in contraband ever on the increase in the late nineteenth century, and now affecting directly the security of their domains, the Ottoman government acquired the added incentive to put an end to it.

The matter took on a serious dimension when the Ottomans lost control over the Eritrean side of the Red Sea to the Italians at the end of the nineteenth century. With a firm foothold at Muṣawwa‘, the Italians not only encouraged traffic in contraband, but used the smuggling of weapons to ‘Asīrī chiefs in rebellion against Ottoman authority as the means for cementing ties both with them and with the Imām of Yemen, and for promoting their own commercial and political interests there.

One might argue then that it is with the intensification of international political and commercial rivalry in the lower Red Sea that we begin to witness an increase in smuggling and piracy, both private and state sponsored.

The International Setting

The two principal foreign powers manoeuvring for position in the lower Red Sea in the nineteenth century were thus the British and the Italians. After decades of futile attempts, the British acquired at last in 1839 a foothold at Aden and by the end of the 1850s were seeking to expand their influence into the highlands for the purpose of promoting British commerce. Indeed, they became actively involved in the political struggles of the Peninsula with the Government of India promoting arms shipment to allies such as the Ṣabāḥs of Kuwait against ʻAbd al-ʻAzīz ibn Rašīd who was locked in struggle with Ottoman backing against both the House of Saʻūd of Nağd and the Ṣabāḥs. They also provided support to Imām Yaḥyā of the Yemeni highlands in his rebellion against the Ottomans.[1]

In the 1880s the Italians were aiming for the Bay of ʻAṣāb in present-day Eritrea while denying the Egyptians any legitimate claim to the area over which they had exercised influence, if not control, for some time. In this undertaking they had the blessing of the British who entertained similar ambitions in the Bāb al-Mandab area.[2]

The rapprochement between England and Italy was of concern to Germany, which country suspected that it might lead to control of the entrance to the lower Red Sea, ensure England of Italian help to expand her influence in the Aden hinterland and support for Italy to build a naval base on the opposite side of the Red Sea. Germany was displeased with Italy because she had not supported the *Baghdad Bahn* project.[3] Chancellor von Bülow notified his ambassador in Rome that Italy, as an ally of Germany, should make no commitment or concession to England in exchange for support in the Red Sea because of her negative attitude towards the railroad scheme. The Italian minister in Berlin alleged that no such deals were in the offing and that it was simply rumour.[4]

That Italy coveted influence in southern Arabia is evident from its naval actions in that region. She missed very few opportunities to castigate the Turkish authorities in the Yemen 'on the slightest pretext' and the British vice-consul in Hodeida wrote to his government urging that they checkmate Italy's overt designs and aspirations in Yemen.[5] They made demands that the Ottomans simply could not meet without compromising their legitimacy and sovereignty. The Italians would in turn respond by dispatching units of their fleet to the

Yemen to menace and intimidate coastal towns like Hodeida, Kamarān, Perim, Mocha, and the island of Farasān.[6]

With Italy threatening to take matters into its own hands and to bombard ports from which pirates and smugglers issued forth, the Ottoman government was pressured into accepting terms imposed by the Italians. They agreed to five conditions demanded by the Italian Foreign Ministry in order to put an end to piracy. According to a telegram dispatched by the Foreign Ministry to Commandant Arnone who was stationed off the coast of Mīdī, the first stipulation called for the destruction of the piratical *sunbūk*s[7] and a joint *zaptnāme* (restraining order) to that effect to be signed with his Ottoman counterpart.

Secondly, Italian corsairs held by the Ottomans were to be delivered within two months to Italian officials stationed at Muṣawwa‘. According to a telegram of 27 October 1318/1900 dispatched jointly by Kāmil and Rušdī Beys, the captives would be released one month after Arnone destroyed the *sunbūk* and the Italian fleet lifted its siege of Mīdī. After their release, Arnone would then sail to Hodeida and receive the Italian captives.

Thirdly, the Ottoman fleet was to track down the piratical *sunbūk*s and wipe them out and the Ottoman navy was to issue orders assigning the necessary warships to Red Sea service. Pirates seized were to be tried and punished to the full extent of the law.

Fourthly, Italy's claim of 19,000 MT$[8] compensation for losses to pirates was to be paid from the revenues of the (Yemen) *vilayet* as authorized by the central government on 6 October 1900. Compensation for those killed in the amount of 6500 MT$ had been authorized by the telegram of 26 October. These two assurances would be delivered to Arnone when he arrived in Hodeida.

Fifthly, the west coast of the Red Sea was also to be rid of piracy and the Italian government would protect equally *sunbūk*s of all nationalities according to established laws, particularly as concerns non-discrimination in levying customs duties. These terms were approved in a special session of the Porte's ministers and communicated both to its officials in Yemen and the Italian government.[9]

Not to be denied, the French staked out a claim to Šayẖ Sa‘īd. They clashed with the Italians when both sought to control Zayla‘. England supported Italian efforts to gain control over the key port of Muṣawwa‘ opposite the Yemeni coast which then was Egyptian territory and a key town for trade with Ethiopia and the Sudan, even though the British acknowledged that it was 'part and parcel of Ottoman land'.[10]

England and Italy were on close friendly relations in this region, albeit England had gained control of Egypt at this time and one would have expected that it would have been in her interest to defend the Egyptian position as concerns Muṣawwa‘. Instead, she looked the other way, ignored the breach of the Treaty of Paris (1856) implied in Italy's occupation of Ethiopia, and Italy thus obtained the 'best plum of the pudding'.[11] Instead of defending it, Col Chemside, governor of the Egyptian Red Sea littoral, handed Muṣawwa' over to the Italians. There were protests from the Khedive of Egypt, St Petersburg, and Vienna, but the Sultan balked at sending warships to undo the action of the British, although he had reasons to fear also the presence of French, Italian and British warships in the area. The inhabitants of Muṣawwa' and of Benlil, whence Egyptian garrisons were forced out, had hoped the Ottoman government would challenge the action but prudence and a weak naval presence decreed otherwise.[12]

Protests to all the capitals of Europe were for naught. Italy argued that the action was necessary both to 'pacify' the land and to counter 'the lack of security'. The German press vehemently opposed Italy's action and supported the Sultan's sovereign rights but to no avail. The Negus, ruler of Ethiopia, was to be appeased by 'rich gifts'. The Italian press alluded to a deal between Great Britain and Italy: the latter would abandon claims to Mediterranean lands while the former would allow her a free hand in the Red Sea.[13]

Piracy and politics

The Italo-Ottoman agreement to control piracy in the Red Sea did not yield immediate results. Within a year the German government was reporting intensified piratical activity on the part of both Arab and Italian-protected *sunbūk*s. In October of 1901 the Italian *sunbūk Dancoli* was sailing with a load of camels from the Arabian coast to Muṣawwa'. She was attacked near the islands of Farasān and pillaged. One crewman was enslaved. Shortly thereafter the *sunbūk Marzūq* carrying 27 pilgrims was attacked while heading in the opposite direction. The entire crew were enslaved. The Italian Embassy in Istanbul lodged severe warnings with the Sublime Porte over such acts of piracy emanating from Arabian shores. The protests of 19, 26 and 28 November and of 2 December 1901 pointed the finger of blame at the chief pirate, one Said Ben Abdul Rahi (*sic*) and to another, Abdul Ben Aubesh (*sic*). The acts were alleged to have been perpetuated within sight of the Ottoman corvette *Beyrut*. It was further alleged that such piracy had been taking place off the coast of Jeddah. The Royal Italian Embassy stated, furthermore, that if the Ottoman government did not take measures to suppress piracy in the Red Sea, Italy would do so itself.

In March 1902 a pirate *sunbūk* manned by 40 men armed with Remington rifles attacked the island of Dahlak. The wife of the Italian *zaptiye* (police officer) was killed, a carabiniere wounded, and a number of native women violated. The incident was reported in detail to the Ottoman embassy in Rome in an aide mémoire and to the Ottoman Foreign Minister Reshid Pasa on 27 April.

In May 1902 the Italian *sunbūk*s *Malac* and *Fulca* were attacked by two pirate ships; one escaped, the other was captured and relieved of its cargo of camels. Three *sunbūk*s were thus attacked in less than three months. But it was not only *sunbūk*s bearing the Italian flag that were assaulted. In the same month of May an Ottoman *sunbūk* carrying two hundred packets of merchandise belonging to Muṣawwaʿ merchants was captured by pirates from the Arabian coast near Cos.

On 27 May 1902 the Porte informed the Italian Embassy of the steps it would take to end piracy in the Red Sea. The measures consisted of sending four steamships of the *maẖṣūṣah* (special) class to the Red Sea but by July there was still no evidence that the measures had been carried out. Then in September 1902 a pirate *sunbūk* with nineteen crewmen and fourteen rifles attacked the village of Dubell (?) on the island of Dahlak near Muṣawwaʿ and carried off booty worth 20,000 MT$, even obliging Arab fishermen to help load it on a *sunbūk* anchored off shore, which they had stolen.[14]

The Italian government was no longer prepared to delay executing its ultimatum of direct intervention to end piracy. The Ottoman ambassador in Berlin, Tevfik Pasha, had sent an urgent ciphered message to his government stressing the need to delay Italian action in view of the fact that the Porte had been conciliatory in the face of the Italian ultimatum and stating that some pirates had been apprehended.[15]

Germany interceded with Italy on behalf of the Ottoman government to settle the problem of piracy peacefully, assuring her ally that more Ottoman gunboats and a cruiser would be sent into the Red Sea to interdict the smuggling of weapons. The Kaiser's government alleged that it could not be proved that weapon smuggling was from the Eritrean coast or that Italy was involved in it. Nevertheless, the German ambassador in Istanbul was instructed to tell the Foreign Minister, Rifaat, that his country and the other three countries involved in the Red Sea (France, Italy and England) were opposed to any form of arms smuggling.[16]

Who Were the Pirates?

The so-called pirates were members of the leading and powerful clans of the Arabian coast. This was evident from the report submitted by Col Riza Bey and Lt Col Rušdī Bey concerning those captured, to wit Muḥammad Ibrāhīm and Salīm Adham and Muḥammad ʿUṯmān as well as the eldest son of Šayẖ Ṭāhir of Mīdī.[17] Upon learning of the Šayẖ's implied involvement in piracy, the Italian government demanded he be arrested and handed over to them and the fulfilment of other demands in the ultimatum, otherwise they would commence the bombardment of Mīdī.

Again in May 1902 an Ottoman *sunbūk* carrying 200 barrels of petrol and 35 packets of merchandise belonging to Muṣawwa‘ merchants was captured by pirates operating off the Arabian coast near Cos.

The Ottoman governor moved quickly to arrest Ibrāhīm, Adham and ‘Uṯmān as well as the eldest son of Šayẖ Ṭāhir and to give chase to their *sunbūk*.[18] The arrest followed an ultimatum from the Italian commandant threatening to bombard Mīdī. Riza informed Arnone that he could not deliver Šayẖ Ṭāhir to him because it would have grave consequences for Ottoman troops, but that he was prepared to have him punished as stipulated in an imperial order from Istanbul. Šayẖ Ṭāhir was of considerable importance in the region and the rebellion that might ensue from his being handed over to the Italians would prove disastrous to Ottoman presence in Yemen. But Arnone insisted and notified the grand council of the *vilayet*'s admiralty that if Ṭāhir was not handed over with 6,500 MT$ in blood money for Italians of Muṣawwa‘ killed and wounded he would provide no guarantee that his ships *Nourallah* and *Césaré* could avoid hitting Ottoman troops when they opened fire.[19]

The Porte dispatched a telegram to Rome to reiterate its position that the right to punish was that of the Ottoman government, not the Italian commander's, and urged that he be so notified in the interest of avoiding belligerency.[20] But before any action could be taken the Ottoman government received a telegram of 'great urgency' from 'Aptullah Pasha stating that Arnone had indeed bombarded and levelled Mīdī, forcing all the inhabitants to flee with only imperial troops remaining behind. The Italian government viewed the whole matter not as a gross violation of international customs but as a natural outgrowth of hostility. The Ottoman Foreign Ministry instructed its ambassador in Rome to notify the Italian government of the event and to urge it put an end to such outrages. However, according to a report in *L'Eclaire* (3 November 1902), relayed from Aden the day before, the Italian government had deemed the guarantees offered by the Ottoman government as insufficient and had issued orders to its commander to bombard Mīdī on 2 November.[21]

The Ottomans were caught in an awkward position. Following their bombardments, and notwithstanding the fact that some of the pirates had been captured, the Italians still insisted it was not enough. They had proceeded to bombard the littoral, only an hour away from Mīdī, three days after they bombarded Mīdī itself. The argument they used: *sunbūk*s carrying the Italian flag were being attacked by the powerful Banī Marwān of the Yemeni coast, who were sufficiently aroused now to attack even the Ottoman camp that same night.[22]

Angered over such high-handed action and Italian refusal to accept assurances of the Ottoman government, the Sultan's government despatched urgent messages to its embassy in Berlin in which Tevfik Pasha was enjoined to prevail on the German Chancellor to intercede with the Italian government in order to obtain the withdrawal of their fleet and negotiate areas of disagreement.[23]

The Ottoman government was fully aware of the fact that the Italians were seeking any pretext to encroach upon the Yemeni littoral using piracy now as the main pretext when they themselves were equally guilty of sponsoring the same from their possessions on the opposite side of the Red Sea. The ultimatum, scheduled to expire on 18 October, had given little time, as designed, for the Ottomans to respond. Instead, they had called upon the German Kaiser to exert pressure on the Italians to hold off until a full investigation could be conducted, the corsairs interdicted and goods taken by them restored to their rightful owners.

Germany, however, had not succeeded in restraining Italy from carrying out coercive measures as her policy objectives clearly aimed at extending Italian influence to Yemen. Promoting her own brand of piracy, in which Italian agents played no small part, was designed to provoke the retaliation of the powerful Arabian tribes of the littoral. It was a part of Italy's overall objective in driving a wedge between them and legitimate authority.[24]

Tevfik Pasha, Ottoman ambassador in Berlin, relayed to German Chancellor von Bülow on 21 October his government's request that Germany exert further pressure on Italy to desist.[25] But the commander of the Italian cruiser *Piémonte* stationed off the port of Hodeida claimed he had not received instructions to desist, further alleging that corsairs had taken loot from the island of Dahlak.[26] The amusing side of it was that the pirates were able to take the loot by *sunbūk*s to Muṣawwa' right past the Italian warship and to get 19,000 MT$ for it. An angered Ottoman commander sought to head off bombardment by having enough time to reinforce his Mīdī garrison with four additional battalions and one battery, hoping in so doing that the Italian flotilla of four warships would sail away.[27]

The predicament of the Ottoman government is perhaps best stated in a report by a marine officer who spent many years in the Red Sea countering slave trade. He describes Mīdī as nearly inaccessible by land or sea. Its chief could call upon 20,000 warriors if need be. He also notes that there was no Ottoman post in the area and that to come upon it by sea would require traversing three and a half miles of narrow winding waterway. To approach it by land would enable the Ottomans to get no closer than 50 miles from it.[28]

To compound the woes of the Ottoman navy in the Red Sea, envious French reporters with no love for Germany were asserting that the Italians, in gaining terms from the Ottomans, albeit not abiding by them, were able to accomplish what a French naval squadron (5 large ships and 2 counter-torpedo boats) were not able to do, namely win compensation for French losses to Mīdī pirates.

Italy's success was attributed to her friendship with Germany and the intercession of the Kaiser.[29]

The British too were questioning whether it was not time for all the powers trading in the Red Sea to act in concert to counter piracy after the Italians had so boldly pointed the way. British shipping had also been subject to piratical raids and it was recognized that the Ottomans were either too weak or apathetic to counter them. The British had extended protection to Ḥaḍramī shipping and to their merchants stationed in Hodeida if they could prove they were born in Ḥaḍramawt or had been established in Aden beforehand. Ottoman authorities, however, refused to acknowledge British right of protection and the argument lasted for three years between the Ottoman and British authorities.

The Ottomans in the meanwhile took special care to protect Ḥaḍramī trading out of Hodeida although they could not extend such protection to al-Ḫawḫah, whence Ḥaḍramīs transported certain quantities of coffee to Aden without paying their share of customs in the absence of Ottoman officials to survey the area. Goods of all kind, especially tobacco, reached Aden without the Ottomans being able to interdict such contraband or collect customs where due. Moreover, there was some understanding with the *mudīr* of Hodeida to let such goods slip through without customs being collected on them. Worse yet, every week large quantities of Maria Theresa dollars, whose import was prohibited, still managed to reach the Yemeni highlands via the ports of Hodeida and Mocha where they were still more popular than the Ottoman *Mecidiye*.[30]

The Ottomans were confronted with the necessity both to patrol over 400 miles of Yemeni coastline and to match and overcome the strength of the tribes engaged in smuggling. A reporter reiterated the strength of the Banī Marwān and their ability to muster 20,000 men armed with Martini-Henri rifles and good breech loaders. He also argued that perhaps the time had come to mount a strong military expedition against them and maybe the Italians should have the support of Great Britain in doing so.[31] Within half a decade Italy and Great Britain found it in their mutual political interest to support each other's ambitions in the Red Sea, an undertaking that lasted until the end of World War I.[32]

The Ottoman Predicament

European encroachments on Yemeni territory and commerce precipitated a formal study and assessment in May 1889, when Mehmet Zia was dispatched by the Ottomans to evaluate the situation at close range. In his report of 27 May he asserted that with Britain and France enjoying footholds on the Yemeni coast and Italy at the opposite end of the Red Sea, new measures were now necessary to deal with the situation in the interest of stabilizing and strengthening Ottoman coastal establishments and developing the mineral and agricultural resources of the Tihāmah.

Zia attributed the deteriorating situation to the near absence of any Ottoman presence in this region, which in turn was due to lack of funds to pay for officials and troops. This, in his view, had led to the prevalence of anarchy and lawlessness in this region, thus inviting intervention by foreign powers who seized the opportunity to cultivate the chiefs of the tribes. Intrigue went on with the disaffected inhabitants who were wooed with arms. England had taken control of Aden by means of converting it into a coal depot and had fortified it. The emir of Laḥǧ had received a battery of artillery from Britain. Her ships sailed at will to Mocha, Hodeida and other coastal areas in and out of Ottoman ports as if they owned them. Italy is in Muṣawwa‘ and ‘Aṣāb, from which ports it smuggles arms into Yemen. It has two to three depots in Mocha. France so far is inactive although for a century or so it has kept an eye on British activities in this area.

Rectifying the situation

After assessing the situation, Zia proceeded to propose fifteen measures for rectifying it, a number of which aimed at specifically preventing foreign intervention and coastal activities affecting the interior. One of these recommended substituting the Ottoman *Mecidiye* currency for the Austrian thaler and removing English currency from circulation. Another urged stationing war ships from Istanbul in the Red Sea to patrol the coast.[33]

A more impressive set of recommendations for reforming the Yemen generally and addressing the situation in the Red Sea particularly was submitted in a thirty-eight page report by Mehmet Nedim.[34] In it he stated that for a number of years Yemen had been insecure both by land and by sea, especially following the introduction of new arms into the country. If the inhabitants were not stripped of them, he argued, the land would never be secure. He recognized the difficulty of patrolling a four-hundred-mile coastline with an average depth of between four and five feet. Large ships could not anchor within two to three miles from the shore and only *sunbūk*s could come nearer. These were the vessels employed in smuggling arms and other goods past customs stations, he stated, with much loss of revenue to the treasury. To stop them would require the use of piercing devices, 250 imperial troops, one small artillery piece and eight steamships to patrol the coast. Smuggling by land from Aden could be stopped, he argued, with the construction of four customs posts along the border with a military outpost at Ḥuǧariyyah to interdict smugglers using the Ḥuǧariyyah–Ta‘izz road.

The pattern of traffic as outlined by Nedim suggests that each September large commercial ships laden with goods from Zanzibar, Java, Basrah, and Iranian coastal cities entered the Red Sea, anchored for a few days after telling Ottoman officials that they were simply passing through, but tarrying long enough for local merchants to learn the content of the vessels. They then sailed to the opposite shore where agents of the merchants bargained for the purchase of the contents then smuggled them across into Yemen and Ḥiğāz at a great loss to the customs revenue of the *vilayets*.

Placing warships on patrol would prevent this type of traffic. Moreover, if the ships were allowed to anchor at all, it should only be after they had been made to unload their cargo and pay customs fees on it.

Farasān and Kamarān islands, being uninhabited, as were some twenty other localities along the coast, posed a danger in that some day they might suffer the same fate as Perim, with the English and Italians using them for off-loading so close to the Yemeni shoreline. Nedim recommended that water be pumped to them and natives from the mainland be encouraged to settle them and till the soil by providing them with implements and tools and, where the land was not suitable for cultivation, encouraging them to take up fishing. The same policy should apply also for the islands off the Ḥijāz. Moreover, the islands of Farasān and Kamarān were rich in high quality cement, where it could be produced at far less cost than importing it which, in itself, was a great saving.

Each year, continues Nedim, Ḥiğāzīs exploited mother of pearl and pearls which they transported to Aden and sold to British merchants. Yemen was bypassed and lost out on another source of revenue. He suggested that these merchants be granted a five-year customs exemption in exchange for unloading these commodities at either al-Luḥayyah or Hodeida in order to benefit Yemeni merchants and the local treasury.

Nedim's report dwells on the commercial value of Mocha as a port which he claims can be entered only by the smaller *caique* vessels. The annual value of import–exports is placed at 20,000 Ottoman liras; besides woven mats and containers, no other noteworthy industry is located there. The Ẓaharī and Mašāliḥa tribesmen of the area earn their keep by transporting commercial goods and salt from the salt mines of the region; the yield of the mines in the area is up to one and a half million kilograms. It is carried by camel into the highlands and across the sea to ʿAṣāb and Muṣawwaʿ, Ubūḫ, Zaylaʿ and Zanzibar.

Villages between Mocha and Hodeida (100 miles apart) engaged for the most part in fishing. With some 45,000 inhabitants, Hodeida was the port par excellence on the Red Sea. Its commerce approximated two million Ottoman liras annually.[35] The export value of coffee beans and their skins alone is listed at one and a half million liras, and most of it is in the hands of foreign traders.

The coinage problem was again noted in his report (p. 15), wherein he states that the country's currency consists of gold coins and Selim *Mecidiyes* (*sic*) only. The need was for the equivalent of five million liras of silver.

Proposed Measures to Control and Interdict

Another proposal to control the Arabian littoral of the Red Sea from ‘Aqabah to Bāb al-Mandab and to prevent smuggling, piracy and contraband traffic was discovered in the Naval Museum library in Istanbul.[36] According to this 22-page draft report, undated but most likely presented after 1906 since it refers to the Ḥiğāz railway, the distance to be patrolled was put at 1,000 miles and a shoreline fraught with natural barriers. At the time of the report there were only a few scattered posts for patrolling and officials appeared helpless to do much about preventing illegal traffic in the Red Sea. The area, furthermore, was largely undeveloped and, where inhabited, there were fewer than a 1,000 residents in any one locality.

Existing posts were located at ‘Aqabah, Yanbu‘, Jeddah, al-Līṯ, Qunfiḏah, Farasān, al-Luḥayyah, Kamarān, Hodeida, Mocha and Bāb al-Mandab. The areas in between were controlled by Arabian tribal chiefs who dominated the shoreline and the traffic, commercial and otherwise, up to Aden and Muṣawwa‘. Enriched by such illicit traffic, their sons travelled to Egypt, Sawākin and centres of foreign trade with motorized vessels further to extend their trading operations.

The report recognized that legal traffic in the Red Sea required security of transport to the key centres of trading, namely Muṣawwa‘, Djibouti, and Aden. To provide protection and security it was necessary to control the shores and bar the entry of weapons and other contraband. It also required preventing the periodical uprising of the tribes settled off these shores. To date there was no evidence of such control. It was imperative at this juncture to despatch both naval and military forces to put an end to defiance on both land and on sea. Such undertakings were all the more urgent in view of the fact that the British, Italians and French had banded together against the Ottoman government and were capitalizing on every opportunity to benefit from any turmoil facing it. Stabilizing the region of the Red Sea was now of utmost importance in order to ensure the security of both the inhabitants and the Sultan's possessions.

Proposals for Controlling Illicit Traffic

The principal influential tribes of the Yemen and the Ḥiğāz littoral consisted of the Zarānīq, Banī Marwān, Idrīsīs and their followers. Their most important political and commercial ports were Ḫawḫah, Ibn ‘Abbās, Ḥabl, Mīdī, Ğīzān,

Šaqīq, al-Nadīm, and al-Barq. Official posts were recommended to be established to control imports at these points.

Developing the coastal area was considered important for controlling what went on off the coast. A ten-point plan was proposed to that end:

1) establish civil, land and sea posts to be manned by religious, yet tough and enterprising men;
2) open offices to enforce government rights and provide general services at such localities as Hodeida, Qunfiḏah, Jeddah and ʻAqabah; such services might include hospitals, water and ice facilities as a favour to the inhabitants from their government;
3) establish telegraphic stations to communicate with the various posts and keep officials informed of needs;
4) construct docking facilities to facilitate entry and departure and construct lighthouses, and lay buoys with kerosene burners to aid in the process;
5) place customs officials at all such ports, not only at the major ones as at present;
6) construct 500–600-ton boats to provision officials and military personnel at such posts, to provide a postal service to them, to touch at different ports, to provide also services to merchants, and to keep an eye on smugglers in the area;
7) construct blockhouses for troops to be stationed at these coastal posts in order to counter the aggressiveness of the Zarānīq, Banī Marwān, Idrīsīs and tribal followers of the *ašrāf*[37] and to ensure the security of the interior;
8) establish a commission headed by civil officials and consisting of military and naval officers who would meet from time to time in order to co-ordinate civil, military and naval activities, enforce security and prevent smuggling;
9) plant armed informants at ports from which smuggling takes place, from Muṣawwaʻ to Djibouti, who would quickly inform officials on the other side of the Red Sea of pending smuggling activities and enable patrolling boats to intercept them, and
10) patrol the coast by sea.

Patrolling the coast by sea

In devising the means of stemming the flow of contraband, preventing smuggling, and reaping customs duties on items escaping such fees, the report recommends adapting such means to the topographic reality of the coastal region.

The region is seen as consisting of three segments: one under control of the Zarānīq who inhabit Ḫawḫah, al-Qāḥ and Ġulayfiqah ports; the second under the control of Banī Marwān who inhabit this section with its ports at al-Wasīm, al-Barq, Šaqīq, Ǧīzān, Mīdī and Ḥabl; the third stretches southward from Ra's al-Muǧāmalah to Šayẖ Sa'īd.[38]

Much of the traffic in contraband, and smuggling, is concentrated in the first segment which stretches along the Ḥiǧāz and Yemeni coast, especially in the neighbourhood of Farasān island and the other smaller ones where pearl and mother of pearl fishermen evade the paying of customs because they operate without licences. The third segment is also the scene of much illegal activity starting from the 'Asīr borderline at al-Līṯ and environs, especially at Ra's al-'Akr where there are strong natural barriers from which armed bandits venture out with their small *sunbūk*s and prey on commercial sea traffic.

In the first and second segments there is an additional complicating factor: the involvement of the Italians and French in this illicit traffic, even the British, in that it issues forth from ports under their control and with vessels bearing their flags, namely from Muṣawwa' to Djibouti. Nearly the entire cargo they transport consists of contraband. They sail, moreover, close to areas within range of ports to which they can flee and where they can count on their own consular officials for protection. Under such conditions they can escape payment of customs duties and render it impossible to prove that they are engaged in the transportation of contraband. If intercepted en route, they count on their flag country to provide a gunboat or cruiser to threaten Ottoman officials and demand their release. The Ottomans have no similar vessels in the area to neutralize those of the Europeans or to put muscle behind their efforts to counter such evasive tactics.

The report stresses the urgent need to patrol off the ports of Ḫawḫah, al-Qāḥ, Ǧulayfiqah, al-Wasīm, al-Barq, Šaqīq, Ǧīzān, Mīdī and Ḥabl where many of the tribal chiefs have the fire arms to keep would-be interceptors at bay with their fast-moving sail boats (*falūkahs*).

The importance of surveillance ships

The first requirement for carrying out the necessary surveillance are gunboats. Motorized *sunbūk*s would fulfil the need. Given weather and strong wind conditions to overcome in the south, these vessels should displace more than 500 tons, be able to carry large guns, and reach ports with some facility. Between al-Līṯ and Kamarān there are many islands, and winds whip up gale-like storms. Water depth before al-Luḥayyah is only 4.1 fathoms and the shore consists of muddy banks and the same characterizes the area at al-Līṯ. The deepest waters measure up to 15.6 fathoms, and are to be found off Ṣabīhah: here larger vessels can be stationed. At nearly two kilometres from Ṣabīhah one can see coral and rocks and warning signs can be posted for ships to navigate around them without much difficulty.

Second, to chase the *sunbūk*s, artillery should be stationed at certain posts along the shore. This would also serve to discourage tribesmen from firing on them. The vessels chasing them should be armed with 15 cm, 57 mm, and 88 mm guns and an 11 mm light piece.

Third, it is imperative to speed the construction of posts and barracks economically and with special funds made available to that end.

Fourth, the principal structure of the barrack should not be above water in order to avoid collapse; it should, however, face the sea; the flank should not be exposed to attack; water depth should be 9.8 feet at the minimum in order to enable ships to dock right up to the edge; the facility should be screened to prevent collision with it below the water level. Officers' and soldiers' quarters should be in a pleasant setting, constructed from baked clay bricks and surrounded by trees. If constructed from planks, the seams of the walls should be caulked (presumably to prevent draughts). Officers' quarters should be above and the messes below, if possible. Messes of officers and sailors should face the sun and be flanked by trees. The flank of the building should have awnings protruding no less than 1.5 feet, and the windward direction should not be blocked by trees in order to enable the wind to fill up the sails of vessels transporting combustible materials.

There are two ways of ventilation: the natural unrestricted flow of air which can be of service in wind sails up to a certain point, and which can be used for natural ventilation; the other is the one generated by electrical devices, which are needed for ventilating officers' and soldiers' quarters as well as their common rooms. Lockers and individual rooms should have fans. Cabins and stern lockers on ships should also have fans. Ships should have a cooling and heating system. They should have also refuse disposal, cleaning and sanitary devices to eliminate contaminants. Baths and storage facilities likely to attract mildew should be located on upper levels. Officers should have their own bathrooms and water basins. Soldiers should have theirs on the superstructure as well as an inside cabin on the upper level.

Fifth, for those who might become ill a hospital facility connected to a bagnio should be installed.

Sixth, the vessels must be both swift and manoeuvrable; to that end they must be equipped with twin screw propellers. They should have a speed of between twelve and sixteen knots. Their engines should be of 'Triple' [expansion] type.

Seventh, the boilers must be able to utilize sea water; so a system of purification is required.

Eighth, the bridge should have mounted on it a cannon which the commandant can quickly fire when needed;

Ninth, they should have speed and capacity to cover 3,000 miles and be equipped with tanks for gas, coal and oil.

Tenth, the commander should be able to steer the steam-driven vessel by hand, thus a wheel should be mounted on the bridge at the stern.

Eleventh, an ice maker capable of producing five kilograms of ice per hour is needed for the purpose of preserving perishable food stuff.

Twelfth, the ship should be equipped to carry a complement of 100 and cover a distance of 3,000 miles at a time; it should have also equipment to distil drinking water at an average of twenty kilos per person in a 24-hour period.

Thirteenth, the flag staff should be visible up to 300 miles with a 60 cm telescope; there should be also a telegraph dispatching facility, and dual observation stands on the command bridge.

Fourteenth, a 15 cm fixed-mounting gun should be located on the bow; an 88 mm at the stern; it would not be suitable to have 57 mm guns below, so one should be placed by the flag at the bow, another on the port quarter; a communication device should be located on the bridge with the gunners at bow and stern; ammunition should be provided: for the 15 cm gun 100 rounds; for the 57 mm: 250; for the 88 mm: 200 rounds, and the 11 mm machine gun: 20,000 rounds.

Fifteenth, adequate electric lighting should be provided both above and below decks independent of the supply to ammunition storage facilities in the interest of security.

Sixteenth, there should be cooling equipment for the ammunition, including fans.

Seventeenth, rescue equipment is required in case of disaster.

Eighteenth, it should have an average size oven for baking bread.

Nineteenth, a dynamo for generating electricity fuelled by diesel is needed; and as few motors as necessary to avoid generating heat.

Twentieth, it should have equipment to repair damage in case of emergency.

Twenty-first, it should be provided with rescue boats to move quickly should storms break out.

Twenty-second, docking stations should be built in the shape of warships in order to discourage attackers and to provide security.

Twenty-third, pursuit vessels should carry smaller motorized boats that can be lowered quickly and give chase to smugglers' boats preventing them from entering safe harbours. They should be constructed in a way to enable quick deployment; they should carry machine guns, ammunition and be equipped also with small hand guns, and be able to pursue vigorously and seize the loads of smuggling boats.

Motorized sunbūks

At the sight of a steam ship or its smoke on the horizon, smugglers and their *caiques* are more likely to return to shore and safe havens than to continue sailing with illicit loads of female slaves. Catching up with them requires thirty-ton motor boats equipped with 37 mm artillery and stationed at or near Qunfiḏah. These are the type of *sunbūk*s that are required because they can move fast against those of the smugglers.

Where to station watch ships

Since the Red Sea stretches over 1,000 miles, it is difficult to establish administrative posts such as the one at Hodeida given the nature of the coast. Ideally, in order to control the coast line one needs to establish policing posts at 100-mile intervals and station a ship at each one. This should be located in a natural place of safety, but unfortunately such places do not exist; they have to be built.

To watch for and intercept smuggling boats, it is proposed to divide up the region as follows to establish stations and areas of surveillance for naval vessels:

Ships	*Location*	*Area to Watch*
1	Bāb al-Mandab	Perim island area
1	Bāb al-Mandab	Ḫawḫah
1	Hayish island	Mocha to Ḡulayfiqah
1	Hodeida	Ḫawḫah to Ra's Kutayb
1	Kamarān	Hodeida to al-Luḥayyah
1	Mīdī	Ibn 'Abbās to Ǧīzān
1	Farasān	Mīdī to al-Barq
1	Qunfiḏah	Šaqīq to al-Līṯ
1	Jeddah	al-Līṯ to Yanbu'
1	'Aqabah	Yanbu' to 'Aqabah

Fuel, water and other necessities for the ships should be provided at the above stations.

Where to have a naval base

What remains is to establish a naval base in order to keep track of ship movement and prevent disturbances. The Red Sea is especially in need of such a base to patrol shores. The port of Abkhur is very suitable because the entrance of its harbour is in the shape of the eye of a bridge.[39] It is curved in form, and the curved length is six and a half nautical miles; 20 at the entrance, 25 in the middle and three and a half fathoms deep at the end; it is 8,500 metres from entrance to the end. Its coast is shaped like a quay, straight up (lit. like a pole) from the water. If needed, a prefabricated dock can quickly be brought in. It is only three to three and a half hours by camel from Jeddah. The climate from Jeddah to this place is good.

Establishing the port occasions no difficulty. It is easily defensible because it can be connected to the Ḥiğāz railroad. It is very important for the Ottomans to have a protective base half-way down the Red Sea. It is equally important for precaution's sake to have such bases at 'Aqabah, Jeddah, Qunfiḏah, and Kamarān in the following manner: a facility at 'Aqabah can be connected to the Ḥiğāz railway system; its entrance protected with fortifications above and on the opposite side of the sea inlet but with a potable water facility for it might be difficult to build. Jeddah is a most important location for the Ḥiğāz on the Red Sea, but to establish a port here would entail exposure to natural hazards, and render transportation thereto extremely difficult and expensive. It would not be possible to establish a naval base here. Qunfiḏah in 'Asīr is a very important location for constructing a base; the weather, water and shore are fine; if possible, it would be convenient to have an ironworks facility there, but it might be a problem to locate a naval base there. Kamarān is likewise an adequate place for a naval base given its pleasant climate. But should war break out, it would be very difficult to defend.

Locating the naval base

If one of the locations chosen materializes into a base, then a number of facilities will have to be established, namely army barracks, docks for warships, and sleeping quarters for up to fifteen persons. It would require also additional space for an up-to-date hospital; for iron and ceramic works facilities; a foundry; a boiler room and a factory for making tools. The base should be able to handle gunboats and mail steamers, and would require also a large floating dock, depots for storing oil, gas and other similar combustibles, besides storage facilities for combat equipment and machines. Water depots would be required, as well as water distilling facilities and machines for making ice.

With the exception of brass, and in the interest of conservation, machinery and necessities generally can be shipped from Istanbul. Because Red Sea trade for the most part is in the hands of Greek merchants, one would have to deal with the one who presents the lowest bid for locally obtained supplies. Communication between Jeddah, the Yemen and Istanbul should be done through a cable company arranged via Sawākin. In order to avoid delays and minimize annual expenditures, a telegraph station should be established.

A model should be made in order to facilitate the process of establishing pontoons, locating suitable positions for port and naval construction facilities, lifts for heavy loads, and, to facilitate entry and departure from ports, suitable lighthouses and light buoys should be planted at proper intervals.

End Results?

The observations contained in the report and the recommendations offered made perfect sense. The problem lies in the fact that time was running out on the Ottoman empire and the realization of such elaborate and extensive time-consuming construction projects was halted by political events, namely the revolution against Sultan Abdülhamit and the intensification of the international pressure on a much weakened Ottoman state.

Two powerful Yemeni leaders worked against Ottoman control of the coast: Sayyid Muḥammad al-Idrīsī and Aḥmad Fatīnī of the Zarānīq. The former proclaimed in 1906 his mission to undo what he termed Turkish misrule. In this he had the support of other Tihāmah tribes: Banī Ǧāmī‘, Wā‘idāt, Banī Qays, Za‘liyyah and Banī Sulayl.[40] By 1907 the powerful Zarānīq tribe of the Tihāmah had been won over, not only to the Idrīsī but to the Italian cause as well. Rising in revolt in the name of religious reform, Idrīsī's movement attracted support as far north as Qunfiḏah. With the capture of the key stronghold of Mahāyil, the capital of ‘Asīr (Abhā) was cut off from Qunfiḏah's port. The Ottomans now were engaged in a struggle to put an end to a revolt encouraged and supported by the Italians.

In the highlands, Imām Yaḥyā's revolt nearly ended Ottoman rule by 1911. No sooner did they come to terms with him than the war with Italy broke out. The Ottomans could hardly be expected to proceed with the measures recommended for reinforcing militarily their positions along a 1,000-mile coast with rebellious tribesmen menacing the Yemeni part of it.

The question of how to control piracy and or smuggling was now superseded by the more urgent one of how to maintain the Ottoman presence in the Red Sea.

Documentary Sources

Germany:

Politische Archiv des Auswärtiges Amtes (Bonn).

Abteilung A. Acten: 'Süd Arabische Litoral des Rothen Meeres', *Türkei*, 76, vol. 10.

Turkey:

Başbakanlık Arşivi (Istanbul).

Deniz Müzesi Kütüphanesi (Istanbul).

Elyazması #167 13s, 'Yemen ve Hicaz Savahilinin inzıbat ve bahren muhafazası hakkında mütalaât'.

Other references utilized appear fully when first cited.

Secondary references

In addition to those cited in the notes:

Marston, Thomas, *Britain's Imperial Role in the Red Sea Area 1870–1878*, Hamden, Conn., 1961.

Notes and References

1. For chronological details see İ.H. Danişmend, *İzahlı Osmanlı Tarihi Kronolojisi*, 4 (Istanbul: Yayinevi, n.d.) 351–58.
2. Cf. Baldry 1976. 'The Turkish–Italian War in the Yemen'. *Arabian Studies* 3: 51–65, where he reports that the British, on the contrary, were alarmed by Italian activity in the Red Sea. He cites *A Report on the necessity of consular establishments in the Red Sea* (FO 195/1375) to help prevent the extension of Italian influence.
3. A 1344. Monts of the German Embassy in Rome to Chancellor von Bülow in Berlin. Rome 22 January 1907. Politische Archiv (henceforth PA) (Bonn). *Türkei*, 76, 10.
4. PA. A 1737. Berlin 31 January 1907 to the German embassy in Rome. *Türkei*, 76, 10.
5. Baldry 1976: 51, citing Richardson to Grey of 25 June 1913. FO 195/2453/1896.
6. FO 195/2060, 2083, 2148 and 2126 as cited in Baldry 1976.
7. A small flat-bottomed boat that was manoeuvrable and elusive when chased.
8. Maria Theresa dollars.
9. Telegraphic Communiqué from the Sadaret (Prime Ministry) of the Ottoman government to the *vali* (governor) of Yemen dated 28 October 1318/1900. Republic of Yemen, Centre for Documentation and Research, document 50690.
10. *Pall Mall Gazette* of 28 February 1885.
11. *Pall Mall Gazette*. For details of the struggle see PA, *Acta-Türkei*, I.A.B.q. 76, i–iv (1858–1885).
12. For details see PA, *Acta-Türkei*, 10 of 4–14 February 1885.
13. PA, vii (20 March and 1 June 1885).
14. Incidents reported to Berlin by the German ambassador in Rome. PA, A 15856, *Türkei*, 165, nr. 2.
15. PA, Constantinople, 29 October 1902. No. 144 in A 15865. Given the strained relations between Istanbul and Rome, Berlin was being used as the centre for communicating Ottoman responses to Rome, the underlying assumption being that Italy would listen to Germany.
16. PA, A 1192. Rome 18 January 1901 to Berlin. *Türkei*, 76, 10.
17. Telegram from Marshall 'Aptullah Pasha to the governor ad interim of Yemen of 15/28 October 1318/1902. PA, A 15993 *Türkei*, 165, nr. 2.
18. Turkey. Başbakanlık Arşivi. Telegrams of Lt Col Rushdi and Col Riza as relayed by Aptullah Pasha to the *Sadrazam* in his 28 October telegram.
19. Telegram of Riza Bey of 17/30 October 1318/1902 from Ṣan'ā'. PA, A 15993, *Türkei*, 165, nr. 2.
20. PA, Annex to 15993.
21. PA, A 16091, *Türkei*, 165, nr. 2.

22. PA, Annex to A 15993.
23. PA, Telegram 392 of 6 November 1902. A 16213, *Türkei*, 165, nr. 2.
24. Communiqué from the sultan's government, Pera 18 October 1902, to the German Embassy. PA, A 15266 in *Türkei*, 165, nr. 2.
25. PA, Berlin 21 October 1902. A 15369 in *Türkei*, 165, nr. 2.
26. Telegram from Constantinople of 20 October published in the *Frankfurter Zeitung* the next day. PA, A 15387 in *Türkei*, 165, nr. 2.
27. Report in the *Frankfurter Zeitung* of 22 October 1902. PA, A 15430 in *Türkei*, 165, nr. 2.
28. Article appearing in the *Daily Mail* (issue of 5 November 1902) under the title 'Action of the Italians' and reprinted in the *Neue Preussische Zeitung* under the heading 'Aus England', issue of 11 November. Copy in PA, A 16327 in *Türkei*, 165, nr. 2.
29. Alphonse Humbert, 'Facheux Rapprochement', *L'Eclaire*, 9 November 1902.
30. Report from Aden (15 March 1908) relaying Ottoman concern over the diversion of trade from Hodeida to Aden and the loss of customs revenue especially in coffee and tobacco.
31. Article 'Italy and the Yemen. Important Action Pending', *The Globe* of 11 December 1902, relaying a report from Rome of 9 December. Copy in PA, Ad to 18060, *Türkei*, 165, nr. 2.
32. See Baldry 1976 51–65 and also Baldry, 'British Naval Operations Against Turkish Yaman, 1914–1919'. *Die Welt des Islams* 19: 1–4, 148–97.
33. Report, 'Recommendations for effecting particular reforms in Yemen' submitted to the Ottoman sultan by former kaimmakam (deputy governor) of Mocha, Mehmet Riza of 27 May 1307/1889 in BA, *Yıldız Evrakı*, no. 437 Kısım 14 Zarf 126, 2nd of 2.
34. BA. *Yıldız Evrakı*, 330 Kısım, 14 Zarf, 126.
35. Exports were valued at 1,610,000 liras and imports at 340,000, most of them from India and Persian Gulf ports. See Nedim's report (14–15) for breakdown of import–export items.
36. 'Yemen ve Hicaz Savahilinin inzıbat ve bahren muhafazası haqqında mütalaât'. Deniz Müzesi Kütüphanesi elyazması, 167.
37. Powerful clans who attribute their descent to the Prophet Muḥammad and enjoy both prestige and power in the lower Yemen.
38. There is no mention of the tribe(s) controlling this section.
39. Ottoman bridges had either round arches or wide-based pointed arches. The 'eye' intended here is the round one.
40. R20/A4F2 as cited by Baldry 1976 54.

Wise Men Control Wasteful Women: Documents on 'Customs and Traditions' in the Kathīrī State Archive, Say'ūn*

Ulrike Freitag and Hanne Schönig[1]

Introduction

The imposing mudbrick palace of Say'ūn, the former capital of the Kathīrī sultanate in Wadi Ḥaḍramawt hosts one of the most fascinating archives of the Middle East. When the British ended their protectorate in 1967, when the sultan was deposed both former Ḥaḍramī sultanates joined the new People's Republic of Yemen, the palace was turned into a 'people's palace' and became an ethnographic and historical museum, as well as housing a library and the cultural administration.

In the 1980s, the former director, 'Abd al-Qādir al-Ṣabbān discovered a number of old sacks filled with various papers in an abandoned room. A passionate historian himself, al-Ṣabbān recognized immediately the value of his find, which was the former state archive of the Kathīrī sultanate. The contents of the archive, which al-Ṣabbān has painstakingly catalogued and which is now open to scholars under the normal conditions for research, concern overwhelmingly the period since the 1850s, when the Kathīrī sultanate was revived, although the oldest existing document dates back to 1622.[2] In this article, we will introduce one particular type of document which is a fascinating source for

* Note on transliteration: we use the system of transliteration of New Arabian Studies unless dialectical terms are used, which are transcribed rather than transliterated. For example, short vowels of dialectical terms are omitted unless there is clear evidence for them.

anthropologists, linguists and historians alike and helps us shed light on the important turning-points in the lives of Ḥaḍramīs earlier this century. The documents, overwhelmingly classified under 'Customs and Traditions' (*'ādāt wa-taqālīd*)[3] are also known as 'Documents of Prohibition' (*waṯā'iq al-tabtūl*).[4] Taking as its point of departure one document, which is here reproduced in facsimile as well as in translation,[5] the article investigates the relation of private and public in a society based on strict gender segregation and social stratification, the function of cultural conservatism in the 1920s and '30s, when Ḥaḍramawt underwent dramatic changes. It also investigates the dress and jewellery used during birth and marriage ceremonies and compares the document to descriptions available from contemporary travellers, thereby expanding on the information available from Serjeant's earlier work.[6]

'The Private is Public'—Female Behaviour as State Concern

The main concern of the documents seems to be that of most worthy statesmen, namely to avert damage from the unsuspecting nation. While the preamble of our document states this in a rather matter-of-factly form, the oldest remaining Kathīrī resolution on this matter, dating from 1341/1923 spells out the full dangers emanating from certain customs which virtually amount to the social disintegration of society:

> [...] the continuation of these repugnant customs will be of harm and cause great corruption āfasādū. It has led and will lead to the migration of the men and leave the country without them, so that their sons will be orphans and their wives widows.[7]

What was it that troubled the notables of 1923 and the members of the National Reform Council (of which we know little otherwise) of 1939? With much love for detail, the documents constitute a concerted effort to control 'conspicuous consumption',[8] consumption aimed at ostentatiously displaying wealth. Such conspicuous consumption played a particularly prominent role during the great life-cycle celebrations of marriage, birth and death, but also on other festive occasions such as the religious holidays, the return of travellers and the like. The documents therefore enlist exactly the types of dress, food and decorations admissible at specific occasions, limiting, for example, the amount of jewellery women may wear during normal visits (paragraphs 1 + 2) or stipulating that no silk may be worn except on specific days of the wedding (para 3). Other documents go further in limiting even the decoration of undergarments which were presumably not on display to normal visitors.[9]

Another major issue of concern is the limitation of wedding and food gifts (paras 4,10,11,13) and, more generally, the containment of wedding expenses as well as those of other life-cycle celebrations such as birth through entertainment (paras 5,6,10) and an expensive dowry (para 16) which apparently had been displayed for visitors (paras 12 + 15). Other documents complement this catalogue along similar lines with detailed stipulations on the number of coffers allowed for the bride (one each for jewellery and make up), the gifts given to a newly circumcised boy (a maximum of 1 riyal and no clothes), and even the kind of (unembroidered) cushions used for furnishing the reception rooms in which tea and coffee were served in defined quantities and prescribed types of glasses (no quality glass or crystal to be used or displayed).[10]

The large number of ordinances, which seem to have started in the late nineteenth or early twentieth century,[11] and the repetition of many of the stipulations indicates that the majority of the citizens of Say'ūn were not overly impressed by the prohibitions. Interestingly, however, there are certain indicators that the laws reflected a felt societal need. Firstly, many of the initiatives seem to have started by the *ahl al-ḥall wa-al-'aqd*, i.e. the notables and later a reform council and, secondly, complaints were launched contesting certain stipulations while implicitly acknowledging the overall project.[12] An undated document consists of a letter by the members of the aforementioned Reform Council to the sultan in which they inform him of popular protests against some of the rules recently past.[13] This letter constitutes possibly a direct response to our document which is the only one referring to a reform council.[14] Besides this short notification, the document also consists of an announcement that—contrary to the earlier restrictions (paras 5 + 6)—the bride's parents would now be at liberty to invite anyone they choose for the *ḥaṭrah* day as well as the *ṣubḥah* lunch.[15] Furthermore, a bride was allowed to wear her silk and jewellery for a longer period and the wife of someone about to embark on a journey—another major social occasion in the Ḥaḍramawt—was now permitted to wear the same, albeit only for one day.

Even such modifications only seem to have secured short-lived application of the rules. An exasperated writer only identified as 'tormented' (*muta'allim*) reported in July 1942 that many of the customs previously forbidden had been taken up once more. Given the current circumstances—the writer is here referring to the economic problems brought about by World War II—which made tight savings even more pressing than it had been before, the writer appeals to the sultan for action. He suggests that a new proclamation be issued, and that a woman be appointed to report on those of her sisters who violate the rules in women's gatherings.[16]

Commenting on a similar piece of legislation from the rival Qu'ayṭī capital of al-Mukallā in 1959, Serjeant observed that these sumptuary laws were passed 'especially in respect of the extravagant demands of women for dress and other forms of ostentation where their rivalry leads their male relatives into expenditure beyond their means.'[17] Are we, in other words, confronted with a concerted effort of men attempting to contain the collective squandermania of their wives? Were the notables perhaps even concerned that poorer women and perhaps even families would go hungry in their uncontrollable desire to show off, not only in terms of dress but also by providing their daughters with the customary *muṣirrat al-banāt*, a bag with sweets which girls were given after readings of the Quran in Ramaḍān. This interpretation which regards women's consumption as an exclusively gender-specific behaviour divorced of any wider social context certainly seems one favoured by Western and Eastern gender stereotypes alike and is a recurrent theme in similar types of discussions. Commenting on the rising cost of marriage in Aden around 1960, Farouk Luqman stated that 'Wives, nowadays, and rightly so perhaps, think of conjugal bliss in terms of the latest bedroom suites, electric kitchen, washing and spin drying machines, air-conditioners and refrigerators [...].'[18]

It is rather clear that in Ḥaḍramawt dress and jewellery is as much an indicator of social status and wealth as in other parts of Yemen and the wider Arabian Peninsula, and plays therefore an important part in the construction of social identities.[19] Similarly, reciprocal invitations and visiting as well as the generous serving of food (the famous 'Arab hospitality') contribute to the establishment and development of social networks as well as to the positioning of individuals within such networks.[20] It is true that much of this does indeed take place in the interior of houses, the notoriously 'private sphere' of Middle Eastern women, who thus decide over many issues linked to the house such as often enough its decoration. Thus, the criticism of the display of various vessels, vases and mirrors in paragraph 12 and of silk cushions elsewhere can be seen as one directed at women. Also, much of the social interaction is carried out by female visiting, although the documents clearly refer to occasions involving men.

This leads to the crucial point, namely that, although much of the criticized customs may seem to take place inside houses and among women, they are eminently public activities in that they go far beyond specificially female or individual behaviour exactly because they are important for the social standing not just of individuals but of families and kinship groups. The behaviour as well as dress of women reflect upon their male relatives, just as marriage expenditure and ceremonies indicate the social standing of the couple to the wider public.[21] This is nicely mirrored by the stipulation (in paragraph 3 of our document) that 'the woman can wear in her house whatever she wants, if no woman is present from outside the house.' Similarly, the social networks created through visits—by men, women and families—as well as through food gifts among relatives are an important part of the 'familial ethos' described by Singerman for Cairene families.[22] Women can therefore be seen as representatives acting as much for their households (*bayt*) as for their individual interests (which are by no means precluded by such an approach).[23] Celebrations—of weddings, births and circumcision, of religious feasts and on the occasion of travel—are crucial and highly visible moments for such mutual visits, which is why their regulation, for example through the limitation of the number of invitees, was of wider concern.

It should have become clear by now that at least certain parts of the interior of the house which are the scene of much of this social interaction, are a very public space indeed. The documents thus serve to confirm, from a historical perspective, vom Bruck's discussion of Middle Eastern (in her case Ṣan'ānī) houses[24] and should help lay to rest the myth of the private nature of these houses, together with that of the private functions of female behaviour.

While the above should explain why female dress and behaviour clearly was a public concern, it does not yet explain the reason why Ḥaḍramīs at least since the late nineteenth century and very much in the first half of this century became so concerned with these matters that a series of laws had to be passed. Here, a look at similar types of legislation might be of use. Sumptuary laws, and in particular dress codes, have a long tradition not only in the Middle East, and have served different purposes at various junctures in the histories of their societies. The first such laws which are known to us date to the Second Punic War when, during a severe financial crisis, the Roman Republic passed the Lex Oppia (215 BC) limiting the amount of golden jewellery and the types of dresses women were allowed to wear. Later Roman sumptuary laws aimed at controlling other public displays of luxury such as banquets, as well as at limiting the use of imported cloth, a motivation which can also be observed in seventeenth century France which was trying to build its own silk industry rather than import British and Italian silk. Mostly, such laws seem to have been directed at controlling social expenditure, sometimes in order to protect the overall economy, at other instances aiming to preserve gender or social boundaries.[25] Often, albeit not always, such laws were linked to dramatic economic and social transformations, such as in the Ottoman case, where the Tanẓīmāt were accompanied by laws aiming at introducing a new, 'modern' dress code. Interestingly, it has been noted in this context that dress codes often indicate a high level of social mobility, something we will return to in due course.[26]

We will argue in the following section that the Ḥaḍramī laws can serve as an indicator for the massive changes which had occurred in the Indian Ocean in the nineteenth century and which touched the heart of Ḥaḍramī society which was in close contact with the wider world through its diaspora.

Cultural Conservatism in a Time of Change

Although we are on very unsatisfactory grounds regarding the beginnings of sumptuary laws in modern Ḥaḍramī history,[27] it would at least historically make sense to assume that they began at some stage after the middle of the nineteenth century, albeit not necessarily for the first time in Ḥaḍramī history.[28] While emigration had been on the increase since the late eighteenth century, it would seem that from the middle of the nineteenth century, significant parts of the diaspora particularly in South and Southeast Asia became seriously wealthy while becoming increasingly involved in Ḥaḍramī politics.[29] This resulted in the establishment, roughly between the 1850s and the 1880s, of the (revived) Kathīrī and Qu'ayṭī sultanates. The political situation was stabilized, for better or worse, by protectorate treaties with Britain (1882-88 and 1918), and while attempts to establish independent polities continue, a number of merchant families began to invest parts of their fortune locally. It would seem that at least some of them also became directly involved in the introduction of luxury goods into the Wadi. Thus, 'Umar b. 'Alī al-Ǧunayd of Tarīm, one of the wealthiest traders of Singapore, has been accredited with the introduction of muslin for men's clothes in the Ḥaḍramawt.[30]

Economically, remittances became a prominent source of income and led to a remarkable rise in imports, which can be anecdotally reconstructed from travellers' descriptions. While von Wrede described Ḥaḍramawt in 1843 as a rather poor place,[31] the Bents, travelling in Ḥaḍramawt in 1893–94 were surprised to find the sultan's palace of al-Qaṭn furnished with carpets from Daghestan and old China dishes and in the government guesthouse in al-Šiḥr Indian furniture.[32] Hirsch's report on his journey in 1893 not only confirms their observations, but also gives us an idea about the imported items available on the major market of Šibām, such as Italian soap, French lights and Dutch porcelan.[33] While the Ḥaḍramawt had for long been integrated into the Indian Ocean economy and imports such as dates, spices, coffee, cloth, lifestock, poultry and wooden poles can be traced back over a long period, the import of luxury items clearly increased from the late nineteenth century. By 1935 Japanese bales, kerosene, petrol and tea, all luxury items linked to a change in lifestyle, had become staple imports and amounted to approximately 13.5% of all imports.[34] This does not include rice, which was slowly becoming the new staple grain, and arms, but also excludes such admittedly rare, but increasingly popular imports as water pumps, coloured glass windows and teakdoors, automobiles and Western style bathroom and kitchen furnishings, all of which were described by van der Meulen and von Wissmann.[35]

One cannot help but recognize a number of the items mentioned in the documents among the above goods, notably the lamps, vessels and silk clothes.

Although the expensive traditionally imported coffee was now consumed in apparently large quantities, which is attested by the import figures as well as by the limitations imposed on coffee consumption (para 14), it was now increasingly replaced by tea. Tea was prepared during gatherings on expensive sets which comprised a number of trays, a samovar, tea glasses and silver spoons, sugar boxes and the like—hence the attempt to limit their spread (para 7). Ostentatious consumption was not limited to the social occasions covered by the sumptuary laws. The beautiful mudbrick palaces which dot the Wadi and are at their most spectacular in Say'ūn and Tarīm mostly date from the first half of the twentieth century, and were criticized at the time. Instead of investing remittances in a productive manner, Ḥaḍramīs invested in buildings which occupied valuable agricultural lands, destroyed the palm groves which were central to the local Ḥaḍramī economy and employed the labour of animals and humans which could otherwise be used productively, complained Muḥammad b. Hāšim, teacher and journalist in 1940.[36]

It would indeed seem that the economically sensible investment of the remittances—instead of their spending on social status—was one of the concerns of the Ḥaḍramī notables. For some time, Ḥaḍramī reformers in Southeast Asia had observed with some concern the way in which the homeland had become dependent on the remittances. Their journals abound with articles on the need to invest remittances sensibly and to reform the Ḥaḍramī economy, and be it only because Ḥaḍramawt might one day be needed as a retreat for the diaspora.[37] Furthermore, a fatwā from the Singaporean *'ālim* Abū Bakr b. Ṭāhā al-Saqqāf from this period, which was printed in Surabaya and found its way to Ḥabbān in the Wāḥidī sultanate, reveals that worries about luxurious wedding spendings might also have concerned less well-to-do Ḥaḍramīs abroad. In a question, al-Saqqāf was asked his opinion about the possibly tribal custom—not mentioned in any of the documents—of covering the legs of groom and bride with the blood of a slaughtered animal on the evening of the *zifāf* or wedding night. Poor people had replaced this by using eggs. Al-Saqqāf stated that, because of lacking *šarī'ah* background, this custom could be abandoned if—one might add, economically—harmful.[38]

Another type of economic and religious explanation for and criticism of the new female fashion was brought forward in the short-lived hand-written journal *al-Tahḏīb* from Say'ūn. In an article entitled 'Evil customs and their influence on the Ḥaḍramī people', an anonymous author argued that the import of female adornments from India, Java, Tihāmah, Naǧd, China and other places showed that Ḥaḍramīs, like other ignorant people, easily fell for the imitation of others.[39] This demonstrated the need for internal reform, all the more so because Ḥaḍramī folly inadvertently supported sinister policies elsewhere: 'Europe and India have launched a fierce war against our country, extracting our wealth from the interior of our houses and attracting our scarce resources by way of their embellished deceptive goods which fall apart as soon as water touches them much like a spider's web.'[40] As indicated above, World War II only exacerbated direct economic concerns.

In addition, it cannot be excluded that a more indirect reasoning underlay the concerns of the notables. In their majority, they were members of the sayyid —and to a much lesser degree of the *mašāyiḫ* and *qabīlī*—stratum and therefore highly regarded in Ḥaḍramī society.[41] Their status had been severely challenged, however, in Indonesia where successful merchants from the *qabīlī* and other strata had achieved political recognition by the Dutch and had started to challenge the old order.[42]

Only one document from 1933 seems to be concerned with the immediate upkeep of social boundaries.[43] In May 1933, it stipulated detailed rules for the jewellery and perfumes admissible for goldsmiths, clearly the group which most easily could produce outstanding pieces for their womenfolk. In addition, it limited the dowry as well as the *mahr* (bridal money) for *masākīn*, the town dwellers who were—from the notables' point of view—the lowest status group but some of whom had amassed considerable wealth through migration.[44] In addition, it seems that prices for craftsmen had been on the increase for some time in the 1930s, which would have been another major source of income for this group.[45]

It could well be that, although only one surviving document deals with this thorny issue, it was one very close to the heart of the legislators. Possibly they feared that increasing consumerism, manifested in displays of wealth, which were irrespective of status groups, would change the perception of social hierarchies in a way dangerous to the *sayyids*. Hitherto meaningful signs of status were threatened to be replaced by quickly changing symbols of wealth, something which indeed seems to be a trait of consumer culture.[46] But the social order seemed not just threatened by consumerism: in the age of migrants returning from overseas diasporas where gender segregation was less strict, and of European travellers arriving in Ḥaḍramawt, the documents reflect a concern to uphold the separate spheres for men and women and outlaw intermingling.[47]

Ḥaḍramī society was not just socially stratified, but also at odds with each other over where to go in a rapidly changing world, which was expressed most clearly in the conflict between *salafīs*, organized in the *Ǧam'iyyat al-Iṣlāḥ wa-al-Iršād* and what might be termed 'traditionalists' who founded the *Rābiṭah 'Alawiyyah*. Although these factions resulted from a conflict among Ḥaḍramīs in Southeast Asia, they found support in the Ḥaḍramawt and can therefore—to a certain extent at least—be used to characterize factions in the Ḥaḍramawt as well.[48] Interestingly, both the sumptuary laws as well as the relevant articles from the reformist press employ an immensely moralizing style.[49] One could even argue that the joint condemnation of the excesses of consumerism was an attempt for both groups to meet and establish some common ground, particularly if men could agree that not any of them but rather their womenfolk were to blame. This would not have been the first historical incidence of this kind, an Ottoman law of 1727 was also quick to blame 'good-for-nothing' women for excessive innovations in dress, thereby bankrupting their husbands.[50] It is interesting to note that this particular form of male bonding might, of course, be partly explained away by reference to the fact that, in Islam, morality is a matter of collective social, rather than individual concern.[51] However, the strong emphasis on a time-honoured and religiously founded morality which is reflected in the preambles of the documents as well as in other literature of the time contrasts rather too sharply with the rapid changes which some of the very people appealing to morality helped to bring about for this explanation to be fully convincing. It would rather seem that the cultural and moral conservatism expressed in the sumptuary laws was the logical balance for the political and economic changes, a way by which the Ḥaḍramīs could 'remain themselves' while at the same time keeping pace with the twentieth century.[52]

There exists an additional, and only partly contradictory explanation for this emphasis on consumer restrictions, which is again linked to the divide between *salafīs* and traditionalists. Burke has drawn our attention to the fact that there exists not just conspicuous consumption, but also 'inconspicuous consumption' and even 'conspicuous refraining from consuming'. He adds that in 'a particular social context, simplicity may be the best way of making oneself conspicuous'.[53] Given the generally more puritan orientation of the *salafīs*, they might well have attempted to combine the economically wise with what they saw as religiously recommended, and have tried to downscale consumption on the basis of religious arguments. An interesting example might be the comment by the Saudi envoy of Kuwaiti origin, 'Abd al-'Azīz al-Rushayd, on the aforementioned *fatwā* regarding the application of blood and eggs to the legs of newly wed couples. Rather than merely agreeing with al-Saqqāf's vague statement that such a custom might prove harmful, he argued forcefully that both the use of blood and eggs were indeed a harmful custom, because it was rooted in the fear of *ğinn* and devils. It therefore indicated that those following the custom feared forces other than God,[54] something abhorrent to any good *salafī* not to mention Wahhābī. It might thus be that puritan attitudes, grounded in a particular interpretation of religion, could serve as a basis for 'conspicuous refraining from consumption', and that the sumptuary laws were an answer by the traditionalists who tried to keep up with what must certainly have been a popular move with the poorer sections of society.

In any case, such arguments seem to have remained largely academic in view of the dominating trend towards more and more, rather than less conspicuous consumption. Only thus can we explain the ongoing concern with the issue, and the constant repetitions of laws which seem to have been not worth the paper they were written on.

A Sample Document (No. 36 of 1357/1939)

Translation

Ordinance on the abrogation of customary habits on the part of the (National Reform Council in Say'ūn). It consists of 19 paragraphs in two pages with Sultan Ja'far b. Manṣūr b. Ghālib's ratification.

Ordinance on the abrogation of customary habits

Praise be to God whose help we seek—this is what the National Reform Council in Say'ūn has decided to abolish of the habits, which are harmful to the country and human kind. This āwas decidedū after thorough investigations and consultations with the people of judgement and authority. It lead to the agreement that the following is the most suitable for the present population and the most considerate towards them all.

(1) Any kind of jewellery is forbidden—except for one necklace (*murriyyah*) (3.3.),[55] an amulet (*rāʻī*) (3.3.), one pair of bracelets (*muṭall*) (3.3.), an anklet (*sumūṭ*) (3.3.) and earrings (*krābū*),[56] rings with stones (*ẖawātim*) and a belt (*ḥizmah*)[57] [crossed out: provided that the belt contains no gold or gilding but only silver].

(2) Amber (*karhab*) (3.1.) is forbidden except [in] a pair of bracelets (*ḥbūs*) (3.3.) for both hands and in the necklace (*šakk al-rāʻī*) (3.3.). It is not possible to insert gold in or to gild (*ḡams*)[58] the necklace (*šakk al-rāʻī*).

(3) Wearing all kinds of silk clothes, even those made out of the cloth *šīṭah*,[59] is forbidden in all garments except on the wedding days *ḡussah* (1.), *ṣubḥah* (1.) and *ẓillah* (1.)—and [for all] except the bride on her wedding days and afterwards, until the day of her first visit (*ẖaṭrah*) (1.). The woman can wear in her house whatever she wants, if no woman is present from outside the house.

(4) Gifts of all kind, whether a sugar loaf (*rūs qub'*) (5.), sweets, eggs and other things are strictly forbidden.

(5) The visit (*ẖaṭrah*) (1.) is forbidden except for the husband and his wife, the father and the mother, the grandfather and the grandmother, the brother and the sister, the paternal and maternal uncles and aunts, the brother-in-law and the sister-in-law and whoever belongs to the husband's household.

(6) Dinner on *ṣubḥah*-day (1.) and lunch and dinner on *ẓillah*-day (1.) are allowed [to be celebrated] in the same manner as the khaṭrah-day (1.): all who[se presence is] allowed there are allowed to be invited here as well.
(7) It is forbidden to equip the bride with a tea set (*'iddat al-šāhī*) (6.1.) and a kerosene lamp (*karhabān*) (6.2.).
(8) The bride is allowed to wear the head's gear (*ḥaml*) (3.2.) and other kinds of jewellery during her wedding days until her [crossed out: first] visit (*ẖaṭrah*) (1.).

page 2: continuation of the Ordinance on the abrogation of customary habits

(9) The use of alum (*šabb*) (4.) on top of henna (4.) is forbidden except for the bride during her wedding days and the visit (*ẖaṭrah*) (1.).
(10) Lunch [after] birth (*wilādah*) (2.) and the return to the husband's house (*wufā'*) (2.) is forbidden for anyone but the husband. It is forbidden as well to send porridge (*'aṣīd*) (5.1.) and meat to the husband's parents.
(11) It is forbidden for the wife's family to send meat to the husband during the feast days.
(12) The bride is forbidden to arrange on shelves and on the walls all kinds of vessels (*flīsāt*) (6.3.) and vases for flowers and mirrors (*manāẓir*) except cups.
(13) It is forbidden for maternal aunts to offer the groom and the bride clothes as gifts during the wedding days.
(14) The coffee (*qahwah*) (5.2.), which the women usually bring in the palm-vessel (*darī*) (6.3.), is forbidden at any time.
(15) The exhibition of the bride's clothes and her household effects [to the women] during the wedding days is forbidden.
(16) The marriage matters (*mu'n*) of the wife consisting of clothes and all the other things that she needs, are provided by her husband, and her family does not [have to contribute anything].
(17) Everything that has been agreed upon in this ordinance is universally applicable to women and girls.
(18) This ordinance becomes effective and [its application] obligatory upon the ratification of Sultan Ja'far b. Manṣūr and his signature on it.
(19) The application of this ordinance starts on the first day of the coming month of Muḥarram of the year 1358 [2 February 1939].

Written at the beginning of the month Dhū al-Ḥiǧǧah 1357 [January 1939]
(the sultan's signature)

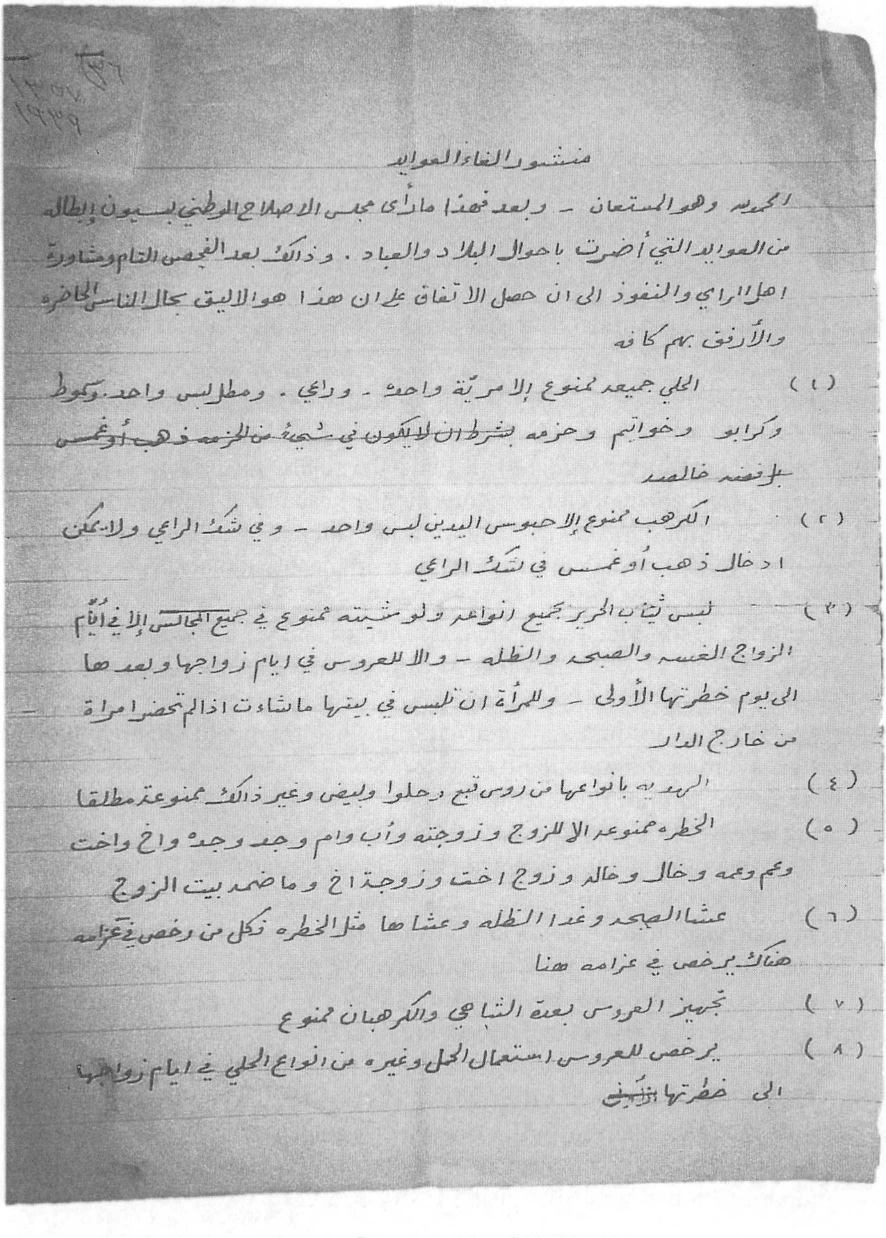

٣٦
١٣٥٧
١٩٣٩

منشور الغاء العوايد

الحمد لله وهو المستعان – وبعد فهذا ما رأى مجلس الاصلاح الوطني بسيون إبطاله
من العوايد التي أضرت باحوال البلاد والعباد . وذالك بعد الفحص التام ومشاورة
اهل الراي والنفوذ الى ان حصل الاتفاق على ان هذا هو الاليق بحال الناس الحاضره
والأرفق بهم كافه

(١) الحلي جميعه ممنوع إلا مرّية واحدة – وداي . ومطل لبس واحد . ومحوط
وكرابو وخواتم وحزمه بشرط ان لايكون في شيء من الجميع ذهب أو غمس
بالفضه فالصد

(٢) الكرهب ممنوع إلا حبوس اليدين لبس واحد – وفي شك الراي ولا يمكن
ادخال ذهب أو غمس في شك الراي

(٣) لبس ثياب الحرير بجميع انواعه ولو مشيته ممنوع في جميع المجالس إلا في أيام
الزواج الغسه والصبحه والظله – وإلا للعروس في ايام زواجها وبعدها
الى يوم خطرتها الأولى – وللمرأة ان تلبس في بيتها ما شاءت اذا لم تحضر امرأة
من خارج الدار

(٤) الهديه بانواعها من روس قبع دحلوا وبيض وغير ذالك ممنوعه مطلقا

(٥) الخطره ممنوعه إلا للزوج وزوجته وأب وام وجد وجده واخ واخت
وعم وعمه وخال وخاله وزوج اخت وزوجة اخ وما ضمه بيت الزوج

(٦) عشا الصبحه وغدا الظله وعشاها مثل الخطره فكل من رخص في غرامه
هناك يرخص في غرامه هنا

(٧) تجهيز العروس بعدة الشاهي والكرهبان ممنوع

(٨) يرخص للعروس استعمال الحلي وغيره من انواع الحلي في ايام زواجها
الى خطرتها ~~الثانية~~

Page 1 of Document 36 of 1357/1939.

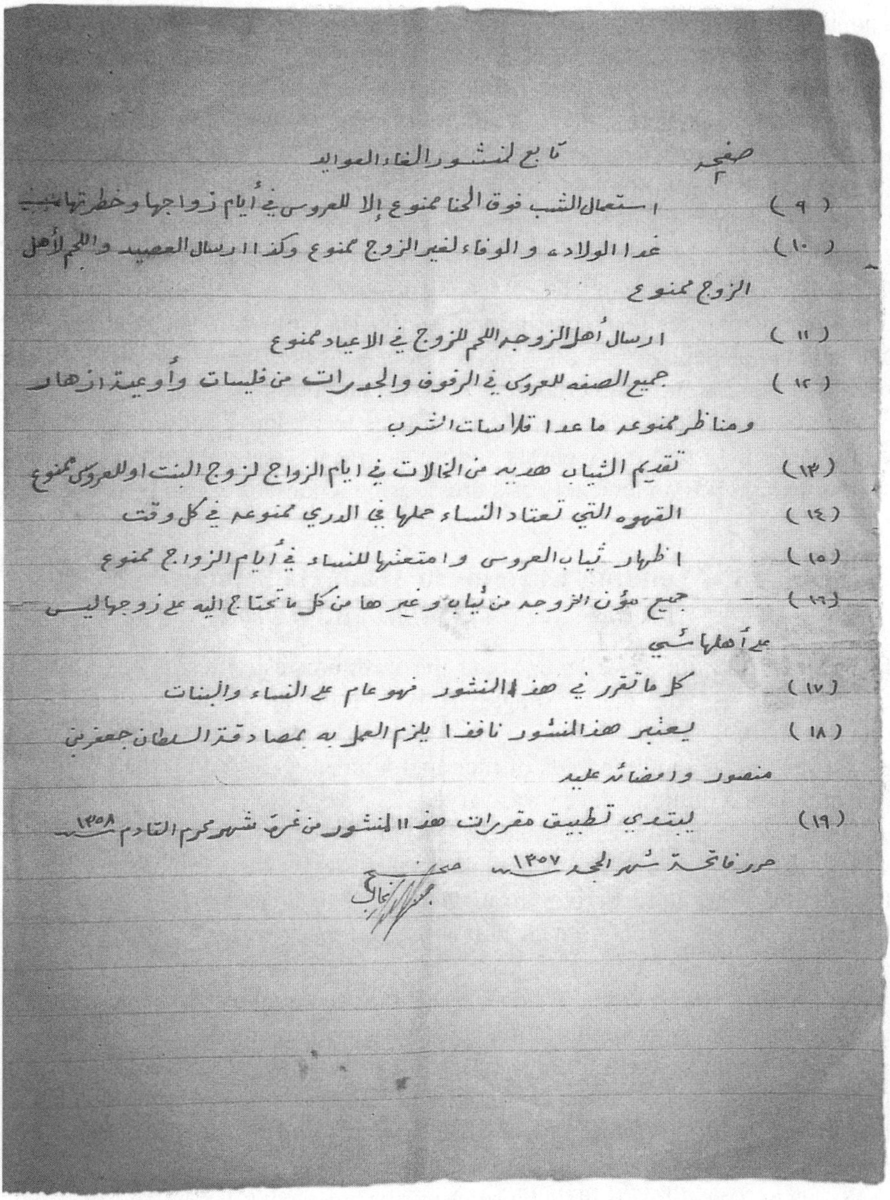

صفحة ٢

تابع لمنشور الغاء العوائد

(٩) استعمال الشب فوق الحنا ممنوع إلا للعروس في أيام زواجها وخطرتها

(١٠) غدا الولادة والوفاء لغير الزوج ممنوع وكذا ارسال العصيد واللحم لأهل الزوج ممنوع

(١١) ارسال أهل الزوجه اللحم للزوج في الاعياد ممنوع

(١٢) جميع الصفه للعروس في الرفوف والجدرات من فليسات وأوعية ازهار ومناظر ممنوعه ما عدا قلاسات الشرب

(١٣) تقديم الثياب هديه من الخالات في ايام الزواج لزوج البنت او للعروس ممنوع

(١٤) القهوه التي تعتاد النساء حملها في الدري ممنوعه في كل وقت

(١٥) اظهار ثياب العروس وامتعتها للنساء في أيام الزواج ممنوع

(١٦) جميع مؤن الزوجه من ثياب وغيرها من كل ما تحتاج اليه على زوجها ليس على أهلها شيء

(١٧) كل ما تقرر في هذا المنشور فهو عام على النساء والبنات

(١٨) يعتبر هذا المنشور نافذا يلزم العمل به بمصادقة السلطان جعفر بن منصور وامضائه عليه

(١٩) يبتدي تطبيق مقررات هذا المنشور من غرة شهر محرم القادم سنة ١٣٥٨

حرر فاتحة شهر الحجة ١٣٥٧ سنة

Page 2 of Document 36 of 1357/1939.

Ethno-linguistic Commentary

The information we possess for life in Wadi Ḥaḍramawt during the 1930s, namely the towns Say'ūn, Shibām and Tarīm, is rather poor and was mainly reported by foreign travellers, such as Philby, Helfritz, van der Meulen, Wissmann, Harold and Doreen Ingrams and Freya Stark. Among those only the latter two give some more detailed and descriptive information concerning the female world, which men hardly had and to which indeed they had no access. Besides Doreen Ingrams' *Survey of Social and Economic Conditions in the Aden Protectorate*,[61] which is a result of her own observation as well as an evaluation of travel reports and other secondary sources, we also have 'insider'-information: the detailed descriptions by the Ḥaḍramī scholar 'Abd al-Qādir Muḥammad al-Ṣabbān[62] in his book on *'Ādāt wa-taqālīd bi-al-Aḥqāf*[63] supply us with a good picture of certain customs of that period.

In the sample document, we find references to wedding and birth traditions with their dowry and gifts, guests and music, meals, tea and coffee, including several paragraphs on jewellery and dress, using a number of local terminology.

1. Wedding Customs in Wadi Ḥaḍramawt: *ġussah*, *ṣubḥah*, *ẓillah* and *ḫaṭrah*

In the travel accounts we learn about the wedding festivities as cheerful and crowded parties, with dance, songs, plenty of food, the exchange of gifts and dressing up of the bride. Doreen Ingrams attended a marriage in a Sayyid-family in Tarīm: 'Every day hundreds of men and women were fed on the traditional rice and boiled mutton, ...Tea was served.'[64]

The wedding festivities consisted of a number of separate acts, the first of which was the *ġussah*.[65] It was held on the first day of the wedding. According to al-Ṣabbān the word derives from *ġassa*, i.e. to enter s.th.[66] Serjeant's informant, however, explains it as a synonym of *ġusl*, which is elsewhere also vocalized *ġasl*[67], the powdered leaves of the tree called *sidr* or *'ilb* (*Ziziphus spina Christi*), which are until now frequently used amongst women[68] to wash body and hair.[69] In former days the Ḥaḍramī groom washed his hair with gusl, a tradition which was in the 1950s, according to Serjeant, substituted by shaving the head.[70] In fact, one of the ceremonies al-Ṣabbān describes is the shaving of the groom's hair.[71] According to Doreen Ingrams writing about the 1940s, the day before the wedding night, the bride's hair was washed with *ġasl*.[72] In any case *ġasl* belonged to a bride's 'cosmetic dowry' as exhibited in the folkloristic part of the museum in the Say'ūn palace.[73]

The morning after the wedding night is called *ṣubḥah* because it is the first morning on which the wife wakes up in her husband's house.[74] The term *ṣubḥah*[75] also refers to the gift which the husband gives to his wife on the first morning and which is said to have been 'a large trunk, with clothes, perfumes, a watch even, and all manner of things.'[76] There was a party held in the harem of the bridegroom's house and 'the bride receives presents from her own and the bridegroom's relatives and from those present at the party. Jewellery, clothes and money are given …'[77]

The first day after the wedding, *ẓillah*,[78] the bride appeared in public, being fully clothed in her most expensive dress. She also wore the wig *ḥaml* (3.2.) and the headband *'iṣābah*. The ceremony started in the morning with drums and trills. In the evening (after the *'aṣr*) a big women's party was held in large enclosures (*ḥawš*) or in the streets near the house. Before the bride sat down on an elevated place or, nowadays, on a chair, she remained standing some minutes so that all women could have a glance at her. On this occasion she also paid the female minstrels (*muštariḥāt*).[80]

Two weeks after the end of the wedding festivities the wife returned to her father's house for the first time. This was called *haṭrah*, meaning a proud walking, because she proceeded in a dignified manner and tambourine and drums welcomed her. The first *haṭrah* was held at the bride's family. For lunch her father invited the relatives of the bride and the family and relatives and friends of the bridegroom and for dinner the family of the husband, men and women. Before the meal, *taḥmīs* (5.2.) was offered and tea (5.2.) was served before and after.[81] Serjeant's informant for Tarīm calls it 'a big entertainment a month after the marriage to which the wife's parents invite all the husband's relatives.'[82]

2. Pregnancy and Birth: *wilādah*, *šammah* and *wufā'*

In the seventh or eighth month of pregnancy the woman went to her father's house for delivery. This event, however, was preceded by a visit of the wife's family to her husband's family to ask for the wife to be transferred. This was a custom among all social strata. Since the 1940s it has been left to languish and finally limited to the first pregnancy.[83]

Directly after delivery there was a small feast: the parents-in-law asked the husband to have the next meal (lunch or dinner) in their house.[84] Twenty days after the delivery, the wife's family was obliged to give a banquet for the husband's family and to send to his relatives the dish *'aṣīdah* (5.1.), which was in this case called *'aṣīdat al-'ishrīn*.

The seventh day after delivery, called *šammah*,[86] was the day of naming the child and cutting his/her hair.[87] There was a feast to which the family of the husband and his relatives were invited.[88] The female relatives, neighbours and friends met between *'aṣr* and *maǧrib* to congratulate the woman in childbed. Upon entering the *maǧlis* they first kissed the woman's head,[89] then they sat down in front of her to ask about her well-being and to wish her health. They were served coffee (5.2.) and water, and aloes-wood (*'ūd*)[90] was burnt in an incense-burner (*mabḫarah*).[91] If the new-born was male, the family invited more people and slaughtered a sheep.[92]

After a certain time (probably 40 days), the woman returned to her husband's house. Again a ritual demand, now on behalf of the husband and his family, had to precede the return. They brought as a present to the wife's house coffee beans (*ǧafal*) (5.2.), sugar, ginger and a sugar loaf (*rās qub'*) (5.).[93] On the then fixed *yawm al-wufā'* ('completion', i.e. of the stay in her parents' house) the husband had dinner with his wife's family, before they returned to his house with the new-born child.[94]

The first day after the wife's return to her husband, a feast was held in his house. The wifes family and her relatives were invited for lunch in return to the feasts they have given. Both sides competed to outdo each other in the lavish display of hospitality.[95]

3. Dress and Jewellery

In the documents one can in general observe a disapproval of luxury of materials and design as well as of abundance. This is quite the contrary to the wishes of Ḥaḍramī women, as was confirmed by Doreen Ingrams: 'The women like to have as many ornaments as they can afford, anklets, bracelets, necklaces, and six or more ear-rings in each ear.'[97] 'Every woman in the Ḥaḍramawt, rich or poor, wears as many ornaments as she or her husband can afford.'[98] Describing a bride in Šibām, Freya Stark remarked:

> I amused myself by counting the trinkets and adornments on one small bride of twelve years … beginning at her head, where she wore gold acorns and an amulet on either side of her parting, and ending at her feet … with a gold anklet aslant over her instep. On her neck she has three rows of small gold beads above a sort of collar called *m'labba*. Below this came a necklace of perforated gold beads alternate with old Greek coins and a British pound among them: a necklace of big round gold beads below; a necklace of amber, a gold necklace rather like an order, with cases for charms and big coins alternate …; another necklace to hold up the great square amulet in front and a longer one for the large crescent moon in gold. European earrings and rings in quantity: lion-bracelets made by Chinese jewellers in Singapore, and a golden girdle.[99]

In Wadi Daw'an she noticed that the bride wore her wedding dress for 40 days: 'Her black gown had a breastplate of solid silver plaited with cotton: her girdle jingled with silver tassels: her bare feet had anklets of gold.'[100]

3.1. Amber

The form *karhab* is metathesis for the correct *kahrab*,[101] today often called *kahramān*.[102] From ancient times, it is known for medicinal use and its protective power.[103] The descriptions in the travel accounts prove that it was a well-liked stone (see also plate 1): 'Gold and amber are popular among the well-to-do.'[104] Amber also was the 'standard piece of jewelry for everyday wear …'[105] in Ṣan'ā'.

3.2. ḥaml

The 'traditional coarse-haired wig[106] with an ornamental hairdress'[107] (plates 1 and 2)[108] was worn at weddings. This 'curious custom' was noted by Doreen Ingrams, who described it as 'an abundant wig, on top of which is worn a head dress embroidered in gold' worn for the wedding night.[109]

Plate 1. Bride's head made up with the head garment and wig *ḥaml*, the crown *'iṣābah* and the amber-necklace *šakkah*. The picture was taken in the exhibition of the Say'un museum thanks to 'Abd al-Raḥmān al-Saqqāf.

*Plate 2**. Bride's head garment *ḥaml*.

3.3. Necklaces, bracelets and anklets

Different kinds of necklaces are mentioned: *murriyyah* (para 1), a longer necklace; a (silver) amulet (*rāʿī*) (plate 4); the necklace *šakk al-rāʿī*: '*šakkah* kind of jewellery, chain for the neck';[110] *šakkah* is also used for the amber-necklace around the bride's neck in the key of Say'ūn museum (see plate 1).

Bracelets are usually worn as pairs, one on each arm: *muṭall*[111] (para 1); *ḥūbs* (para 2), singular: *ḥabs*, *ḥibs*.[112]

The anklet *sumūṭ* (para 1) has elsewhere (e.g., document No. 18 and al-Ṣabbān[113]) the spelling *ṣumūṭ*. Landberg gives *ṣumt*, pl. *ṣumūt* and translates: bracelet massif.[114] Al-Ṣabbān, however, explained it as an anklet,[115] which was confirmed by the silversmith in the palace of Say'ūn, to whom we gave a list of words and asked him to bring the designed jewellery.

* Plates 2–4 with the kind permission of Ḥadsan ʿUmar Ḥadsan Bā Ḥadšwān, Say'ūn.

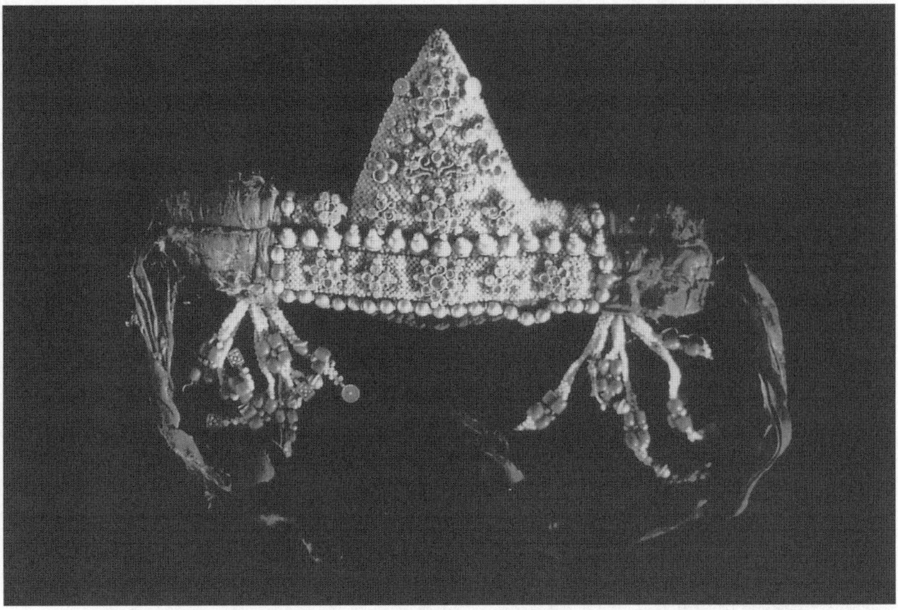

Plate 3. The bride's crown *'iṣābah.*

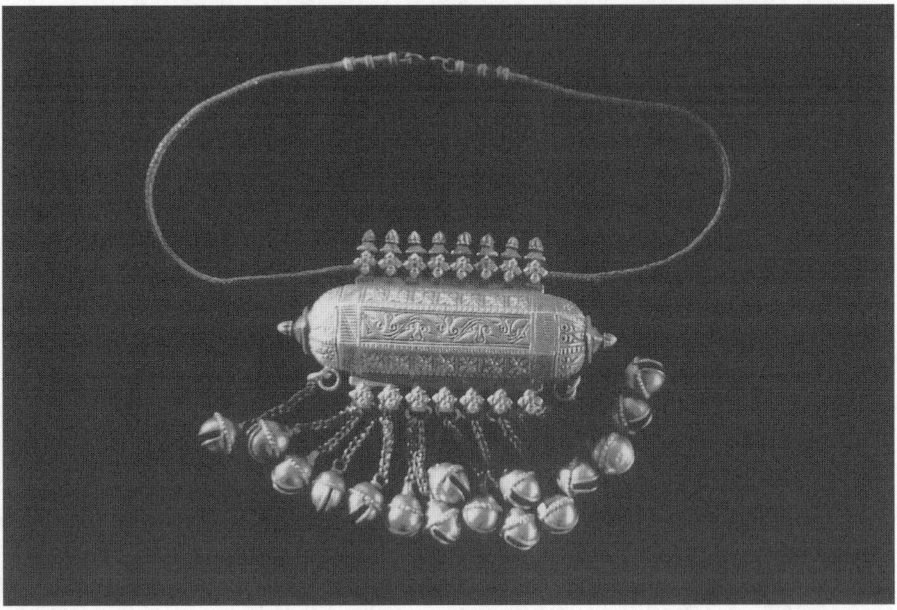

Plate 4. Silver amulet *rāʿī.*

According to the travel accounts, anklets seem to have been very popular. Freya Stark notices in the harem of Sultan ʿAlī b. Manṣūr in Say'ūn: '… golden anklets on their feet'[116] and in al-Ḥuraydah 'the usual click of anklets …'[117] Doreen Ingrams mentions that in Ḥaḍramawt 'A silver anklet with bells is worn on one leg when they dance.'[118] And at the occasion of *ʿīd al-fiṭr* in Say'ūn she observes: 'Always there was dancing … two guests at a time stood up and stamped their feet so that the bells on their anklets tinkled.'[119] Helfritz states on the rural population that the women are overloaded with jewellery, among others wearing thick anklets.[120] Some pictures taken also show the girls wearing this piece of jewellery.[121] Interestingly, a whole document (No 48 of 1360/1941) is devoted to the prohibition of anklets, where however they are called *ḥuǧūl.*[122]

4. Traditional Cosmetics

Doreen Ingrams gives an overview of the range of colours, used for face decoration:

> … the women paint their faces a bright yellow and their eyebrows and nostrils scarlet. A green line may be drawn down the nose or painted in a design on cheeks or forehead. In other places they paint the upper half of their faces yellow and the lower green. A broad red band is sometimes drawn down the centre parting of the hair. Kohl is universally used for the eyes … Henna is popular among all classes for painting designs on hands and feet, and a black paste called Khudhab123 is used for this purpose as well. Among tribeswomen and beduins tattooing the face and hands is popular.124

The use of cosmetics was and still is more plentiful than we can assume from the documents,[125] which only mention henna (*ḥinnā'*)[126] and alum (*šabb*)[127] to blacken the henna.[128] Similarly al-Ṣabbān's remarks are very poor in this case: immediately after *laylat al-qabḍah* (i.e. the day the girl is told that she will be married and to whom)[129] the bride gets decorated: the *naqqāšāt* (*muḥanniyāt*)[130] prepare the henna, i.e. they mix it with water. The bride's hands and feet are painted with different ornaments. The henna is sprinkled with lemon juice. When hands and feet are painted red, as a second step, its colour is turned black by using alum *šabb* and sal ammoniac *šayḏar*:[131] *Šabb* is pulverized, mixed with water and smeared on the parts of the henna-painting which shall become black. Then some drops of water are given on *šayḏar* which is then put onto henna and alum. Alum and sal ammoniac fix the henna so that it remains for a long time.[132] Traditionally in Wadi Ḥaḍramawt also the bridegroom's feet were painted with henna.[133]

Al-Ṣabbān's description has not been verified till now. For the blackening-procedure which we observed in Wadi Ḍahr, the henna-painted hands or feet are rubbed with powdered sal ammoniac *šādir* mixed with a little water. Then you smear in oil melted potash *huṭum* on it. This paste remains about one hour before it can be washed. Only the henna-painted skin becomes black.

5. Wedding and Food Gifts

Gifts of all kinds usually given are forbidden, which is mentioned rather often (here: paras 4, 10, 11, 13, 14), explicitly: clothes in general (para 13); food, such as sweets and eggs (para 4), meat (paras 10 and 11) and *'aṣīd* (5.1.) (para 10), coffee (5.2.) (para 14), sugar and especially sugar loaf (*rūs qub'*) (para 4), which is imported from India.[134] In contrast to the tradition mentioned by al-Ṣabbān, sugar loaf being a guest's gift at the occasion of *wufā'* (2.), the document forbids it among other food (para 4), which might be due to the general disapproval of foreign influences.

5.1. 'aṣīd

We can assume the frequent custom of exchanging meat and the *'aṣīd* (5.1.) on several occasions, because it is strictly forbidden in various documents (here: paras 10 and 11). The importance of *'aṣīd* is emphasized by al-Ṣabbān, who describes its ingredients (wheat flour, in water soaked dates)[135] and production in detail.[136] It is a traditional dish in Arabia from ancient times.[137] Serjeant quotes a Ḥaḍramī prose text (*maqāmah*): *al-Ḫuṭbah fī al-aṣīd*.[138]

5.2. Coffee and tea

Serjeant wonders that an ordinary term concerning coffee '*ku'dah* ... A coffee *dallah*[139] or kettle' appears in a word list given by a sayyid from Tarīm, and suggests that it must have 'some specific application in Ḥaḍramawt.'[140] In fact, as we learn from our documents and the very long and detailed remarks in al-Ṣabbān,[141] the coffee- and tea-ceremonies play an important role during the festivities, whereas coffee has a much longer tradition.[142] According to al-Ṣabbān[143] coffee entered the Wadi for the first time in the middle of the eighth/fourteenth century. This seems to be confirmed by Landberg, who suggests the introduction of coffee into the Yemen considerably before the ninth/fifteenth century, which is usually given as a date.[144] According to D. Ingrams, *qišr*, the infusion made from the outer coffee husks was the commonest drink in the Protectorate.[145]

Also the tradition of bringing coffee beans (*ǧafal*)[146] was combatted (document 39), although this was a custom at all sorts of visits.[147] It reminds one of the presentday custom of every guest's bringing his own *qāt*, a tradition which proves that it is a precious commodity. *Qāt* is thus not only cultivated on the former coffee plantations, but has also become a substitute for drink on social contexts.[148]

Al-Ṣabbān mentions that on the occasion of *šammah* (2.) the female visitors were offered *taḥmīs*,[149] roasted coffee: the beans were ground, roasted and then presented to the guests to smell them before they are prepared to drink.[150] Ingrams describes it as being part of the *ṣubḥah*-meeting, when bride, bridegroom and their fathers assembled[151] as well as a part of the etiquette of receiving visitors.[152] The prohibition to bring coffee (para 14) seems to refer to this tradition. Assisting a wedding ceremony at the bridegroom's house in al-Ḥurayḍah (Wadi 'Amd), Doreen Ingrams noticed the custom that several of the guests threw handfuls of coffee beans on a mat in front of him and she learned, that 'only those who have been invited to lunch tomorrow and the beans will be used for their coffee' do this.[153] It is also 'customary for travellers to offer a handful of coffee to the host on entering a house.'[154]

Tea entered the Wadi only last century, but it quickly replaced the coffee in many circumstances.[155] It has become very popular because of the relations to the East Indies (see also 6.1.).

6. Household Utensils[156]

6.1. 'Iddat al-šāhī

Tea is prepared in a samovar, which is part of the *'iddat al-šāhī* 'tea outfits', consisting of the samovar, a number of small china teapots, glasses, trays, spoons, sugar-cutters … tongs for picking the charcoal and a basin of water for rinsing out the glasses.'[157] Even today the *'iddat al-šāhī* often is the dominant equipment in the scantily furnished Ḥaḍramī houses.

6.2. Karhabān

Metathesis for *kahrabān*.[158] This is an imported kerosene lamp, which was used in the Wadi until they got electricity.[159] The bride usually receives it with the dowry.[160]

6.3. Vessels: flīs and darī

Flīs is a receptacle made of *ṣhd* (?) for sugar (here: *sunkar*[161]).[162] I knew in Ṣan'ā' small flat (diameter of about 5–6 cm, 2–3 cm high) receptacles made of soapstone (*ḥaraḍ*) and called *fals*. They are used for *buḫr li-l-mā'*, the incense which flavours the water the *qāt*-chewers drink during the *qāt*-sessions. They are as well used to mix the solid *ḫiḍāb* lump with water to get the liquid gall-ink for body-painting *naqš*.[163]

Al-Ṣabbān notes a local vessel *darǧih* made of palmleaves and produced in Šibām and al-Šiḥr.164 The orthography darī might be according to the Ḥaḍramī pronunciation of ǧīm = yīm.[165] Al-Ṣabbān mentions it as well in the Dalīl among the coffee set.[166]

Notes and References

1. The Deutsche Forschungsgemeinschaft generously supported both of us during our fieldwork in the Yemen in 1996. Earlier versions of parts of the article were published by U. Freitag in German under the title 'Dokumente zu 'Sitten und Traditionen' im Sultanspalast von Say'ūn, Hadhramaut', in Andreas Eckert and Gesine Kr,ger (eds), *Quellen zur außereuropäischen Geschichte*, Münster: Lit Verlag 1998, 10–22 and by H. Schönig, 'Some Katīrī documents on 'ādāt wa-taqālīd', *Proceedings of the Seminar for Arabian Studies* 28 (1998) (in print).
2. For a discussion of the contents of the archive, see the brochure issued by the archive and H. Schönig, 'Some Katīrī documents …', note 1 above.
3. At least one such document of May 1933 can be found in the uncatalogued folder *Bayānāt al-dawlah alKatīriyyah.*
4. 'Abd al-Qādir al-Ṣabbān, *'Ādāt wa-taqālīd bi-alAḥqāf*, I (completed, according to preface, Mukalla 1980), 114. II is still an unpublished manuscript.
5. al-Hay'ah al-'āmmah li-l-āthār wa-al-matāḥif wa-al-maḫṭūṭāt, Say'ūn branch, Qism al-Tawṯīq (hitherto referred to as QT), Document IV: 36 (1357/1939).
6. R.B. Serjeant, 'Recent Marriage Legislation from al-Makallā with Notes on Marriage Customs', in R.B. Serjeant, *Customary and Shari'ah Law in Arabian Society*, Variorum reprints: Great Yarmouth 1991. For 1937 or 1938, a reference to similar legislation in al-Siḥr is made by Harold Ingrams, *Arabia and the Isles*, 3rd ed. London 1966, 311, but without further investigation into the topic.
7. QT IV:3, dated 12 Ramaḍān 1341/28 April 1923. The document is reprinted with some minor changes in al-Ṣabbān, *'Ādāt wa-taqālīd* …, I, 114f. Almost the same vocabulary is used in the article ''ādāt al-sū' wa-aṯru-hā fī al-ša'b al-Ḥaḍramī', al-Tahḏīb 1:3, 1. Šawwāl 1349/19 February 1931, Cairo 1961 (reprint) 54–57, here 55.
8. Roger S. Mason, *Conspicuous Consumption: a study of exceptional consumer behaviour*, Farnborough 1981. For a discussion of the term, cf. Peter Burke, '*Res et verba*: conspicuous consumption in the early modern world', in John Brewer and Roy Porter (eds), *Consumption and the World of Goods*, London and New York 1993, 148–161.
9. QT IV:3, para 2.
10. Besides the already cited documents, cf. QT, documents IV:5 (1.8.1931), IV:18 (May–June 1933), IV:20 (December 1934), IV:34 (2.11.1938), IV:39 (30 April 1939).
11. Serjeant, 'Recent Marriage Legislation …', 472. This dating is confirmed by

al-Tahḏīb 1:3 (1931), 54, which refers to attempts over the last quarter of a century to control female decorum.

12. This is confirmed by the fact that two of the surviving Ḥaḍramī journals of the time, *al-Tahḏīb* and *Nahḍah*, also take issue with the 'harmful customs', *al-Tahḏīb* 1:3 (1931) and *al-Nahḍah* 3 (mid June 1942), 1, 6 and 4 (mid-July 1942), 2.
13. QT IV:43, consisting of a letter of the members of the *Maǧlis al-iṣlāḥ* to the sultan and an announcement (*i'lān*) on certain changes.
14. Of course there is always the possibility of yet another ordinance which has not been preserved.
15. For an explanation of these as well as the other ceremonies discussed, see the ethno-linguistic section of this article.
16. *al-Nahḍah* 4, end of *Ǧumādā al-ākhirah* 1361 (mid-July 1942), 2.
17. Serjeant, 'Recent Marriage Legislation ...', 472.
18. Farouk Luqman, *Love, Matrimony and mental Health in Aden*, Aden Chronicle, Fatat al-Jazira Press, n.d., 23. For a general comment on this topic, cf. Amanda Vickery, 'Women and the world of goods: a Lancashire consumer and her possessions, 1751–81', in Brewer & Roy, *Consumption*, 274–301.
19. See, for example, Martha Mundy, 'Ṣan'ā' Dress, 1920–75', in R.B. Serjeant & Roland Lewcock (eds), *Ṣan'ā'. An Arabian Islamic City*, London 1983, 529–541; Anne Meneley, *Tournaments of Value: Sociability and Hierarchy in a Yemeni Town*, Toronto etc. 1996; Aida S. Kanafani, *Aesthetics and Ritual in the United Arab Emirates. The anthropology of food and personal adornment among Arabian women*, Beirut 1983 and Soraya Altorki, *Women in Saudi Arabia. Ideology and Behavior among the Elite*, New York 1986; Gabriele vom Bruck, 'Elusive Bodies: The Politics of Aesthetics among Yemeni Elite Women', *Signs* 23:1 (1997), 175–214.
20. On the issue of food, cf. Mai Yamani, 'You are what you cook: cuisine and class in Mecca', in Sami Zubaida & Richard Tapper (eds), *Culinary Cultures of the Middle East*, London and New York 1994, 173–184.
21. Altorki, *Women in Saudi Arabia* ..., 64f., Mundy, 'Ṣan'ā' Dress', 537 and Dale Eickelman, *The Middle East. An Anthropological Approach*, 2nd edit., Englewood Cliffs 1989, 172.
22. Diane Singerman, *Avenues of Participation. Family, Politics, and Networks in Uurban Quarters of Cairo*, Princeton 1995, 42.
23. Singerman, *Avenues* ..., 43, cf. Meneley, *Tournaments* ..., 60.
24. Gabriele vom Bruck, 'A House Turned Inside Out', *Journal of Material Culture* 2:2 (1997), 139–172.
25. 'Dress Code', *Encyclopaedia Britannica* 1996 (CD Rom edition).
26. Donald Quataert, 'Clothing Laws in the Ottoman Empire', IJMES 29:3 (1997), 403–425.
27. There exists no information besides the already mentioned note by Serjeant.
28. Increasingly, the beginnings of modern consumer culture are now backdated to the early modern period and Burke, '*Res et verba*' demonstrates the feasibility of this for East Asia as well as Europe. It is therefore not unlikely that a trade diaspora like the Ḥaḍramī one was affected by such changes already before the nineteenth century.

29. A general survey of this history as well as country-related case studies can be found in Ulrike Freitag & William Clarence-Smith (eds), *Hadhrami Traders, Scholars and Statesmen in the Indian Ocean*, Leiden 1997.
30. 'Abd al-Qādir al-Ǧunayd, *al-'Uqūd al-'asǧadiyyah fī nasr manāqib ba'ḍ afrād al-usrah al-Gunaydiyyah*, Singapore 1994, 168f. For an account of wealthy Ḥaḍramī traders in Singapore, see U. Freitag, 'Arab Merchants in Singapore: Attempt at a Collective Biography', in Huub de Jonge and Nico Kaptein (eds), *Arabs in Southeast Asia*, Leiden (forthcoming).
31. Adolph von Wrede, *Reisen in Ḥadhramaut, Beled Benī 'Issa und Beled al-Ḥadschar*, Braunschweig 1873.
32. Theodore & Mabel V.A. Bent, *Southern Arabia*, London 1900, 112f., 202.
33. Leo Hirsch, Reisen in *Süd-Arabien, Mahra-Land und Hadramūt*, Leiden 1897, 205. Adolf Grohmann, *Südarabien als Wirtschaftsgebiet*, II, Brünn etc. 1933, 82f. in his account of the trade of the Ḥaḍramī ports which was written in 1918 draws heavily on Hirsch and other nineteenth century sources.
34. This has been calculated on the basis of the figures given in Harold Ingrams, *A Report on the Social, Economic and Political Condition of the Hadhramaut*, London 1937, 71.
35. D. van der Meulen & H. von Wissmann, *Haḍramaut. Some of its Mysteries Unveiled*, Leiden 1932.
36. *al-Ikhā'* (Tarīm) 2:9, April 1940, 2.
37. *al-Dahnā'* (Surabaya) II:14. Cf. *al-Irshād* (Surabaya) 5, 15 July 1920, *Ḥaḍramawt* (Surabaya) 167, 18 October 1928 and 345, 29 August 1932 and *al-Qistās* (Surabaya) 5, March 1923.
38. No title, the envelope states Siapa = siapa minta ini kitab bisa dapet vrij dari Toko Singapore (whoever wishes this book can obtain a free copy from the Singapore shop), Maṭba'at al-waḥdah, Surabaya, 6 pages. This pamphlet was found by R.B. Serjeant in the Sibblī library in Ḥabbān in 1947 (handwritten comment Serjeant's on the cover). I would like to thank Prof. Yasir Suleiman for the permission to consult this document from Serjeant's papers in Edinburgh.
39. *al-Tahḏīb*, 1:3, 54–57.
40. Ibid. 55.
41. On the social stratification see Sylvaine Camelin, 'Reflections on the System of Social Stratification in Hadhramaut', in Freitag & Clarence-Smith, 147–156.
42. There exists evidence that not only the sayyids, but also qabīlīs felt threatened by the rise particularly of the masākīn. PRO, FO 371/5235/E3283, British Consul-General, Batavia to Foreign Office, 26 February 1920.
43. QT, document from the uncatalogued series *Bayānāt al-dawlah al-Katiriyyah*, of Ṣafar 1353/May 1933. It is reproduced in al-Ṣabbān, 'Ādāt, 116f.
44. A famous example are the Bin Lādin, one of the wealthiest families of Saudi Arabia.
45. See Mikhail Rodionov, 'The Labour Code of the Sultan b. al-Manṣūr al-Kathīrī', *New Arabian Studies* 4 (1997), 196–204.
46. Mike Featherstone, 'Consumer Culture, Symbolic Power and Universalism', in Georg Stauth & Sami Zubaida, *Mass Culture, Popular Culture, and Social Life in the Middle East*, Frankfurt 1987, 17–46.

47. QT, IV:5, Letter of a number of sayyids to Sultan ʿAlī b. Manṣūr (Say'ūn) dated 16 Rabīʿ al-awwal/1 August 1931, and IV:39, paras 3, 7.
48. Cf. Alexander Knysh, 'The Cult of Saints and Religious Reformism in Hadhramaut' and Natalie Mobini-Kesheh, 'Islamic Modernism in Colonial Java: the al-Irshād Movement', both in Freitag & Clarence-Smith, 199–216, 231–248.
49. Cf. Ulrike Freitag, 'Dying of Enforced Spinsterhood: Ḥaḍramawt through the Eyes of ʿAlī Aḥmad Bā Kathīr (1910–69)', *Die Welt des Islams* 37:1 (1997), 2–27 and her forthcoming study of the Ḥaḍramī reform movement.
50. Quataert, 'Clothing Laws', 409.
51. On this issue, cf. Nazih Ayubi, *Political Islam*, London 1993, 42–47.
52. Clifford Geertz, *The Interpretation of Cultures*, New York 1993, 320.
53. Burke, '*Res et Verba*', 149.
54. No title, 5f.
55. C. Snouck Hurgronje, *Mekka in the latter part of the 19th century*, Leiden 1931, 135, gives mûriyya.
56. ʿAbd al-Qādir al-Ṣabbān, *Personal communication* with H. Schönig in November 1997: silver or golden earring.
57. Moshe Piamenta, *Dictionary of post-classical Yemeni Arabic*, 2 vols, Leiden 1990, 1991, I, 93a.
58. R. Dozy, *Supplément aux dictionnaires arabes*, 2 vols, Beyrouth 1991, II, 227b: *gamasa bi-al-dhahab* dorer; cf. Piamenta, *Dictionary*, II, 360a: *gmz*—to glitter, to shine.
59. al-Ṣabbān, *Personal communication*: light cloth for women's dress; cf. Dozy, *Supplément*, I, 808b: *sīt Hindī* and *sīt Yamanī* for '*indienne*, toile de coton peinte'.
60. Serjeant, 'Recent Marriage Legislation', 478: *mu'an wa-shu'ūn al-a'rās* with the translation: 'matters and affairs of marriages'.
61. [Asmarra] 1949.
62. There are many more Ḥaḍramī scholars dealing with local subjects, but as their scientific works do not often pass beyond manuscript form_as Serjeant has already remarked, *Prose and Poetry from Ḥaḍramawt*, London 1951, IX, note 1—we rarely get access to them.
63. *Wādī* (or *Arḍ* or *Bilād*) *al-Aḥqāf* is the popular name for the Ḥaḍramawt in South Arabia: al-Ṣabbān, *ʿĀdāt wa-taqālīd*, 9–10. See also the detailed exposition in Carlo de Landberg, *Etudes sur les dialectes de l'Arabie méridionale*, I: *Ḥaḍramoût*, Leiden 1901, 148–160.
64. Doreen Ingrams, *A Time in Arabia*, London, 1970, 67.
65. Serjeant, 'Recent Marriage Legislation', 493 notes the term *gussah* in Arabic letters erroneously with *sīn*.
66. al-Ṣabbān, *ʿĀdāt*, 95.
67. Thus Serjeant 'Recent Marriage Legislation', 493, note 1 referring to Carlo de Landberg, *Glossaire Daṯînois*, 3 vols, Leiden 1920–49, III, 2369 and my own observations.
68. And men, as U. Freitag was told by ʿAbd al-ʿAzīz b. ʿAqīl in al-Mukallā.
69. See Hanne Schönig, 'Vielfältige Nutzung des *ʿilb*-Baumes. Ein Nachtrag', *Jemen-Report*, Jg. 29, 1/2 (1998) (forthcoming).
70. Serjeant, 'Recent Marriage Legislation', 493 and 497f.

71. al-Ṣabbān, *ʿĀdāt*, 95.
72. Ingrams, *Survey*, 102.
73. See Schönig. 'Vielfältige Nutzung', plate 2.
74. al-Ṣabbān, *ʿĀdāt*, 135, note 160.
75. Piamenta, *Dictionary*, II, 275a/b also gives *ṣubḥiyyah*; Dozy, *Supplément*, I, 814a also gives *ṣabāḥiyyah*.
76. Serjeant, 'Recent Marriage Legislation', 478 with note 2 and 485.
77. Ingrams, Survey, 103.
78. al-Ṣabbān, ʿĀdāt, 136, note 166: It is pronounced with ḍ, but ṭ is correct, perhaps ẓ?—a place surrounded by walls. He himself uses both *ẓillah* and *ḍillah* (64f.). The term refers to different objects, which provide shade, e.g. the large hats women wear during field work (Piamenta, *Dictionary*, II, 313a). Serjeant's informant quotes ẓallah: 'The invited guests rest in the shade of a large tree outside the village where the marriage is to take place. They fire off their rifles as a greeting, and to inform the villagers of their arrival. The villagers issue forth from their village to welcome the *maʿāzīm*, firing their rifles in reply, and escort them back to it' ('Recent Marriage Legislation', 493); al-Ṣabbān, *ʿĀdāt*, 64f. mentions it as well in the birth context: a public feast for women in the afternoon and evening of the wufā' (2.) on a wide place. All women who wish can participate, there is drum music and dances are performed.
79. Ibid., 103: *ʿuṣābah*—like a crown; 134, Anm. 148: It is given this name, as it is bound around the head with silk ribbons. It is allowed to be worn by the upper social classes only.—Piamenta, *Dictionary*, II, 329a: 'Frontlet band; a headband in which fragrant herbs are stuck'. According to L.A. Mayer, *Mamluk Costume*, Genève 1952, 71: a piece of cloth, which was wrapped around the head like a turban. Heather Colyer Ross, *The Art of Arabian Costume. A Saudi Arabian Profile*, Fribourg 1981, 167: 'Head circlet made of silver, leather and silver, reeds and copper wire, etc. worn by men and women.'—According to the information board in the Say'ūn museum, it is also called *ʿiṣābah sağīrah* in contrast to *ʿiṣābah kabīrah* which might be used as a synonym for the head garment *ḥaml* (3.2.).
80. al-Ṣabbān, *ʿĀdāt*, 108. For the *muštariḥah* see Serjeant, 'Recent Marriage Legislation', 488.
81. al-Ṣabbān, *ʿĀdāt*, 110f.
82. Serjeant, 'Recent Marriage Legislation', 492.
83. al-Ṣabbān, *ʿĀdāt*, 52f.
84. Ibid., 60.
85. Ibid., 61.
86. This part of the birth festivities is not mentioned in our document.
87. al-Ṣabbān, *ʿĀdāt*, 59.
88. See also Ingrams, *Survey*, 99.
89. al-Ṣabbān, *ʿĀdāt*, 58; *šammah means taqbīl*. Cf. Dozy, *Supplément*, I, 784a: rencontre, embrassement; Landberg, *Etudes*, I, 625.
90. One of the most expensive fumigating materials, more precious than frankincense.
91. al-Ṣabbān, *ʿĀdāt*, 57f.
92. Ibid., 60.

93. Ibid., 62. In the document: *rūs qub'* (para 4).
94. Ibid., 63.
95. Ibid., 64.
96. The museum exhibits concrete illustration (clothes, jewellery, coins, tea-, coffee- and kitchen-equipment in general), some of them being mentioned in the *Dalīl matḥaf al-'ādāt wa-al-taqālīd al-sa'biyyah* by al-Ṣabbān (2nd ed., [Say'ūn] 1986).
97. Ingrams, *Survey*, 94.
98. Ibid., 96.
99. Freya Start, *A Winter in Arabia*, London 1940, 5f.
100. Freya Stark, *The Southern Gates of Arabia*, London 1940, 110.
101. Lane, 2635a: *kahrab* and *kahrabā* or *kahrubā* from Persian *kāhu rubā*.
102. Dozy, *Supplément*, II, 503b.
103. Lucien Leclerc, *Traité des simples par Ibn el-Bëithar*. Notices et Extraits des Manuscrits de la Bibliothèque Nationale et Autres Bibliothèques, 3 vols, Paris 1877–1883, No. 1982.
104. Ingrams, *Survey*, 96.
105. Mundy, 'Ṣan'ā' Dress', 537a.
106. See al-Ṣabbān, *'Ādāt*, 103: '*quṭn manqūš maṣbūġ bi-al-sawād ka-al-ša'r al-aswad*'.
107. D. Ingrams, *A Time*, 67f.
108. Plate 2 shows the jewellery without the wig.
109. Ingrams, *Survey*, 102.
110. Piamenta, *Dictionary*, I, 262b.
111. al-Ṣabbān, *Ādāt*, 67: *muṭall* is a bracelet put around the new-born child's arm.
112. Landberg, *Glossaire*, I, 337.
113. al-Ṣabbān, *Dalīl*, 28 (ṣmṭ).
114. Landberg, *Etudes*, I, 86.
115. al-Ṣabbān, *Personal communication* and al-Ṣabbān, *'Ādāt*, 146, note 14 (*smṭ*).
116. Stark, *Gates*, 175.
117. Stark, *A Winter*, 141.
118. Ingrams, *Survey*, 96.
119. Ingrams, *A Time*, 29.
120. Hans Helfritz, *Vergessenes Südarabien. Wadis, Hochhäuser und Beduinen*, Leipzig 1936, 60.
121. Stark, *A Winter*, before 85; Ingrams, *A Time*, after 36.
122. See the translation of this short document in Schönig, 'Kaṯīrī documents'.
123. On *ẖudab* (*ẖidāb*) see Schönig, 'Yemeni Women's Traditional Cosmetics (I): Bodypainting (*naqš*) with Gall-ink (khidāb)', *Yemen Update*, Bulletin of the American Institute for Yemeni Studies 38 (1996), 10–15 and Schönig, 'Traditional Cosmetics of Women in Yemen. The black dye *khiḍāb*: Traditional and modern ways of fabrication', *Proceedings of the Seminar for Arabian Studies* 26 (1996), 135–144.
124. Ingrams, *Survey*, 96. Her information is partly taken from Freya Stark (*A Winter* and *Gates*), who often goes into more detail.
125. See also the enumeration of concrete substances in Serjeant, 'Recent Marriage Legislation', 497f.
126. *Lawsonia inermis*. It grows up to 2200 m in the 'Tihama foothills, lower

escarpment, higher escarpment': A. al-Hubaishi/K. M‚ller-Hohenstein, *An Introduction to the vegetation of Yemen*, Eschborn (GTZ), 1984, 198. J. Fleurentin/J.-M. Pelt, 'Repertory of drugs and medicinal plants of Yemen', Journal of Ethnopharmacology 6 (1982), (85–108), 98: Cultivated at 300–1000 m.

127. Synonyms are *šabb al-fuwād*: Armin Schopen, *Traditionelle Heilmittel in Jemen*, Wiesbaden 1983, 169, and *šabb yamānī*, Piamenta, *Dictionary*, I, 243a/b.
128. The translucent white alum-stone is also used in the armpit.
129. For this purpose she is seized (*qbḍ*) and brought to a certain place (al-Ṣabbān, *'Ādāt*, 87f.).
130. Until today there are always four *muḥanniyāt* called to the bride, one for each hand and foot.
131. In Yemen also *šādir*, see Schönig, 'The black dye *khiḍāb*, 136.
132. al-Ṣabbān, *'Ādāt*, 88.
133. Ibid., 92 and 131, note 81.
134. Ibid., 71, note 39: *rās qub'*—sugar in the shape of a pyramid, i.e. a sugar loaf.
135. Piamenta, *Dictionary*, II, 329b: porridge, legume or cornflour gruel.
136. al-Ṣabbān, *'Ādāt*, 61f.
137. R.B. Serjeant, Aḥmad Qaryeh, Annika Bornstein: 'Food and Cookery', in Serjeant and Lewcock, *Ṣan'ā'*, 542–558, 551a/b, who also quote some proverbs dealing with *'aṣīd*. They, however, refer especially to the former North.
138. Serjeant, *Prose and Poetry*, 25–33.
139. Landberg, *Etudes*, I, 55: cafetière.
140. Serjeant, 'Recent Marriage Legislation', 493.
141. al-Ṣabbān, *'Ādāt*, 152–162 and al-Ṣabbān, *Dalīl*, 48–52.
142. There are a lot of publications on the history of coffee, which originates from Ethiopia, and on the harbour al-Mukhā, which has given Mocha its name. See among others: Hans Becker, Volker Höhfeld, Horst Kopp, *Kaffee aus Arabien. Der Bedeutungswandel eines Weltwirtschaftsgutes und seine siedlungsgeographische Konsequenz an der Trockengrenze der Ökumene*, Wiesbaden 1979; C.G. Brouwer, *Al-Mukha: Profile of a Yemeni Seaport, 1615–1640*, Amsterdam 1996; Landberg, *Etudes*, II/2, 1055–1078; Eric Macro, *Bibliography of Yemen and notes on Mocha*, Univ. of Miami Press, Coral Gables, Florida 1960; Wolf Mueller, *Bibliographie des Kaffee, des Kakao der Schokolade, des Tee und deren Surrogate bis zum Jahre 1900*, Bad Bocklet u.a. 1960; Antoinette Schnyder-v. Waldkirch, *Wie Europa den Kaffee entdeckte. Reiseberichte der Barockzeit als Quellen zur Geschichte des Kaffees*, Zürich 1988.
143. al-Ṣabbān, *Dalīl*, 48.
144. Landberg, *Etudes*, II/2, 1072.
145. *Survey*, 157.
146. *ǧafalah*—coffee with husk (Piamenta, *Dictionary*, I, 70a); *ǧafal* 'est le café qui est encore entier (la cérise encore entière) et n'a pas encore été conquassé' (Landberg, *Etudes*, I, 86; see also Ibid., II/2, 1056).
147. L.W.C. van den Berg, *Le Hadhramout et les colonies Arabes dans l'archipel Indien*, Batavia 1886, 68.
148. See Horst Kopp, 'Die Landwirtschaft des Jemen. Vom Mokka zum Qāt', in Werner Daum, *Jemen*, Innsbruck, Frankfurt/Main, ^{2}1988, 365–369 and the poem 'Der

Qāt und der Kaffee' in Aviva Klein-Franke, 'Die Juden im Jemen', in Daum, *Jemen*, 256–275.

149. Literally: coffee roasting. Actually with *ṣād*, but according to Landberg, *Glossaire*, I, 494 also with *sīn*.
150. al-Ṣabbān, *'Ādāt*, 58.
151. D. Ingrams, *A Time*, 68.
152. D. Ingrams, *Survey*, 157.
153. D. Ingrams, *A Time*, 55f.
154. D. Ingrams, *Survey*, 157.
155. al-Ṣabbān, *Dalīl*, 52.
156. See note 91.
157. D. Ingrams, *Survey*, 158. See also al-Ṣān, *Dalīl*, 53.
158. Comparable to the metathesis of *kahrab/karhab* (amber), see 3.1.
159. al-Ṣabbān, *Dalīl*, 44.
160. al-Ṣabbān, *Personal communication.*
161. Landberg, *Glossaire*, vol. III, 1990: Ḥḍr = *sukkar.*
162. al-Ṣābbān, *Personal communication.*
163. See Schönig, 'Bodypainting (*naqš*)', 12.
164. al-Ṣabbān, *'Ādāt*, 71, note 39.
165. Landberg, *Etudes*, vol. I, 539: g — prononcé y, demi-voyelle.
166. al-Ṣabbān, *Dalīl*, 51.

The Small Long-handled Axes of Oman*

David Insall

The small long-handled axe (*ğerz*) still carried today in the Musandam has been compared with similar small axes found in excavations at early sites in eastern Arabia, indicating 4000 years of cultural continuity. This paper describes how small long-handled axes have traditionally been carried throughout most of Oman and are still in use in some regions. They fall into two groups: the '*maḫğān*-type' having a very long shaft, carried only by *sāwiyāt* (women of the mountain bedouin) of the Eastern Ḥajar range, and the '*ğerz*-type' with a shorter handle, carried mainly by men on camel back throughout the deserts of central, southern and western Oman. Unlike the *ğerz*, the *Maḫğān*-type are purely

* In this paper the short 'a' is spelt as a short 'e' in a number of words, in accordance with the pronunciation widely used for this letter in Omani dialect. Thus '*jabal*' is spelt '*jebel*'; '*banī*' is spelt '*benī*'. Other features of transcription are j for *jīm*.

The assistance of the following is gratefully acknowledged: HE Sayyid Mohammed bin Ahmed Al-Bu Sa'īdi (His Majesty The Sultan's Personal Adviser for Historical and Religious Affairs), Sheikh Mohammed bin Ahmed bin Hadeyah Al-Mahri ('Bin Hadeyah'), Mr Mohammed bin Khalfan Ash Shu'ayli, Mr Ali bin Salim Bait Sa'īd, Sheikh Sultan bin Sa'īd Al-Hindi Al-Wahibi, Mr Mohammed bin Sa'īd Al-Gahafi Al-Wahibi, Mr Bakheit bin Mohammed Al-Muqaymi, Mr Sa'īd bin Ahmed Al-Hassayni, Mr Ali bin Sa'ad Al-Muqaymi, Mr Ali bin Nasser Ar Rasibi, Mr Salim bin Nasser Al-Musherfi, Mr Abdullah Sa'īd As Sa'adi, Mr Sa'īd bin Ali Al-Harmali, Mr Subeyh bin Hafidh Ar Rahbi, Mr Salim bin Saif Ar Rahbi and many others who contributed information about Omani axes; Professor P.M. Costa of the University of Bologna for encouraging the study and commenting on this paper; Dr Paul Yule for providing sketches and details of axes found at Samad Ash Shan; Dr Shahina A. Ghazanfar for providing the latest information on *Acacia gerardii* and *Ziziphus hajarensis*.

This paper is dedicated to the memory of the late Sheikh Majid bin Sa'īd Al-Muqaymi, who strove tirelessly to bring help to his community, but sadly died in 1995, unable to witness completion of the final kilometre of the road to Jaylah.

functional with no ceremonial role. Thus the 'axe culture' appears to have survived, not merely in Musandam, but throughout almost all regions of Oman.

Background

In December 1994 Professor Paolo Costa gave me a copy of his paper in which he recounts the puzzlement of archaeologists at the small size of the axes found at sites dating from the second to the first millenium BC in eastern Arabia (Costa, 1993). Of those described, some were considered to be too weak to be efficient working tools and were probably meant to be used for ceremonial purposes, though others were simpler and sturdier, giving the impression that they were actual weapons, 'perhaps charged with a ceremonial and symbolic meaning.'

He then draws a comparison with the small long-handled axe or *ğerz* which is still carried by the people of Musandam at the northern extremity of the Sultanate of Oman where it flanks the Strait of Hormuz. This axe, now primarily carried for ceremonial purposes, he concludes, 'can usefully be compared with the small excavated axes of which it can be considered to be the latest descendant. In its use we can therefore see 4000 years of cultural continuity.' In the Appendix he describes the *ğerz* as 'undoubtedly a unique implement with no parallel in Arabia.' A small long-handled axe he had seen carried in northern Yemen was larger than the average *ğerz* and was a working tool used primarily for cutting wood. Professor R.B. Serjeant later drew his attention to a battle axe found in the Wāḥidī Sultanate in Yemen, but the shape of the blade was quite different from that of the much smaller *ğerz*. (Vincent, Jr., 1991 and Costa, 1993, 172.)

This prompted a search through diary notes made in the 1970s and 1980s. In 1981 during a helicopter visit to the remote village of 'Amq Bi'r high in the Wadi Ṭīwī in the Eastern Ḥajar range of mountains in Northern Oman, some 220 km south east of Muscat, I recorded seeing a shepherdess (*sāwiyah*) of the Benī Muqaym leave the village with a child in a basket slung over her back: 'Against her other shoulder, she carried a small long-handled axe remarkably like the *ğerz* of Musandam.'

The *Maḥğān*-type Small Axe

Distribution. Enquiries confirmed that women of several of the tribes in the mountains to the south and east of Muscat as far as Ṣur, generally described as the Eastern Ḥajar, used to carried such axes, although very few do so nowadays. The tribes whose women carried them included the Nuwayrah and Na'ab of Jebel al-Aswad; eastwards the Hanāẓilah of Jebel al-Abyaḍ; the Sa'ādiyyīn of

Shenah; the Raḥbiyyīn north of Ibra (but with shorter shafts); the Benī ʻĪsa, Benī Muqaym, the Benī Ḥaṣayn and Benī Suba‘, who live in the high mountains between the Wadi Ta‘in and the watersheds of Wadi Ṭiwī and Wadi Shāb further to the east, as well as al-Rubāh and the Benī Ǧadānah in the upper watersheds of the Wadi Suwayh, Wadi al-‘Arabiyyīn and the Ḥayl Selmah area. On the other hand, women of the Raḥbiyyīn, whose flocks graze the foothills at the western end of the Eastern Ḥajar, are said not to have carried them.

Geography and Culture of the Eastern Ḥajar

Little has been described of the 'habitat' of the *Maḥǧān*-type small axe. This most remote and inaccessible region includes the so-called Jebel Benī Jābir, one of several plateaux rising to over 2000 m at their highest point. During the late 1970s and throughout the 1980s it was progressively opened up to the rest of the country. Initially a helicopter administrative and 'flying doctor' service was provided, also enabling provisions and building materials to be flown in. Later, graded roads were built, enabling drinking water to be delivered, children to travel to school, more extensive health and veterinary services to be provided, and livestock to be taken further afield for sale. Once Oman's most remote *falaǧ* settlement, some 25 km distant from any vehicle access, a road now reaches to within 1 km of the village of Jaylah at the head of the Wadi Shāb.

The rolling upper lands are relatively barren, with scarce springs or short-term catchments deep in the sheer ravines which furrow them. An important tree, found in the Eastern Ḥajar, the *ṭiyū* (*Ceratonia oreothauma*), is to be found here, as well as other plants and animals endemic to Oman. The flora and fauna of the region reflect both northern influences from Iran and Pakistan, including relict species from the days when the Strait of Hormuz was a land bridge, and African influences, evidenced by relict plant species which suggest that the monsoon climate of Dhofar extended much further north than it does today. (Ghazanfar, 1995, pers. comm.)

The people rear goats and sheep, as well as their many donkeys which still provide a main means of transport for carrying goods and, yoked in trains of six, water to seasonal settlements away from the roads. Although more permanent houses have now been built where there is vehicle access, those who derive their living from livestock rearing still move seasonally according to the available grazing. They are tough and fit, with remarkable agility as rock climbers, often scaling the steepest pitches barefoot. In 1982 the author visited the Burūǧ Kibaykib, the now well-known 'tower tombs' dating from the second millenium BC, in a walking party which included HE Khalfan bin Nasser al-Wuhaibi (then President of the Consultative Assembly, and now Vice-President of the State Assembly), HE al-Liwa Bakheit bin Sa‘īd al-Shanfari (Assistant Inspector-

General of Customs) and Mr Kamal bin Abdurredha bin Sultan. During the donkey-borne picnic lunch by the towers, a group of bedouin children scrambled up the 8 m high near-vertical outer wall of one of the tombs as if it was a staircase.

Legend has it that a man called Kibaykib built the towers.

> It was long ago in the age of Jahiliyyah. Although he was part-*ğinn*, he lived there alone and never troubled anyone. He ate donkey meat, which he cooked on hot stones in a hole in the ground, just as we make medebi today. You can still see the place. He had a magic sword, a thunderbolt, which could cut anything in two, even iron and rocks. He used it to cut rocks to shape the stones with which he then built the towers.
>
> He often slept at a place called Nawm, in one of the towers. He would crawl in through the narrow entrance and could then stand up inside.
>
> One evening a bedouin of the Sa'ādiyyīn called Qadāḥ visited the spring-fed pool of 'Ayn Nagab to bathe. It is near to Gabiyatayn and has a large mango tree which is still there today. As he came down he saw the lady spirit *(ğinniyyah)* who lived there and owned the land. She was bathing naked in the pool. He crept up from behind her and seized her, held her tightly in his grip, drew milk from her breast and drank it. In shock and surprise, she declared, 'Oh! I accept you. You are a son amongst my sons, drinking my milk. Otherwise I would have killed you, annihilated you. However I now want you to go and get hold of Kibaykib's sword. I'll tell you where the pagan is hiding. You'll find him at *Ramiyat Sīr* (also '*Ruwāmi Sīr*'), but you must know his special trait. If he is lying down and his eyes are closed, then he is awake, but if his eyes are open, he is asleep and you can take the thunderbolt. You will see this from its glowing light because he always keeps it near his head.'
>
> Qadāḥ then went to the place, saw the glow of the thunderbolt and Kibaykib lying by it. His eyes were open, which meant that he was asleep. So he crept up and grabbed it from him, but it then made a noise. Kibaykib woke up and then ran off at great speed, bounding like a leopard. Swordless and afraid, he went up and over the high jebel and down into the Wadi Sūq. Although unable to keep up with him, Qadāḥ followed him. When Kibaykib turned on him to try to get the sword back Qadāḥ would run to a water pool for safety, because Kibaykib was afraid of water. Then Kibaykib took up residence in a small cave in a cliff which is still there today, commanding the main route through the Wadi Sūq, which lies between Ṭiwī and Ibra. Those who came from the west brought dates and those from the east brought fish. Kibaykib would rush out and steal their goods, so that he could eat. The people became fed up with Kibaykib's behaviour. They told Qadāḥ: 'Either you give back Kibaykib his thunderbolt so he can go back to his towers, or else you must kill him with it.'
>
> Qadāḥ decided to kill Kibaykib. Waiting until he was out in the open near his cave, he then cut him into two halves. His head and shoulders fell dead nearby, but his legs and the rest of his body ran a long way, until they too fell dead. That is why he has two graves, both called Qabr Kibaykib and several kilometres apart.

(Sheikh Mājid bin Sa'īd al-Muqaymi and Bakheit bin Mohammed al-Muqaymi, 1981, pers.comm. Sa'īd bin Aḥmed al-Ḥasseini, 1998, pers. comm.)

About six years ago Sa'īd bin Aḥmad was walking with Sheikh Mājid at a place overlooking the Ramiyat Sīr towers. They saw a light glowing at the foot of one of them. It was nothing like a fire or a camping cooker. They thought that someone was trying to attract their attention, perhaps needing help. When they reached the place the light had vanished and there was no sign of anyone having been there.

As one has come to expect with an unwritten bedouin legend passed by word of mouth amongst different communities, a different version exists amongst the Benī 'Īsa and was recorded at al-Sumayyah, beyond the downstream end of the Wadi Ta'īn.

> There is an old belief that if a woman sleeps naked, she risks being raped by the Devil and will give birth to a deformed or bedevilled child. Kibayti (*sic*) was born deformed, having only a stick-like body, but huge powerful arms and legs and was about three metres tall. He looked like the image of the Devil. He was armed with a thunderbolt, which he had grabbed during a thunderstorm when lightning struck open water. In these circumstances a thunderbolt does not disappear into the ground but remains for a few seconds on the surface of the water, long enough to be picked up by hand. If pointed at anything, it will cut it in two, including a human being. When not in use, it can be kept alight provided it is buried in flour with the glowing tip exposed above the surface. He used it to threaten people and rob people of the provisions which they brought across the mountains between Ibra and the Wadi Beni Khalid. However, provided they gave him food he would not harm them.
>
> He used to hide in one of three of the towers, which he built, sleeping in a different one each night to avoid detection. One night a local man searched the area with a group of friends and spotted the glowing tip through the small entrance at the base of one of the towers. He saw Kibaytī asleep, crept up and grabbed the thunderbolt, which he turned against him, cutting him in two. Kibaytī screamed 'Cut me more', but another man said 'No, two halves is enough to kill a devil. Wait for quarter of an hour' and Kibaytī died. The thunderbolt was kept alight by the Sa'ādiyyīn for a number of years in a container, replacing the flour every year. However, one day there was not enough flour, sickness befell the village and they found that the thunderbolt had vanished into the ground, leaving the earth scorched.
>
> (Sa'īd 'Alī Nāṣir al-Harmalī, 1997, pers. comm.).

Where there are permanent springs feeding date gardens, such as at Jaylah, houses are built of rock with earth mortar, *ṭiyū* wood often used for the lintels. Sometimes they are plastered with locally made *ṣarūj*, a cement made by baking limestone over palm log kilns, which was also traditionally used to build and line the open irrigation channels. However factory-made cement is now generally brought in for this purpose today. Many of the older houses have tiny doorways, particularly those used primarily for storage of possessions when their owners are away grazing flocks elsewhere and outside the season of the date harvest. In this respect they may be compared with the *bayt al-qafl* of the Šiḥūḥ of Musandam (Costa, 1993, 16) (Plate 1).

It is a region with a distinct cultural heritage, where dialects still differ between the tribes. The Benī 'Īsa mountain bedouin pronounce the letter '*ğīm*' as the Russian 'zh', calling the settlement of al-Ğurr 'Lazhur' and that of Ğabiyatayn 'Zhobtīn', identical to the pronunciation of the same letter in Morocco and Algeria, but quite different from that of their immediate neighbours, the Benī Muqaym and the Sa'ādiyyīn, the latter pronouncing it as the soft 'y' of the Ğa'alān.

It is also the home of the third type of Omani traditional flute, a single pipe open at both ends with four finger-holes, which is held vertically and blown across the open end at the top, in the same way as pan-pipes. It was first seen amongst the Sa'adiyyīn, the Benī Muqaym and the Benī Ḥasayn and tape-recorded by the author in 1981.

Plate 1: A Sa'ādi *bayt al-qafl* at Šebekah, Wadi Sūq, Eastern Ḥajar.

A fine tradition of handicrafts still exists there, including the weaving of equipment to saddle the donkeys. Ḥamdān bin Sālim bin Rashid al-Muqaymi, the last maker of bronze donkey bells died in 1981, but happily his brother Ḥāfiẓ has recently taken up the craft in the same workshop in the remote village of al-Ḡomb in Wadi Shāb. He also makes steel tools, such as tweezers, awls, hand saws and axes. A second axe-maker is Khamīs bin Muḥsin bin Khamīs al-Muqaymī of Jaylah, who also lives at Qaron (more correctly spelt 'Qarān' but pronounced 'Qaron' in the local dialect of that region) and al-Ḡomb, dependent on the season and the grazing.

The Qaron *Maḥğān*-type Small Axe (*ḥosīn*; *qadūm*)

Many messages requesting the manufacture and purchase of a small axe were passed without success. Finally in April 1996 a secondhand one was bought from the father of a girl who was just setting out with the goats in the early morning, the axe resting against her shoulder.

The shaft is fairly new and the axe-head bright through daily use. The overall width of the blade is 3.5 cm. The main dimension, from the edge of the blade to the outside of the eye, is 7.9 cm. The width of the band around the eye is 1.5 cm and its thickness varies from 4 to 5 mm. The eye is elliptical, between 2.1 cm and 2.6 cm internally, with a small v-shaped recess, only 7 mm deep, towards the blade. (Plate 2).

It is clearly hand-forged, showing a few irregular hammer marks on the surface of the blade. The outside surface of the band bears fine parallel cracks at right angles to its circumference, apparently from forging and bending at slightly too low a temperature or at too great a speed. This indicates that it was formed by bending a flat bar through 360 degrees, but there is no sign of the join on either side of the blade. It is apparently made out of one piece of steel and weighs 90 gm.

The blade is blunt, although its smoothness at the cutting edge suggests that it may have been sharpened during or since manufacture. It is clearly not used today for cutting wood. The extended 'hook' in the profile of the lower point of the blade differs from that of any others described.

The shaft measures 1.535 m overall in length, tapering very slightly from 1.9 cm at the head to 1.5 cm at the other end, both ends being slightly bevelled. It only deviates from perfect straightness along its full length by 5 mm. Two shallow diagonal notches have been cut to fit the slight taper on the blade side of the eye. A single wooden wedge is in place to secure the head to the shaft, which, like the one seen at Jaylah, is narrower than the eye.

The knotty hardwood shaft is made from *qaṣm* wood, a tree new to science, recently described and given the name *Ziziphus hajarensis*. There are some

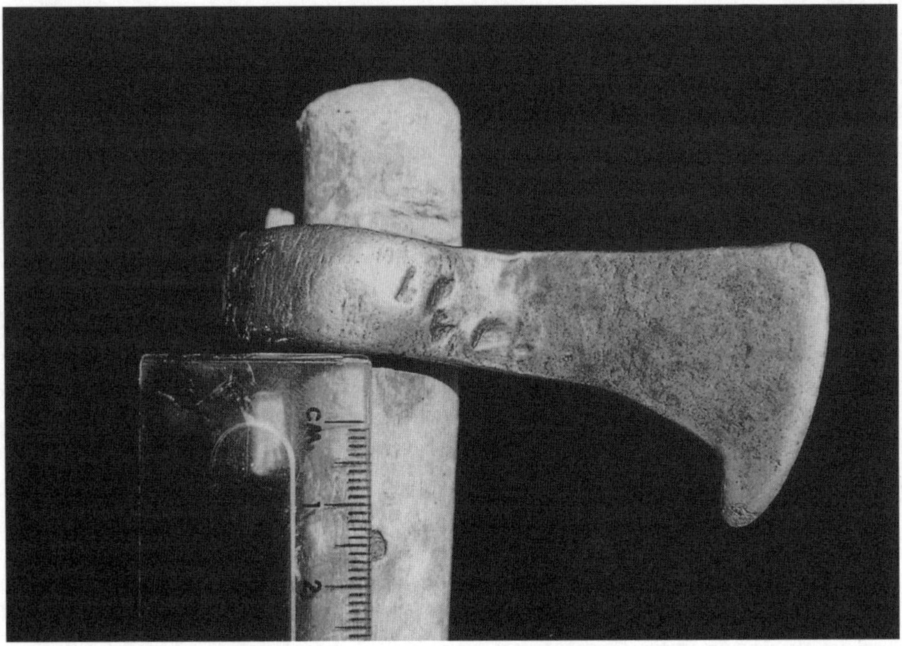

Plate 2: The Qaron axe, showing wooden wedge, hand-forging indentations and bending cracks.

39 knots over the surface area, spaced with even density throughout. The leaves of *qaṣm* are similar to those of *Ziziphus spina Christi*, but the tree is spinier, with small crab-apple-like fruits whose thin outer flesh is eaten locally. The large hard nuts inside are crushed and, traditionally, the small kernels ground to a flour, made into a paste and cooked or eaten raw. It is important to the diet of the Arabian *tahr* (*Hemitragus jayakari*), the endemic mountain goat which occurs in the region. (Munton, 1985, 23)

The Jaylah Small Axe

Some weeks later I photographed an axe that I had seen at Jaylah. It had been fitted with a new shaft replacing a broken one. As it differs from the first one, the details are given below.

The overall width of the blade is 3.2 cm. This is remarkably close to that of the 2nd Millenium axe (2.9 m) excavated from a tomb at al-Khadhrah, near Samad al-Šān, some 100 km to the west of Jaylah, but only 30 km from Yaḥmadi where the Jaylah axe may have been made (being identical to that from Shenah). (Costa, 1993, 153) However two more recently found in grave excavations at

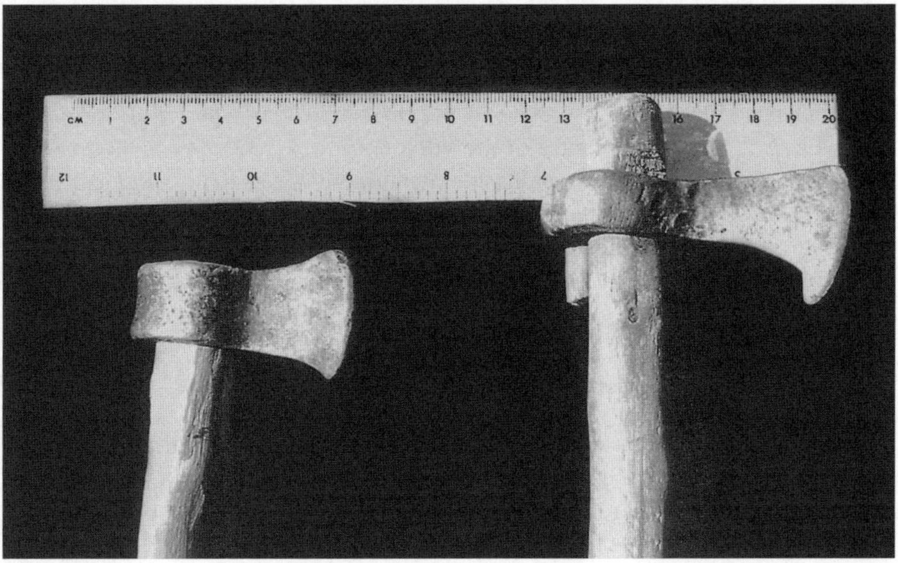

Plate 3: The Jaylah axe (left) compared to the Qaron axe (right).

Samad al-Šān, one dated *c.*200–400 AD, more closely resemble the *ğerz*, having long narrow blades and hammerheads opposite the blade. (Yule, 1994).

From the edge of the blade to the outside of the eye is 6 cm (the al-Khadhrah axe is 7.9 cm). The width of the band is 19 mm, its thickness varying from 4 to 6 mm. The eye is almost round, between 2.1 cm and 2.3 cm, with the wedge-shaped recess 3 mm deep. A line extends from this recess on the upper surface, towards the blade edge to a point 10 mm from it, but off-centre by about 1 mm, showing that it was forged from a single flat bar. It weighs 98 gm.

Also made of *qaṣm* wood, the new shaft is 1.340 m long, tapering from 2.1 cm to 1.5 cm, off-straight by 1 cm and with 33 knots. As the thick end fits the axe, there is no wooden wedge. (Plate 3).

Unlike the Qaron axe, there is no pronounced hook, but the lower radius of the blade has a sharper curvature than the upper one. With a similarly blunt blade, it is heavier and stubbier than that from Qaron, but more closely resembles that excavated from al-Khadhrah.

The Shenah Small Axe

An identical axe head without a shaft was photographed in 1997 at Shenah, a saucer-shaped plateau containing a group of villages of the Sa'ādiyyin, to the south of al-Sumayyah and outside the main massif of the Eastern Ḥajar. This axe was said to have been made by a smith of Yaḥmadī, near Ibra, although there used to be two Siyābī brothers who were the smiths in Shenah. One is still alive but now blind. They worked in the open under a large *sidrah* (*Ziziphus spina Christi*) tree in the centre of the village.

The rim of the Shenah plateau has its own high peak, al-Kol, rising to 1350 m above sea level, which contains the only known population of the endemic *ṭiyū* tree (*Ceratonia oreothauma*) outside the main massif of the Eastern Ḥajar. Within the plateau are several hundred unsurveyed beehive tombs, as well as a major collection of rock art sites shown to the author in 1997.

Uses

A demonstration of the use of the Qaron axe was given. It was raised to a *ṭulḥah* tree (*Acacia gerardii*), the thick-trunked and gnarled acacia species dominant at higher altitudes of the region. The blunt blade was gently tapped against a branch causing leaves to fall, so that they could be collected on a mat and fed to goats and sheep. The hook at the lower end of the blade was said to be used to pull down the branches so that the nutritious fruits (*karamūs*) of the tree, when in season, could be gathered by hand for feeding to the flocks. It was also said that in former times when the sun was hot in the middle of the day and there was a severe drought, a shepherdess could use the axe to cut a few shoots from the top of the tree and feed them to the starving animals. She would then be able to settle down and rest.

It is also said that traditionally the Ḥanāẓilah *sāwiyah* would carry it as a weapon, to defend herself against attack. Whilst sitting down to eat, she would not lay it on the ground but rest it against her shoulder as a warning to any would-be intruder that she was armed. The menfolk (*siwān*) of the region, on the other hand, carry on their belts a sharp and functional wooden-handled knife, sometimes decorated with silver, as elsewhere amongst the mountain siwān of Northern Oman. It is replaced by the silver sheathed curved dagger (*ẖunǧar*) by the better-off or on more formal occasions.

A few scratches on the surface of the shaft and a partial split near its base, suggest that it has also been used to beat trees. This method is common throughout other regions of the Sultanate, where a long pole with no metal head or hook is used to strike acacia branches over woven mats or cloths to gather the leaves, avoiding cutting off the branches. The action is described as *maẖbāṭ* (striking) and the stick is called the *maḥǧān*. (ʻAlī bin Nāṣir al-Rāsibī, pers. comm.) This action is however frowned on and traditionally forbidden in many areas, as it damages the tree by breaking the bark and releasing moisture.

A *maḥǧān* seen at Shenah consisted of a long wooden pole about 4 metres long, with a stout wooden hook made by cutting a side branch at the junction at the thicker end, made of *sidrah* wood (*Ziziphus spina Christi*) (Plate 4). The hook is used to lower the branches to assist browsing, to make *karamūs*-gathering easier and to enable the branches to be shaken, rather than beaten, so that some of the leaves fall to the ground. A four-handled woven mat is used to collect the fallen fodder, which is then carried by threading the pole through the loop handles. A similar implement, called maqseyp is said to be used by Jibbāli shepherdesses in the mountains of the southern governorate of Dhofar. This one is chosen on the tree, the green wood bent progressively for up to a year to make the hook and is finally cut when it is ready. ('Alī bin Sālim Bayt Sa'īd pers. comm.) 'A date-palm leaf mat and a staff with a hooked head:– they said, "household furniture"' forms part of an old Omani proverb implying that everyone has things in proportion to his position and capacity. (Jayakar, 1987, 37).

Others commonly seen in northern Oman are of similar length, but have no hook, suggesting that they are only used for *maẖbāṭ*, the *karamūs* falling during the operation and the branches never lowered for browsing animals.

Plate 4: A hooked *maḥǧān* at Shenah.

The Legend of Hayl Selmah

The legend of Hayl Selmah describes an event at Hayl Selmah just three kilometres to the north of Qaron. One version related to the author in 1981 is as follows:

> Selmah, a bedouin girl aged about thirty, one morning penned her goats in an enclosure near Hayl Selmah and went off on a long journey to fetch some dates, rice and other food (*zād*). Late that afternoon she returned to find that all of her seven two-month-old kid goats had been killed by a leopard. He was lying there asleep, guarding them and waiting until they were high enough to eat. She then wrapped a pair of trousers over her neck and body, with a spiky thistle (*kanab*, *Echinops spinosissimus*), to protect herself and went up to him with her axe raised high, shouting 'You're despicable! You're an abortion, for doing this!' He got up, came forward and struck her with one paw on her body and the other in her eye. At the same moment she swung down the axe and split the leopard's head right down the middle.
>
> Later, relatives found them both dead in one another's arms. To honour her bravery, God made seven stars come down from the sky, creating the seven *hosilāt* or sinkholes. The largest, called hosilat maqandelī, has since been explored and found to be the second largest known underground chamber in the world. From that time it had been publicized under a new name of Majlis al-ginn, although the record has now been set straight. (S. Hanna & M. Al Belushi, 1996, 67–74). The other five are called: H̱osilah Manqodh, H̱osilat al 'Adāb, H̱osilah Ḥanṭawṭ, H̱osilah beyn Laḥiyūl and H̱osilat 'Aqabat H̱osil. (Names recorded in the hand of Sheikh Mājid bin Sa'īd al-Muqaymi, 1994).

Today's *Maḥǧān*-type axe is not sharp enough to split a leopard's head in two, and there are no longer any leopards in that region, but its potential role as a personal defensive weapon cannot be ignored: in 1993 a woman of al-Rubah at the village of Sawqah some 15 km to the north west of Hayl Selmah was attacked and injured by a wolf at the edge of the village. She was not carrying an axe.

Discussion

Unlike the *ǧerz*, this axe appears to be purely functional with no ceremonial role, but its functions are reported to include personal defence. It appears to have no special name amongst the communities so far visited, beyond the general colloquial name for an axe of any size in the eastern Ḥajar region, *h̠oṣīn*. The derivation of this word, however, could suggest a more warlike role for it, being close to the verb *ḥaṣa*, meaning to emasculate. However one source at al-Sumayyah said that the Jebel Siwān called the small axes *qadūm* and the larger axes *ẖoṣīn*, whilst the villagers below referred to both as *ẖoṣīn*, the small one *ẖoṣīn sāgīr* and the large one *ẖoṣīn kabīr*.

The pronounced hook on the blade of the Qaron axe appears to replace the hook of the hook-type *maḥgān*, but additionally gives it both cutting and defensive capabilities.

Whether simple or ornate, the *ğerz* always has a hammer head opposite the blade edge, unlike some axes excavated from early tombs. The *maḥgān*-type axes do not have one. In this respect they appear to be closer relatives of the ancient axes than the *ğerz*.

The Camel-borne small axes (*qadūm*; *fa's* [Arabic]; *mansayp* [Mahri])

Distribution. Within days of completion of the final draft of a paper about the axes so far described, I met a man of the Jenebah from central Oman who was carrying a Sḥūḥī *ğerz*. Although made in Musandam, he had bought it from a friend in the UAE. When asked why he carried it, he said that there were similar axes amongst the Āl Wahībah and the Jenebah. A man of the Āl Wahībah then took me to a settlement near Sarab, to the north of Duqm, where he showed me one which had been made by an Omani smith at Sanaw. He then arranged for the same man to make me a new one.

The picture then developed rapidly. It became apparent that most if not all of the bedouin tribes of the desert regions had traditionally carried small axes when travelling by camel. Apart from the Āl Wahībah and the Jenebah, they were said to have been carried by the Mahrah, the Duru‘, the Manāsīr, the ‘Awāmir and all the tribes of what is now the UAE, but not in the mountains of Dhofar. One was seen at the home of a Maserfī family near Bilād Benī Bū Ḥasan in the Ja‘lān. It was one of a set of four axes of different sizes, Omani-made and of high quality. All had been given new shafts made of steel pipe, welded on to the axe (Plate 5).

Description of the camel-borne small axes

Although axes are made to individual order, the small ones generally vary little in size or shape. Those seen, as well as some described, all have hammer heads opposite the blade, like the *ğerz*. The smith makes the axe but his client makes the shaft.

The shaft of the Wahībī axe is 55 cm long and made of *gāf* wood (*Prosopis cineraria*) (Plate 6). The measure used by the Āl Wahībah for the overall length is the length of one's arm plus the width of two fingers. That carried by the eastern Mahrah is measured as the distance from the tip of the elbow to the tip

Plate 5: Set of four small axes belonging to the Maserfī family in the Ja'lān.

Plate 6: A new Wahībī axe.

of the knuckles of one's clenched fist, about 36 cm. Shafts are also made of *sidr* wood (*Ziziphus spina Christi*), favoured for it strength.

The blade of the Wahībī axe weighs 170 gm, or nearly twice that of Qaron. The blade is slightly curved with a maximum width of 4.8 cm, and the distance from the tip of the blade to the flat of the hammer head is 8 cm. The diameter of the eye is 2.2 cm, its depth 1.3 cm and the minimum thickness of the band round the eye is 6 mm. The lower flank of the blade has a sharper radius than the upper one, giving it the same hooking facility as the *Maḥǧān*-type axes. There is no sign of any join to indicate from what shape of metal it was forged. The black finish suggests that it was finally quenched in oil.

Uses

The *qadūm* was carried in the camel bag (*harag*) on all long journeys and used for cutting bites fodder from the upper branches of *gāf* trees (*Prosopis cineraria*) for the camel. It was also used for polling these trees, mostly in the winter months, to stimulate growth of the lower branches ensuring that they remained accessible to browsing camels and to travellers on camelback. The practice is now forbidden by law, as a general measure to protect all trees from overuse and excessive damage.

One source, Bin Hadeyah, quoted an old saying amongst the bedouins: 'He who hasn't an axe won't get wood. He who has no land won't live. He who doesn't have onions doesn't live'. He described how you could stop for a rest during a long journey, use the axe to chip a few pieces of dead wood to make a fire and relax. At night when the camels were cold they would use the axe to cut fruits from the trees for them. His axe, made at Ḥabbī, near Bahlā, was of such good steel that once when he went to Saudi Arabia on pilgrimage many people there wanted to buy it. He preferred one a little broader than many, about the width of the palm of his hand (c. 9 cm blade width), and kept it very sharp. It was used for slaughtering camels or 'wild and awkward cattle', as well for butchering the meat and smaller bones. Heavier axes were used for cutting the large bones. 'It was not carried as a status symbol: years ago it was said, 'He who carries not a *ẖunǧar* is not a man.' The *ẖunǧar* was the means of defence, as well as the knife and the gun, not the axe.'

Places of Manufacture

There were, and still are, smiths making axes to order in the principal areas where the bedouin traditionally come during the date harvest or to visit or trade in the *sūq*. Sanaw, Adam, the towns of the Ǧa'lān, Ṣalālah and Ḥabbī (near Bahlā) are all centres where the *qadūm* can still be made and all the axe-makers are Omani. Bin Ḥadeyah described the Awlād Amīrī of Ḥabbī as being the finest of all. His family, the Mahrah of Šelīm in the Governorate of Dhofar, always had theirs made there. 'They were better than those made in Ṣalālah.' He described a type of steel called '*mashah fawrah*', presumably referring to the quenching process after forging. This was the best of all: 'It could cut iron as well as wood.'

Discussion

The *qadūm* of the desert tribes has a shorter shaft than the *Maḥǧān*-type axe of the mountains, so that it can easily be carried on camelback. Its traditional use is mainly as a cutter, the hook-like lower curvature making it easier to draw down branches so that they can be held and cut.

Essentially a sharp tool, it has a wide range of cutting uses. This, combined with the hammerhead opposite the blade, the shorter shaft and the sharper curvature at the lower flank of the blade, brings it close to the typical Shuḥī *ǧerz* in design. However it has a wider blade than the *ǧerz*, as well as a shorter distance between the hammerhead and the blade tip. Unlike the *ǧerz*, the qadūm is not reported to have been decorated and has no ceremonial role. Nor was it normally used as a weapon for defence or in conflict.

Other Axes and Other Areas

Larger axes, generally called *ẖosīn* (but latterly also *fa's*), are used throughout Oman for cutting timber, thinner longer and heavier ones being used to split thick logs and tree stumps.

There remain areas with no history of small axes. It has been reported that *siwān* of the Benī Riyām and other communities in the Jebel al-Akhdhar did not carry them. Nor has any evidence of their use been found in the western Ḥajar range, northwards from the Jebel al-Akhdhar to the northern border. In the upper Wadi Saramī, Wilāyat Habūrah, a tool called a *maqsal* was described as having been used in a similar way to the *Maḥǧān*-type axe. It consists of a sharp knife fixed to the end of a long pole, a pruning tool but not an axe.

Conclusions

It now appears that small long-handled axes have enjoyed a widespread traditional use throughout large areas of Oman and, reportedly, amongst tribes of the UAE. They are still made and are still used, albeit no longer to cut green timber.

The discovery of similar axes in excavations over a wide area of Oman and the UAE supports a view that the axe culture has survived several thousand years of cultural continuity, not merely in formerly isolated areas such as Musandam, but indeed throughout most of Oman and the UAE.

The *Maḥǧān*-type axe may be a longer-handled functional distant cousin of the *ǧerz*, perhaps from the same bloodline as that found at Qidfa (Costa 1993, Plate 1b). On the other hand, the camel-borne *qadūm* appears to be a non-ceremonial, non-combatant functional first cousin of the *ǧerz*.

No attempt has been made in this paper to explain the apparent absence of small axes from Jebel Dhofar, the Jebel al-Akhdhar or the western Ḥajar, because new evidence may yet be found. Just as the *ǧerz* was until recently thought to be 'undoubtedly unique with no parallel in Arabia', so also the Qaron axe appeared to be the end of the line of enquiry in 1996. One thing is certain: Oman still holds many surprises for the researcher.

Bibliography

Costa, P.M. 1991. *Musandam, architecture and material culture of a little-known region of Oman*. London.

Costa, P.M. 1993. Musandam—An ethno-archaeological appreciation. *NAS* 1: 153–174.

Hanna, S. & Al-Belushi, M. 1996. *Caves of Oman*. Muscat.

Insall, D.H. 1996. History in place names. *Historical Association of Oman*. NL 3: 2–4.

Jayakar, A.S.G. 1987. *Omani Proverbs*. Cambridge.

Munton, P.M. 1985. The ecology of the Arabian Tahr (*Hemitragus jayakari* Thomas 1894) and a strategy for the conservation of the species. *Journal of Oman Studies* 8: 1, 11–48.

Vincent, R.K., Jr 1991. The *jerz*, the unique small axe of Musandam. In Costa, P.M., *Musandam, architecture and material culture of a little known region of Oman*. London.

Yule, P. 1994. *Die Gräberfelder* in Samad Ash Shan (Sultanat Oman) Materielen zu einer Kulturgeschichte. Unpublished Habilitation thesis. University of Heidelberg.

Frontispiece: Aden (Lopo Sõares' Fleet) 1521 (see Plate 30 below).

Four English Artists at Aden 1839–1847

*Eric Macro**

Twenty years have passed since I took what became a special walk—westward down Piccadilly. Turning left into St James's then into Bury Street I found myself in that haven of treasure, the Martyn Gregory gallery. There, luckily, I found Patrick Conner, the well known art critic and writer. To him I am more than grateful, for it was he who introduced me to the gallery's collection of William Prinsep watercolours. He also spoke to me at that time about Bellairs' watercolours of the Middle and Far East. Then and there I decided to undertake the research, the results of which now appear in these pages.

As I have indicated later, my interests lay particularly in the topographical aspects of the paintings and the fact of finding *any* paintings of Aden undertaken

* *Acknowledgements:* I have later mentioned my gratitude to Patrick Conner in a niche of his own because it was he who had been professionally concerned with some of the paintings which I have dealt with here. Harry Philby and Harold Ingrams first set me this project in London in the dark days of 1945. Brian Doe and Charles Beckingham followed quickly with a continuing encouragement. Half a century went by before I could fit the plan into my schedule. I hope that those first two mentioned scholars from their desert in the sky, will approve the results of their patronage. In the USA Sam Zwemer took a lot of trouble to see that I did not stray, right up to the end of his days in the middle of this century. Carl Rathjens was ever generous with his wisdom: when at last in 1945 the world allowed us to communicate, I was able, in his home in Hamburg, to become one of his ever grateful pupils. In Aden, Reginald Champion, Tom Hickenbotham and Ken Trevaskis gave me the benefit of much of their experience. Had it not been for Bob Serjeant's superior scholarship, watchful eye and long friendship, I could not have later come under the exemplary surveillance of such a highly qualified and watchful Arabist as Jack R. Smart.

[Anglicized names have been used to a greater extent in this text. Transliterated names, in order to fit in more easily with this, retain j for *jīm*, sh for *shīn*, etc. Edd.]

in the 1830s. I am particularly interested in the artist as a draughtsman. That is why I have not concerned myself greatly with colour, other than in exceptional circumstances. I am interested more in the accurate portrayal of size, shape proportion and location. It may be that, by looking at pictures in a certain way, I have distressed the art critics. So be it. If a charlatan is one who, *inter alia*, uses artists' work to challenge or verify topography, architecture or other such situations, then I am he. But I would not decline the gift of a Reubens to hang in my little house on the hill. Perhaps I have taken too strict a view of artists' licence. Smith put too many islands in that bay; Jones paints coconuts on date palms; Robinson paints the praying Muslim facing away from Mecca and Brown has a two-humped camel in South Arabia. None of our four subject artists has committed any such anachronism.

Alas, there is only one error in any of their pictures. Strangely, it occurs here in a watercolour, the painter of which we would not expect to waver. If anyone finds that licence has been taken or that a picture is one which has been concocted to suit the artist's whim, doubt is cast upon the worth of the painting to the historian. Perhaps we are looking here at the difference between history and the historical novel.

My examination of the Prinsep pictures in London was an interesting experience; there I had found the first subject of my title. Bellairs was an obvious second. The third, Rundle, was, like Bellairs, an officer of the Royal Navy. Both were accurate. Rundle makes you hear the crack of the rifle-fire and the officer screaming 'charge'! We hear the slushing of the landing craft's keel ploughing its way through the wet sand, and finally coming to a halt up on the dry beach. Last but not least, our anonymous Army Officer. He was not much of an artist. However his sketches please me but would not, I imagine, receive the approbation of the masters. Fair enough, but I understand what he is saying to me with his brush and what he is saying is reasonably accurate.

Two of our four Englishmen, Prinsep and Bellairs were in Aden as transient ship's passengers. Rundle and the Army Officer both served there in a military capacity. The events leading to the British occupation of Aden in 1839 and Aden's role as a way-station on the 'overland' route to India, are both part of the history of how Aden became British and how and why our four artists went there.

Rather than include those historical comments on the overland route in the story of the four artists I have thought it tidier to relegate them to an appendix at the end of the book. There are a number of extracts from the Army Officer's observations on Aden during his service there, which I considered would be appropriate for inclusion. These I have selected from his *Historical and Statistical Sketches of Aden* [1848] and placed them as the second appendix.

Introduction

Some years ago, during the course of a lecture at Cambridge, I spoke about the importance of the study of paintings and drawings in the context of historical and topographical research.[1] If some of this exhortation fell on stony ground, at least the converts became an inner cabinet of enthusiasts. One, perhaps unseen, advantage was that, hopefully, none of those disciples would become the Gilbertian model of a modern arm-chair historian. At about the same time, there appeared in England a number of English watercolours of Aden scenes, painted during the first half of the last century. These provided incentives for further study. Some of the paintings[2] were of Aden and Egypt, and knowing both territories well, I was asked to examine and comment on them. My interest lay in the depiction of the land and seascapes, and the man and nature made alterations to both of them. It is often now possible to go inside a building or sit on a wall in Aden and place your own easel where those saints had trod and painted their pictures, well over a century ago. One attractive aspect of those pictures is that some were, not surprisingly, painted by Englishmen, William Prinsep and Walford Bellairs, (to name only two) representatives of the people who, at that time, most frequently passed that way. At this period two other English artists, James Rundle and an anonymous British army officer, painted views of Aden. Each of the four artists were in Aden within eight years of the other.

I have thought it of interest to make a brief examination of how such a small nation as England came to expand her trade and later her territorial possessions, leading to her establishment of such a large communications system in the East.

By the time that the Normans had annexed England in 1066, founding for her a permanent ruling dynasty, more new blood in the form of certain western European tribes had settled in the south and east of Britain. The strength, both ethnically and numerically, of the indigenous Britons and the remaining Roman blood, helped the later Norman conquerors of the island to build a new nation. Barely two centuries later it could have been all but annihilated had it not been for the death of a major Asian potentate five thousand miles away.

Mainland Europe herself did not realize how near she had been to extinction in 1242. Highly disciplined, organized and well commanded, the Mongol army under Ghengis's grandson Batu, thundered west across the plains of Asia into eastern Europe in 1241, annihilating as it went a large Polish-German force at Liegniz in Silesia and 85,000 Hungarians. Batu however, now an absent candidate for a vacant throne following the Great Khan's death, raced with his army back to the royal capital at Karakoram.

As the Mongol threat abated so were the more enterprising of European merchants encouraged to embark upon long overland expeditions into the centres of Asiatic trade. In 1252 the most famous of them, the Polo brothers, Nicolo and

Maffeo, set out from their native Venice on that epic journey to China. Returning there sixteen years later, they took with them in 1271 Nicolo's son Marco. Based at the Court of Kubla Kahn, Marco Polo travelled the length and breadth of China for a further sixteen years on behalf of the Khan. Stunned by the enormity of Asian wealth, splendour and power revealed by Marco Polo on his return to the Adriatic towards the end of the thirteenth century, some countries of Europe, of which England was prominent in the field, began to seek out means of trading direct with the orient.

1. Building British Trade to the East

England's early trading

Venice and Genoa had long retained the monopoly of oriental trade because the westbound caravan routes from Asia terminated in the Levant or on the Black Sea. As the superior naval power in the Mediterranean, Venice which provided shipping for at least one Crusade, had enjoyed exclusive trading privileges with the east for a period of two hundred years. This momentum was to decrease with the onset of the sixteenth century and the rise of the Portuguese, English and Dutch abilities each to build up a trade by sea with the East.

The existence of Venetian commercial superiority in the Mediterranean had not however discouraged England and some other nations bordering the north eastern Atlantic, from venturing, much later, through the Pillars of Hercules to go about their business in new waters. Those western European nations endowed with direct access to the Atlantic Ocean, were to become the first great seafaring nations of the 'western' world. Fortunately the Norman rulers of England had always been conscious of the need for external trade and for the maintenance of both mercantile and military fleets.

Traditionally England had taken part in the exchange of goods across the Channel with mainland Europe, particularly with Flanders and Aquitaine. After 1066 exports of tin and lead had continued and sale of wool to Flanders increased until the beginning of the fifteenth century when the cloth trade began to replace that of wool. From about 1330 wheat was sent east across the Channel, dried and salt fish went to Gascony and coal came from Newcastle even then, in the last quarter of the fourteenth century. All the foreign, trade in England had been controlled until about 1245 by German merchant organizations (the Hansa) and sometimes the Flemish, established in England, the Baltic and Flanders. Gradually a considerable trade was built up with Genoa and Venice but, this time, all the business and shipping arrangements remained in the hands of the Genoese, who came to Southampton, and of the Venetians, who brought their goods to London.

At that time English ships did not venture further than the confines of the North Sea and the Channel. Enterprising English kings however eventually came to appreciate that the concept of nationhood embraced a flourishing overseas trading system operated by a efficient merchant fleet. The population had doubled during the century and a half after the Conquest and, in spite of the decimation brought about by the Black Death and the French Wars, the rulers of England soon began to assemble their own private fleets, armed, prepared for action and stationed in five ports (the so-called Cinque Ports) along the south coast. These fleets contained the first ships of the Royal Navy and they used the first English naval bases suitably fortified and provided with docks, arsenals and anchorages. England's loss of Normandy prompted King John to found Portsmouth as a Royal Navy base in 1204. In that century the Cinque Ports increased greatly in power. Edward I saw to it that trade and industry were subjected to national control and in later years the king decreed that 57 ships be maintained at his pleasure in the Cinque Ports. Merchant ships were subject to the royal requisition without notice or payment. Edward III lost his cog *Christopher* to the French in 1338 but although he achieved a personal victory against them in 1340 at Sluys in his cog *Thomas*, he did not follow up his successes by building a permanent Royal Navy.

The English in the Mediterranean

Theatregoers attending a premier at the Globe theatre in south London in the early months of 1602 heard an old witch from the stage, recite in the opening words the now much quoted: 'Her husband's to Aleppo gone, master of the *Tyger*'. Perhaps the audience wondered what this had to do with the *Macbeth* which they were about to see. Shakespeare's reference to the *Tyger* going to Aleppo was no fiction. She had sailed to that Levant entrepot some nineteen years previously and the voyage serves to illustrate the type of pioneering journeys undertaken by the English toward the end of the sixteenth century. The *Tyger*, perhaps unknown to her captain, disembarked a certain Ralph Fitch near Aleppo. Adventurers went there to join other English commercial explorers of Asia, all seeking to trade with the East. The [English] East India Company was founded in 1600, and by 1609 the first English ship, the *Ascension*, had dropped anchor at Aden. English merchants were now starting to travel far afield in search of business. In February 1583, the *Tyger* took Ralph Fitch, John Newberry and four others to Aleppo on the first leg of their pioneering trading venture to India and the East Indies. Three years later the *Tyger*, (captain, Thomas Rickmans) owned by a London alderman, dropped anchor in Alexandria harbour. It is, recorded that the obliging Rickmans conducted an English visitor, Lawrence Aldersley, to 'Pompey his pillar … a mighty thing of gray marble ...'. The ever generous Rickmans also took Aldersley to the pyramids, presumably those of Gizeh which 'bee high and in forme 4-square'.

Portugal in India

Later the traveller John Evesham took passage aboard the *Tyger* (still captained by Thomas Rickmans) leaving Gravesend on 5th December 1587 bound once again for Alexandria and now also for Cairo. But voyages undertaken by European ships like those of the *Tyger* were beginning to lose their original purpose. It became no longer necessary either to challenge or to circumvent Venetian control of the movement of oriental merchandise into Europe. At the end of the fifteenth century commerce on the great ocean sea lanes was well under way and most nations of the north-eastern seaboard of the Atlantic were not slow to take advantage of the opportunities available. The Portuguese, in the person of Vasco da Gama had, in 1498, long since reached India by sea and had enjoyed almost a century of direct trade between Lisbon, the Algarve and the orient.

England changes course

The western European market for eastern wares had rarely been fully satisfied. Towards the end of the sixteenth century, English merchants trading in oriental goods were beginning to find that they could no longer fulfil the demand for eastern products by their usual reliance on the Mediterranean as their source of supply. That great sea was no longer safe for commercial shipping. Oriental goods obtained there were now too expensive. One result was the rather late ability of the English to make a purposeful voyage around the Cape in 1601. (The Dutch had already done so). By 1609 the English were trading in Arabia and India, later in the Far East. Nevertheless, English ships were still attracted to the Mediterranean.

The British and Aden

During the past 150 years much effort has been expended in discussing the reasons—some would say pretexts—advanced by the British and Indian governments to justify their occupation of Aden in 1839. Such an exercise constitutes a dreary, aged and unprofitable post mortem, signifying nothing: but it is a tale often told. Whatever anti-imperialist or otherwise thinking historians may say, 129 years of British colonial rule gave Aden its finest hours, the like of which it had never seen nor has yet regained, Arnold Toynbee's patronizing quips notwithstanding. Here at Aden, if more platitudes are in order, was the budding Hong Kong of the Middle East, an Aden where, since 1967, one still hears some unsolicited hankering after the good old days of the old colonial administration, democratic institutions and all. In the 1830s and 1840s other potential invaders had been close at hand, lurking at the bottom end of the Red Sea and ready to pounce. If the French, still smarting under the adversity of Napoleon's misfortunes, had been quicker off the mark, they could have eventually rejected Djibouti. So also could the Italians have improved upon Massawa, Mogadishu and Assab, in favour of Aden's cheaper and far superior natural facilities, a mere 120 miles or so from the narrow, and, at that time strategic, entrance to the Red Sea. In any event, the French were soon to cast covetous eyes upon Shaykh Said, Socotra and Perim, all without result. Any of these British rejects, would have been unsatisfactory in any event.

At mid-century, Aden's development was progressing well and by 1920 it had long been a flourishing way-station on the short sea route from Europe to the Far East and the Pacific. Its administrative and military requirements in those days were minimal: a squadron of Royal Air Force aircraft, (in the 1920s and 1930s) some Gunners, some infantry and some local levies being adequate for keeping the peace.[3] The main function of the colony was, originally, to refuel and re-provision passenger, freight and warships and to serve as the Royal Navy base from which the Senior Service would patrol the British shipping lanes. Aden was unique in Arabia. No town in the whole of the Peninsula had progressed so well and no other Arabian port was visited by so many Europeans during the early and middle years of the nineteenth century. It had stolen al-Mukhā's thunder.

Turkish control of the Mediterranean and the Red Sea trade

Meanwhile the Turks, after consolidating their power in the eastern Mediterranean generally, had tightened their hold over the western end of those land trading routes from the east which, crossing north Arabia, Mesopotamia and Persia, debouched into Asia Minor, the Levant and Sinai. In order to maintain their control, the Turks prohibited any Christian ship from sailing into the Red Sea beyond al-Mukhā, under the pretext of denying the unbeliever any access to the area of the holy places of Islam. The matter of the land trade routes, vital in the Turks' view, was not mentioned. This edict kept European shipping away from Suez and consequently from bringing its merchandise to Egypt's Red Sea port. Thus the Turks not only monopolized the Suez trade but, by having power over an unencumbered land area from Constantinople to Aden, were able to exercise their authority over the commerce which came westward out of Asia. Aden had so far remained a commercial backwater.

British India and her communications

The creation of a British Indian empire was no surprise. Its military control and commercial prominence extended over the sub-continent well into the twentieth century. By 1800 the Government of India was seeking help from Whitehall to speed up communications between the two countries via Egypt and the Red Sea. An eighteen month wait for a reply to a letter from Calcutta to London created great dissatisfaction in government and commercial circles in Calcutta, Bengal and Bombay. The Indian government had demonstrated that a route via Egypt and Europe to England would more than halve the communication time between England and India. Needless to say, this plea to London fell initially on deaf ears and in any event the Turks continued to disallow any sea communication between British India and Egypt. However, by the last quarter of the eighteenth century, at a time when the Turks' power in Asia and their influence in Europe was rapidly declining, ships from British India were beginning to appear at Jeddah, or in the Suez roads, with little or no objection from the Turks. Calcutta, Bombay and Bengal were now bringing greater pressure to bear on an indifferent London to establish a route from India through Egypt to Europe along which government dispatches could travel both ways and at speed.

The rise of 'Alī Bey

As the last quarter of the eighteenth century approached, the Turks do not appear to have appreciated their own weakness in Egypt. By 1766 the Mamluk Beys, who ruled Egypt on the Turks' behalf, became dissatisfied with their lot. They overthrew the resident Turkish Pasha and sent him packing, back to Constantinople. 'Alī Bey, the ringleader, rapidly disposed of the other beys and emerged as the ruler of Egypt. From that time, with the help of Warren Hastings (Governor General of India), James Bruce (explorer of Ethiopia) and George Baldwin (erstwhile but energetic British Consul in Cairo), British ships started to arrive in the Suez roads. Most were from Bengal or Bombay and were able to have their cargoes and dispatches offloaded, transported to Cairo and if necessary to Alexandria. From there passengers, goods and mail could be sent to most parts of Europe, very often through ports in the Tyrrhenian Sea or the Adriatic.

Aden and the long struggle for the route

The back door to Egypt was only slightly ajar and negotiations on all sides were to prove difficult. Many political problems had to be resolved before any route throughout Egypt could be firmly established: Muslim Arabia, Sudan and Egypt almost encircled the Red Sea and lay athwart the narrow junction between Africa and Asia. Wars and revolutions intervened and years passed when no international discussions were possible. The intrusion of Christianity was resented by the Turks who were conscious that only with their help could the length of the journey of the infidel from Bombay or Bengal to London be reduced by 63% if Turkish-ruled Egypt was to be used as a highway between the Red Sea and Europe. The Turks also resented England's increasing power to exert pressure on Egypt to shorten the India-England journey. Egypt was not always easy to get at politically. She was often engulfed in either revolution or foreign occupation. Consequently negotiations were impossible over long periods. However as we have already noted, auspices seemed brighter in 1770. From that time, the occasional British ship was allowed to offload at Suez and some maritime surveys were undertaken by British ships in the Gulf of Suez and the northern reaches of the Red Sea. At that time the birth of the overland route was still over half a century into the future, a time when the first steamship sailed from Bombay to Suez, having refuelled at Aden on the way.

It had become a foregone conclusion in India and among English officials in Cairo that a route would eventually be established between Bombay, Suez, Cairo and Alexandria. A re-supply point for the new steamships, which were planned to ply between India and Suez, was essential. It was at this new staging post, that the English amateur artists, Prinsep and Bellairs found themselves in the 1840s with their pallets close at hand. The choice of the port of call, not surprisingly, was the ancient port of Aden. At that time Aden was reluctantly serving out its third year's apprenticeship as a member of the British Empire and had, up to that time from 1829, already served the British as a coaling station. Here was a stifling, barren and volcanic outpost, initially with a mixed population of 600 Arabs, Jews and Somalis which, in spite of itself, was to progress well under the Bombay Government and the Crown for 128 years as the homeland of so many stalwart empire builders. The English artists to be discussed were four, among the thousands of soldiers, sailors and passengers who made short stops at Aden whilst their ships recharged their bunkers.

Included here is the story of four of those people who did just that in the pioneer steamship era. It is both an examination of their pictures and an enquiry into how those artists came to be there. When, in 1847, one of the four passed through Aden, he was making a journey, the itinerary of which (as far as his way through Egypt was concerned) had been agreed between the English and the Egyptian governments only eighteen years previously. At that time the route was still in the process of creation by the new steamship interests, individuals who created special travel agencies, those who provided wheeled vehicles to supplement camels and donkeys, people who constructed hotels and staging posts and provided food—and shipbuilders who made barges and steamers to fit the narrow waterways between Cairo and Alexandria. It did not of course all happen overnight. In the event, it had hardly reached its zenith before it was replaced by an Egyptian State Railway line and later the Suez Canal.

The lethargy of England

These activities, albeit intermittent but constituting the birth-pangs of the 'overland route' to [and from] India, continued until Napoleon's occupation of Egypt just before the turn of the century. The movement to institute this transportation system which would cut out the slow sea voyage from India to England via the Cape was, by 1780, already emerging in India and was encouraged by the few who occasionally represented England in Egypt, officially or otherwise. The lethargy of the British government emerged with characteristic indifference. By 1793 it had completely lost interest in all matters Egyptian. The enterprising British consul was recalled by means of a curt and unwarranted piece of official correspondence. All the pioneer diplomatic work done by those on the spot was wasted. In 1798 Napoleon occupied the Nile delta and Nelson's fleet kept the French army locked up in Egypt having destroyed the enemy fleet at Aboukir. Of that famous naval action the hero was the French Admiral Brueys. Shot almost in half, he crouched on his quarter-deck amid the raging inferno which was his flagship *L'Orient.* His blood, running down the scuppers into the sea, had turned purple from the dye of his uniform. Nearby, still alive, was his captain's ten year old son Casablanca, inevitably awaiting his ordeal by fire. Eventually there was a terrific explosion as *L'Orient* was blown to pieces. Nelson gave no quarter but Napoleon lived to fight another day. Another thirty years were to pass before the overland route was to become a reality and Alexandria, the location of this bloodthirsty battle, was to thrive again with the help of a number of French and English favourites of the ruling pasha.

Muḥammad ʿAlī, ruler of Egypt

The campaign to eject the French from Egypt was a bungled, time-consuming operation and ended in a Pyrrhic victory. The English sent an army through the Mediterranean and at separate times, two different squadrons of warships round the Cape, one in command of an admiral, another of a commodore. Bombay sent a unit of soldiers to garrison the island of Perim and a squadron of Royal Navy ships from the East Indies Station to the Red Sea. All in all the force comprised a total of seven separate military contingents. By the time that the two squadrons from England arrived on the scene, the war had long since finished. General Abercromby the army commander had been killed in action and his body taken back to Malta in a warship. Napoleon had deserted his troops—generals and all—and was comfortably back in Paris before the British attack began. Some will say that he was 'recalled'. Meanwhile the quest for the overland route had once again sunk into oblivion during the time taken by Egypt to sort out its affairs after the French evacuation. One thing was certain, Egypt would pay no further homage to the Turks. Finally in 1811 the Albanian born Muḥammad ʿAlī set himself up as the new dictator. He now began to cooperate with many European powers and by many of them he was courted. He liked the English and was attracted to the idea of the overland route. In 1829 he agreed to the formal request, delivered to him by J.J. Barker, English Consul-General in Cairo, that English mail, freight and passengers might move through Egypt in either direction between Suez and Alexandria. *Now* London started thinking seriously about steamships and coaling stations.

The advent of steam navigation just at this time in the Indian Ocean in the form of the steamer *Hugh Lindsay* (1829) was thus the first to implement the Muḥammad 'Alī–J.J. Barker agreement. On the Bombay–Suez leg of the route, al-Mukhā and rarely al-Mukallā were used as coaling stations in the very early days. Aden already had stocks of coal but labour shortages dictated that some ships after 1829 had to use al-Mukallā temporarily. Very quickly, however, Aden wisely solved its labour problems.

2. Rundle and the Army Officer

Earlier pictures of Arabia

The artists, whose pictures will be discussed later, were not of course the first to paint or sketch views and people in the Arabian Peninsula. Illustrations of some Arabian Red Sea ports had already appeared by the early part of the nineteenth century, Jeddah and Wajh are examples. The establishment in the 1830s of the canal, river and desert route from Alexandria to Suez and the introduction into the Indian Ocean of seagoing steamships during the same period, brought artists, mostly amateur, to Aden. Al-Mukhā had been a subject for European artists from 1680 onwards and continued to be so until the 1830s. From that time, when steamships were sailing between India and Suez, Aden (still independent until 1839)—not al-Mukhā—was chosen as the coaling station. The number of new pictures of al-Mukhā diminished, those of Aden increased. It is not difficult to compile a record of artists who drew or painted in South Arabia over a period of more than three centuries. When historians examine these artists' work, consideration of the artists' *technical* skills is unnecessary. Rather, the more important aspects will be the accuracy of their presentations and what they tell us about the history of their subjects. Fifty or more non-photographic pictures of south Arabia are accessible but less than twenty 'new' paintings will be dealt with in varying degrees of detail in these pages. Of that accessible fifty, 52% are of al-Mukhā, 32% of Aden and 16% of other parts of Arabia; the actual figures are respectively 26, 16 and 8. Between 1517 and 1680 five Aden pictures were known, whereas only three of al-Mukhā had appeared. From 1680 al-Mukhā rapidly shot ahead as the use of the Red Sea by European ships became more frequent and the coffee trade expanded. From 1517 to 1838 (the year prior to England's acquisition of Aden) pictures of Aden known to exist numbered seven whilst the number, during the same period, of al-Mukhā was 26, almost four times as many. A glance at the history books will indicate the reason. Al-Mukhā had been used by European ships since Portuguese times. Aden had always been an Indian Ocean backwater in spite of a few visits by the English East India Company during the seventeenth century. Suddenly during the eight years between 1839, when Aden became British, and 1847 at least ten general pictures of the port were executed and published. Al-Mukhā declined rapidly and the volume of artists' work followed the historical trends, but, over the years, the detail of that work had recorded some history. By contrast, we shall discuss in detail in the next two chapters, some previously unknown paintings of Aden from the nineteenth century. They had been executed by William Prinsep and Walford Bellairs and were brought to public notice in 1984 and 1985.

During a period of over half a century I was in and out of a number of areas of the Arabian Peninsula, its remote and offshore islands and the seas surrounding its coasts. Most of that time was spent in the southern half of that great land mass. What an artists' paradise it was, and how necessarily neglected by artists it had to be. I was not of that eminent fraternity but had always held the view that most pictures are made by man to hold back time for a brief moment, in order to record the results of decisions or activities which became a part, however minuscule, of history. For 'early' pictures of South Arabia we must thank the Victorians, those well brought up middle and upper class Britons whose educational routine included, recitation, elocution, music, sketching and painting. Certainly we must not scoff at them for that. After 1839 those were among the people, who visited Aden en route to England or India and who gave us many of our first 'modern' pictures of this other rock of ages.

The birth of a new Aden

Those who disembarked at Aden in the early 1840s found themselves in a mountainous promontory covering an area of about eight square miles and joined to the Arabian mainland by a low-lying sandy isthmus. By the middle of the nineteenth century, the peninsula had come to support a substantial Asian and British population in three townships. The most populous was Crater the site of the original town which was located on the east coast, facing east across Front Bay. At the far north west was the site of the future Tawwāhi which was to be, later in the century, the location of business premises, the government secretariat and the all important coal dump. The third settlement was Ma'allā located on the north coast about three and a half miles east of Tawwāhi; here ocean-going dhows had been built for hundreds of years. The population of the peninsula was 600; by 1900 it had risen to 40,000.

After 1829 the tiny population of Aden gradually became accustomed to the visits of British passenger steamships plying between India and Egypt. Such was the scarcity of labour on the peninsula that the coaling operations, which took place there initially off Ṣīrah Island[4] east of the town of Aden, had to be moved temporarily two hundred and fifty miles eastward to al-Mukallā on the Ḥaḍramawt coast. However, after the English took Aden nine years later, on 19th January 1839, the population began to increase steadily as the frequency and regularity of the British shipping operation progressed. The presence of the new civil administration and the military garrison soon attracted business and labour to the settlement, labour whose presence was now instrumental in confirming Aden as *the* coaling station between Bombay and al-Quṣayr and Suez. Aden's officials and businessmen soon adapted themselves to the mounting number of transient passengers and crews disembarking from the newly acquired Indian Navy steamers. Governed for the next fifteen years by Captain S.B. Haines, an old Aden hand, the settlement, however ill-prepared and ill-equipped it found itself, was glad to have the business.[5]

Books published about the India–Aden–Egypt voyage in the third and fourth decades of the nineteenth century were legion and often a little trite. Frequently they were narratives produced 'at the urgent request of my friends' and with introductions couched in terms of coy reluctance and mock modesty. It seemed that these rather self-conscious diarists had rapidly unpacked their journals on return to England or India and revised them to satisfy those much courted pressures to publish. There were, of course, exceptions[6] and had it not been for all those steamer writers we should have had to rely almost entirely upon the Aden and the Bombay Governments' records for the history of the subject.[7] From modest beginnings emerged the traffic generated by the new passenger steamers which were to call at Aden in the years which followed. The number of European visitors increased. They were mostly British and they spent a day or two at the new settlement whilst coal was taken on. Some early descriptions survive of this tedious activity, undertaken in an atmosphere of choking, clinging and all-pervading coal dust. This function, of course, moved from Ṣīrah when the coal dump no longer existed there. Its new position was at the west end of the peninsula at a location in what became Tawwāhi the area later known as Steamer Point. For many years Steamer Point was ill-defined geographically. As coaling became a commonplace and onerous operation in the eyes of the passengers, so diminished the number of their narratives of what was then a novelty. To read these early descriptions of the coaling operations at Aden in the 1830s is to realize that the process did not change in a hundred years. Over a century later, in the 1930s and 1940s I witnessed the holds of ocean-going ships anchored in Back Bay, or offshore, still being charged with coal dispensed from hundredweight sacks, borne up a plank from a coal lighter on the backs of Somali coolies.

The situations of both James Sparkhall Rundle and of an un-named 'Army officer' were different to those of Prinsep and Bellairs. Both of the latter were westbound transients from India. Narratives of their visits follow. Rundle was second in command of the flagship of the British fleet which captured Aden in January 1839. The Army officer was British and was stationed in Aden during 1846 and 1847.

An Army officer's early sketches. Aden c.1846

Military people of the 1839-49 decade, based at Aden, or fighting up its beaches like James Rundle, seemed unable or disinclined to record their experiences in detail or to draw or paint what they saw. Fortunately, there were exceptions. One of them, Rundle, is mentioned elsewhere. Another studied the Aden of the mid-1840s in some detail, and, like Rundle, made sketches of parts of the new British acquisition. Whilst the Army officer may not be considered as an artist of the calibre of our two main subjects, one, at the most two, of his five sketches may be considered of historical interest. There were few other artists of any consequence, whose work on Aden has come to light.

On the morning of 27 February 1846 the schooner *Scotia* disembarked at Aden a verbose and observant British Army officer with an enquiring mind.[8] He was to be stationed at Aden for two years but his name, rank and regiment are not yet known. From the papers which he left, he appears to have returned whence he came after serving the traditional (later mandatory) two year tour of duty in Aden. Alas, the British military system in the new and subsequent garrisons did not change; it reigned supreme for the century and a quarter of its existence, and was enjoyed by many thousands of soldiers and airmen. We would not normally be concerned here with the detail of those five anonymous sketches by the Army officer, had they existed alongside other contemporary pictures of the same territory. The two sketches of the Turkish Wall drawn by the Army officer (not included) are uninspiring. One of them shows soldiers and tents, the other shows soldiers and horses. They could be at Aldershot or Camberley. The 'View of the Island of Seerah and Camp, Aden'.

Plate 32 shows Ṣīrah to be disconnected from the mainland, as it was in those days. It shows the remains of the fortifications, (some of them from Albuquerque's time) in the right places and a Union Jack flies, for good measure, at the summit. The foreground (mainland) shows flat sandy ground with the inevitable outcrops of black rock—the site of the original Camp at the south east of Crater and to the north of Ḥuqqāt Bay. The sixteen or so assorted buildings, all military and both administrative and domestic, are excellent in the precision and variety which they display. The rock outcrops have long since been blasted away by the skill and the gunpowder of the Sappers. Regrettably the original location of the Ṣīrah coal dump is just out of sight in this picture, but it is known to have been exhausted and rapidly relocated to Steamer Point at about that time. I found minute traces of coal at the site of the Ṣīrah dump near Maqilein a hundred and twenty years after it had been exhausted.

'Steamer Point, Aden' (Plate 31) is not very enlightening. The viewer is looking west across Back Bay to Little Aden, the latter of which is too close and *much* oversized. The artist was sitting about one hundred yards from the shore and there are two tents and some buildings in the foreground. All of the buildings are of wood and three of them have outside walls of lattice-work, allowing passage of air, stifling as it was—another system which did not change in over a century. Otherwise, anchored in the roads are three small dhows, two ocean-going sailing ships and a minute paddle-steamer just getting under way.

There is a much better picture however, and it is 'View of Aden' (Plate 33). To the 'uninitiated', it could, of course, be anywhere. Aden was a widely dispersed colony particularly in those days. Such a vague title means nothing to the stranger. It is in fact a view of buildings in a very limited part of Crater at its north-east end and a short panorama extending north-east to the Main Pass. The artist would have sat very near to the Salāmah minaret (it being off the picture to his left) and looked to the Main Pass at his far right in the distance. It is a very useful sketch because it shows, unexpectedly, a high volume of domestic and commercial buildings spreading from the west of Temple Cliffs and seaward toward what became the Esplanade and Queen Arwā Road. The *sayl*-bed, bearing any overflow eastward from the Tanks to the sea, is clearly shown and there is even some piping to guide part of the flood water. The road still follows the track which it traces in the Army officer's sketch. Until 1967 it was called (appropriately) Saila Road and crossed Esplanade Road at the Eastern Bank and the Chartered Bank. The Main Pass archway had been completed between January 1839 and the end of 1847. The building of the fortification works rising left and right from each side of the top of the arch, seems to have already begun.

James Sparkhall Rundle

Rundle was second-in-command H.M.S *Volage* (captain: N. Smith) at the British capture of Aden in 1839. Of Rundle's Aden drawings, sketches and watercolours, three have a topographical significance. In a group of three others (not included), one is a long-distance view of Aden's Crater settlement taken from Main Pass. Very little detail of the settlement is discernable. Another is of tall ships manoeuvring off the Aden peninsula. A third is equally uninteresting to the geographer—more ships exercising.

The original sketch by Rundle of the initial landing of the British invasion force (Plate 34) at what became Front Bay, Aden, is clear and full of action. Rundle wrote on it. 'Sailors and Troops Landing'. How modest! *He* led them over the side! British and Indian Army soldiers are landing from the ship's boats. Sailors are running through the surf and up the beach with fixed bayonets, to scale what there remains of the sea wall. The Arab soldiers of Aden, they find, are as brave as they are. This sketch shows that the sea wall reached from south to north, right across the bay. There were two sea gates, the southern was arched, the other, approximately central and having two unconnected 'posts'. No detail is given to the sea wall, neither does any exist on the few and modestly outlined town buildings.

Rundle's second picture illustrates either the same invasion or another part of the action viewed from approximately the same position in the bay and is titled 'Storming of Aden' (Plate 35). There is more action here: the smoke of battle is everywhere, soldiers are helping or dragging their dead, dying and wounded comrades back to the boats or out of the line of fire, only to return themselves to the battle. Somewhere an officer holds his sword high as a rallying point, indicating the direction of the next charge. Matelots, their all-white uniforms creating perfect targets, are wading through the water, dragging the soldier-laden ship's boats in-shore to ease each jump over the side. Still the tough petty officer continues to haul the troop-laden boats ashore and up the beach, the keels ploughing a slushy furrow past the breakers and through the damp, undulating sand.

The two landing-operation pictures are praiseworthy but regrettably they give us little topographical information; nevertheless, at least they confirm that *some* of the sea wall existed in 1839, however poorly maintained. Rundle did well. Who could produce such action pictures so quickly having charged into battle, rifle or pistol in one hand, Union Jack in the other? I have nine drawings of the Aden sea wall going back to 1517 from 1800; not one is similar to another. At present I am engaged on an analysis of each of these pictures in an attempt to discover *any* similarities between them. I hope also to discover whether it is possible to produce any sort of an alignment of the wall. The sea wall is now gone for ever (200 years ago) unless some archaeologist can trace its junctions with the rocks of the mainland to the north and south, and excavate its foundations, long since built over.

Rundle's drawing of the 'Sultan's Palace' (Plate 36) acquired a pretentious title. The 'chief' of Aden assumed the title of sultan but from all accounts his residence was hardly a palace and it was in a hopeless state of disrepair. Interestingly enough, an exterior portion of it appears in one of Prinsep's watercolours—not surprisingly—as the 'palace' held a central position in the town of 600 people. This drawing shows a large flat area around the building, which the military had taken over. In the foreground a matelot talks to two smart soldiers, one with his back to us, another side-view. The uniform detail will please military historians. All three have white trousers, the soldiers, white cap covers, trousers, bandoliers and epaulettes. They seem to be keeping an eye on their piled arms, all three with fixed bayonets. Prinsep recorded the latter military detail at the guard post at Jabal Ḥadīd two years later. Soldiers from one of the Indian regiments are cooking a meal with the help of a smoking bonfire not far away, but at a safe distance from four bell and four ridge tents pitched in the square. A seventh picture by Rundle (not included) shows soldiers standing on a flat piece or rock at Ṣīrah island.

Rundle has taken great care to record what he saw. Although not under Haines' command, he may have been of help to the political agent. However, it is most likely that Rundle returned to Bombay aboard H.M.S *Volage*. He was, after all, Captain H. Smith's second in command. The quality of the sketches by Rundle (1839) and by the Army officer (1847) vary considerably. They provide interesting comparisons with the work of our principal subjects, Prinsep (1841) and Bellairs (1847).

3. Prinsep at Aden

The artist as a historian

In general, topographical descriptions published by those early steamship passengers about their Aden sojourns, were poor. This is not surprising as their visits normally lasted only about forty hours. The very few studies undertaken on the rise of the Aden settlement are based almost entirely on personal experience and on the Aden and Bombay government records. Published historical studies, in which contemporary pictures have been used, appear to be lacking.[9] Whilst recognizing that there is an amount of apocryphal content in early engravings or paintings of topographical subjects, I have long advocated the use of early pictures for the study of development of Arabian towns. Al-Mukhā is a good example. Many views of Aden etc. drawn or painted from ships offshore during the nineteenth century, appear dull and unintelligible.[10] They often feature dark grey mountains on the horizon of a dreary grey seascape—valueless either as works of art or as research material. Most are reminiscent of a view of the Albanian coast on a foggy night from the Corfu channel or of the Outer Hebrides in a heavy rainstorm.

Fortunately not every overland traveller (as the Bombay-Suez passengers were called)[11] took up his pen at the insistence of his persuasive friends. Some took up their brushes of their own volition. Eight generations later we are grateful that they did. Regrettably most of their results were not published, or remain in private hands and, of those which were published many fall into the Outer Hebrides category. However in those days most well educated people sketched and painted. Unfortunately we shall never know the number of Aden pictures in private collections and it is mostly quite by chance that they become known and are recorded. They are rarely if ever studied. If they are recorded and are accessible they are, it seems, never analyzed. In other papers I have said that the search for records of 'western' visitors to Arabia before 1900, who have left worthwhile original material, is an unending quest. Fortunately that search continues to bear fruit.

Two travellers painting at Aden

We are dealing here, particularly with two English amateur artists, whose work I first came across in London. One was a member of a family well known to students of nineteenth century India who painted in 1841, whilst he was travelling west on his own account; the other, in 1847 also going west, was an officer of the Royal Navy. Six of their paintings will be discussed: five by one artist and one by the other. Both of them painted in Aden during the overland route era already mentioned and each was born in 1794.

The aim here is to consider the six paintings and evaluate them in terms of accuracy and their effectiveness as historical documents.

William Prinsep (1794–1874)

The man credited with the foundation of the Indian indigo trade in the eighteenth century was an East India Company servant, John Prinsep. The fifth of his seven sons was William.[12] He (John) also had a daughter. William, a successful banker, worked with his younger brother, George, in a Calcutta business house, Palmer and Company. With some of his brothers, William in his younger days had taken drawing lessons from George Chinnery. At the age of 47 he and his wife left Calcutta to travel to England. It was probably his first visit there and he made the standard 'overland' route journey from Calcutta to Pointe de Galle in Ceylon, Bombay, Aden, al-Quṣayr and thence to the Nile, Cairo and Alexandria. Although we are aware of all the names of the steamers on that route at that time, we do not know which of them took Prinsep from Bombay to Aden and on up the Red Sea. It would have been one of the ships of the Indian Navy fleet detached by the Bombay government to be used in an entirely civilian capacity and almost exclusively for the transportation of members of the British Indian community. Naturally, officers of the Indian Navy were extremely indignant at being made to serve aboard these ships in any rank, not the least as captains. They also strongly objected, having been taken off military duty, to operating a floating and mobile public hotel in addition.[13] The alternatives were to resign or be dismissed from the Service, both unattractive prospects in a foreign land. Much to their relief, in January 1845, the Peninsular and Oriental Steam Navigation Company, using their own ships, took over the 'line', motivated no doubt by the resultant acquisition of the lucrative monopoly of carrying Her Majesty's mails.[14]

Prinsep arrived in Aden in early December 1841[15] and must have spent his whole time painting the five (Aden) pictures which survive him. No sea captain wished to keep his ship in the heat of that port any longer than it took to refill his coal bunkers. Prinsep's stay therefore was brief. His pictures were all pen and ink watercolours and are all in varying degrees pleasant and interesting scenes, particularly to those who are familiar with the subjects. His five Aden watercolours are discussed below. At this time British Aden was three years old.

'Landing Place at Aden' (Plate 14)

The title is a little inexact, although it is true that he would have landed at the general location somewhere in the picture. The view is of the whole of what became known as Ordnance Bay which measured, in those days, about half a mile between its two extremities. The territory behind its crescent shaped beach is clearly shown. Prinsep may be forgiven for his title, after all *he* landed there and in those days these topographical features had not been named. Certainly they are not named on the map of the period. It is not possible to discover where Prinsep landed merely by looking at his picture, but knowledge of the local landscape, coastline and the early history of Aden's development enables us to locate where he first set foot there and where he erected his easel. The landing place, the western extremity of the Tawwāhi beach which was used from the early, but not the first, days of the overland route, was the site on which Prince of Wales Pier was eventually built. Later there was a jetty for shallow draught boats; in 1841 there was just a gently sloping beach. On the pier for many score years there stood a very ugly ten feet high four legged metal shed. It was a corrugated-iron roofed hut without walls and had been erected initially to provide shelter for the saluting canon under the control of the harbour master. Before any pier was built, from a ship anchored in Back Bay, passengers were rowed toward the shore. When the boat grounded the men jumped overboard into the water and walked through the surf to dry land. The women were carried ashore on the backs of Arab or Somali boatmen, thus perhaps exploding the myths about the reticence of our much respected Victorian women. However, it must be admitted that later, plans were provided under which the women could disembark on to dry land from the row-boats.

At first sight Prinsep's picture seems difficult to identify. It appears as a semicircular bay surrounded by high mountains. Closer inspection however enables us to locate exactly where he sat to paint. A check of his outline of the mountains against the sky with reality reveals his accuracy. More important, it shows that up to the end of 1841 there were no buildings between what became Prince of Wales Pier and the eastern limit of Ordnance Bay. This region, less than thirty years later, was a thriving business and domestic area in the shape of a crescent which fitted between the shoreline and the mountains behind it. The pier was named Prince of Wales Pier and the new collection of buildings, Prince of Wales Crescent, in commemoration of a visit to the settlement by the heir to the throne. British passengers continued to land at the pier and shop at the Crescent, both under the royal name, for 120 years.

To return to Prinsep's painting; the starboard bow of the dhow points to where the road eastward to al-Ma'allā begins (it has some traffic in the picture). The veiled woman is standing on the spot where the first Government and (separately) the P&O coal dumps (or 'grounds' as the Aden administration called them) were created. These dumps were located a few yards north west of the plot on which the first Cowasjee Dinshaw building[16] was erected at the west end of the block no. 11 in the Crescent. The woman is looking at a piece of high land behind which the Rock Hotel was built in the 1950s. To the right of and behind the pony lies a primitive weighing scale, used no doubt in the process of imposing duty upon the incoming dhow traffic. The structure behind the scale appears to be a small wooden hut with a yard enclosed by a stake fence, all of which most probably did duty as a customs house. Ideas that this building might have passed muster as a 'hotel' must be discounted, and the temptation to embark here upon a history of hotel building in Aden resisted.

Not so many years ago a painter sitting where Prinsep sat and, facing in the same direction, could see only a few yards. His view would have been blocked by buildings and the trees in Scott Gardens[17] surrounding the statue of Queen Victoria which stood between the town buildings at its back and the original and natural shore line seen in the painting. A mere thirty-six years later, the flat land seen in the painting had been completely built over and some buildings were beginning to appear in the valley to the east at the side of the town and also upon the hillside behind. A sizeable foreshore was however still retained for many years. An important aspect of this picture is that it shows accurately the bare shell which nature had provided as a site for a new town on the west side of the peninsula, a town which was to administer the port of Aden in all its complexity and which would spill over to the flatlands towards Ma'allā to the east and to those areas fronting on to Post Office, Sapper and Telegraph Bays to the south and to the east.

'View of Aden with Jebel Shamsan' (Plate 17)

Prinsep noted that there was a 'Fortified Gorge leading to the town (left): Aden (centre): Road from the landing place (right)'. The words Aden (centre) are meaningless (there are no buildings or town in the picture) unless they be interpreted to mean that the town of Aden lies behind the mountains in the middle of the picture. The clues to the location of this picture are as follows:

(a) a track runs along the shore of (another) crescent shaped beach which covers the entire width of the picture
(b) the high mountains, right centre
(c) the lower mountains, centre
(d) the track to the left being entered by two camels and drivers
(e) the high ground on the extreme left
(f) the high ground on the extreme right.

First, to deal with Prinsep's phrase 'Fortified Gorge …' etc. The fortified gorge, Main Pass, is over 4000 yards to the left (east) of the picture. No track to the Main Pass from the west was 'fortified' as Main Pass was. The only bay en route to the Main Pass was the next one (a) east of Ordnance Bay and was formed by the promontories of Jabal al-'Aynī (f) to its west and Ras Hujayf (e) to its east. Its name was French Bay. The track (d) runs between Ras Hujayf (e) and Jabal Hujayf the lower mountain (c) in the centre, Jabal Shamshān (b) is accurately outlined and positioned in relation to the foreground. Prinsep's perspective is not quite right. The bay which he has drawn here he shows to be smaller in relation to the background than the bay in his previous picture. In fact the reverse is true. From where he sat facing south-east at the foot of the promontory of Jabal al-'Aynī he could not have seen camels at that distance certainly not in the detail shown, unless his eyesight was exceptional or he used a pair of binoculars. Not many years later the first of many structures were to be built on those shores to the left of where the camels are. Here was constructed a pier for the vessels of Messageries Maritimes, the reason, no doubt, for the bay receiving the name of French Bay. Further towards the point of Ras Hujayf were built large installations to accommodate the coal stocks of both Messrs Luke Thomas[18] and of Messrs Cowasjee Dinshaw. Between the donkey and the men in the foreground, another, coal depot was laid down, that belonging to Messrs Edaljee Manackjee.

Prinsep confuses us here by using the phrase 'fortified pass leading to the town'. Such a one existed to be sure, not in this picture but some distance away. Haines would almost certainly have had a small guard in the Hujayf cutting—it was easy and economical to defend but it does not seem that Prinsep intended to signify this. He was a bold artist to paint this desolate scene but his landscape and other details have been presented accurately. Certainly it would not have attracted any military person to volunteer to serve in Aden, considered by misguided soldiers and airmen as a punishment station.

'Aden Harbour' (Plate 18)

By now Prinsep had travelled four and three quarter miles from the 'landing place' and was sitting facing west at a location about twenty yards or so north of Barrier Gate—a name which explains itself—at the south-west end of the isthmus. The high ground on the left is Jabal Ḥadīd. The location is easily identifiable (although Prinsep has taken a good deal of licence here in order to make another dull view look attractive). The immediate clue is the cluster of islands and in particular the characteristic hump-back shape of Slave Island, the largest of the group. The further island, Quarantine Island, was eventually supplied with a jetty. That nearest to the shore, Qalfatain Island, is much too near the beach. It was in fact over half a mile from the land. Between it and Slave Island is Qays al-Ḥammāl. All four islands are bigger than they appear in the painting, and they have all, long since, been built upon. The dhow building yards which had traditionally been at Ma'allā since time immemorial, were, forty or more years ago moved to Slave Island's eastern beach.

Later still Slave Island was enlarged with spoil from harbour dredging. Eventually it became a junk yard for old motor cars and boats. Prinsep would have turned in his grave, had he been confronted with the modern Slave Island. Otherwise the three islands in the foreground are too much in a straight line. The two smaller islands south of Slave Island form a line north west which is at about a fifty degree angle to the line of Slave Island.

Prinsep's coastline here is very untrustworthy. There was no bay on this strip of coast whatsoever, particularly not in the Barrier Gate area. The seascape is of Back Bay, on the north and west of the peninsula, which soon replaced the anchorages at Ḥuqqāt Bay and Front Bay to the east. Fronting on to the latter is Aden town (Crater). Ships could not anchor in the shallow water to the east of the islands in Back Bay but did so off-shore along the north coast of the peninsula and particularly off the west end of it. The large bay bounded by Little Aden to the west (seen in the distance) was shallow and it was unwise for ships of large draught to venture too far north into it.

There is some interest in the picture nevertheless. This soldiers' uniform is as correct as it can be in a small picture and the rifles are piled correctly and in a manner still current over a century later. Some regiments were not however allowed to pile arms with bayonets fixed as the Sepoys here have done. One tent was probably for sleeping and the other for stores including food and ammunition. One wonders what the bucket was for: scraps for the mobile dairy animal perhaps? (the ubiquitous goat walking northward with her Arab master) or merely an early example of the desert lily?

This part of the coast was hardly ever built upon. There were however fortifications and an officers mess existed here for many years after Haines' time. Prinsep wrote on this painting 'Sandy promontory connecting with the province of Yemen right'. He is correct of course but this does not appear in his painting because he is sitting on it and it is behind him to the north. He is also right in implying that Aden's connection with the mainland is tenuous. In those days the isthmus was often inundated particularly at high tide.

The stone structure to the right (west) of the gate appears to be a (military) pill-box. Either Prinsep has forgotten to paint in the rifle slit towards the north, from which direction would come hostile attacks, or the structure had some other purpose (than a gate post) which is not apparent. If he had never been a soldier perhaps he would not have thought of it in any event. Nevertheless in spite of the inaccuracies the picture is an attractive one. The licence taken by Prinsep in this instance shows itself in the bunching up of the islands and in his bringing all of them too far south toward the shore. His easel would have been just north of Barrier Gate with Jabal Ḥadīd in the mid-distance to his left.

At this point the road goes north to what was the Royal Air Force Station, north-east to the old Seedaseer Lines and south-east to the coast. The 'bay' is far too sharply curved; if he saw one it would have been one of very large radius. He has drawn almost a semi-circle whereas this part of the coast is little more than a series of straight lines. Despite his excesses, he has made an attractive picture of an uninteresting scene.

'Aden, the Plain and Town' (Plate 19)

From Barrier Gate Prinsep would have re-traced his steps southward until he came to the fork in the trackway which took him to walk eastward up the hill to Main Pass. He would have seen this pass five hundred yards off to his right as he travelled through Ma'allā on his way to Jabal Ḥadīd and Barrier Gate. Main Pass was a narrow defile (smaller than the Siq at Petra) which provided the main landward access to the Crater where the town of Aden was and is located.

To the left (north) of his picture are the Manṣūrī Hills; in the centre (east) is the sea which comes up to the beach of Front Bay. The hills to the right of the sea form an outcrop of the Shamshān range which, at that point, marches down to the sea[19] just south of Ṣīrah, then an island, now joined to the mainland by a sand-spit causeway. The volume of buildings which Prinsep shows in the town is surprising. The impression given is of a good sized mud- or brick-built settlement. It is surprising because thirty six months previously Haines had found the

Crater, to contain a motley crew of 600 people living in matting huts scattered about the area consisting of a large ruin field. The portion of the uninhabited part of the Crater at the time when it was occupied by the British garrison, was located nearer to the shore and also on the heights of the Manṣūrī Hills along the so called Turkish Wall fortifications. Thus the habitations shown can only have been occupied by local civilians. The indication of a large and apparently flourishing town is not easily explained.

In the foreground to the right of the squatting Adeni (?) is the lower end of the Kushāf valley which contained good wells. Here military installations are starting to appear alongside some government buildings particularly those of Haines' civil engineers who, not unnaturally, are constructing their own buildings first. On this hillside was built the first Residency with its attendant supporting buildings. The road leaving the town on the left leads north-west through the Main Pass gate which was already surmounted by a bridge and some fortifications. This road is now the main route (now Queen Arwā Road) leading out of Aden town. The smaller road to the right, also leading out of the town area but not the Crater, still exists, curving round the spur of Temple Cliff to the site of the old Residency. Now that hillside is littered with the components of an enormous shanty town.

The perspective of the picture is very satisfactory. It gives a good impression of what Queen Arwā Road looked like a century and a half ago and demonstrates that it had not then benefited from the already existing invention of Mr John Loudon McAdam.

'The Bazaar at Aden' *(Plate 20)*

From where he sat, just inside the Crater not far from the Main Pass, painting his fourth view of Aden, Prinsep rode 1900 yards south east along (to use the modern Anglicized road names) Queen Arwā Road to the junction of the tracks which later became the Esplanade and Ḥuqqāt Bay Road. From there it was but a short distance from the tall minaret which he had already seen to the south east from his position just south west of the Main Pass and which he had included in his painting of the Crater. This, the Salāmah minaret, is situated to the south-east of the modern Post Office building. Much earlier in the century the Treasury building and then Law Courts stood on that modern Post Office site. The minaret which dominates Prinsep's picture has no mosque, it is just the central feature of a general collection of people, animals and tumbledown buildings. The Post Office, the Treasury and the Law Courts buildings mentioned above would have stood on the site behind both the minaret and the furthermost of the pair of buildings in the right foreground of Prinsep's picture. It is easy to locate his easel on this occasion as midway between Ḥuqqāt Bay Road and the

Esplanade at the north-west end of what was the camel market and which became the stadium or sports ground. 'The Bazaar at Aden' is an unenterprising title for this picture which is little more than a typical oriental jumble of items to be expected in such a scene. There are no signs of wares exhibited for sale except possibly some water jars and the ubiquitous *'angarīb.* The minaret has not changed since Prinsep's time. It was built 220 years ago[20] as part of an earlier mosque and has long since been neglected. It disintegrated through poor maintenance and the decline in population.

The interest of the picture is twofold. The artist has made what is probably the only known representation of an Aden building dating back to the last quarter of the eighteenth century (the Salāmah minaret) which can still be seen today and in its original location. Secondly the castellated building on the far left of the picture could well have been the Sultan's house which Haines took over in January 1839 as his administration offices, albeit in a dilapidated condition. One of Rundle's[21] drawings (of the palace) and another of his from seaward show a very similar house and Haines' 1837 map of Aden specifically fixes the Sultan's palace close to the minaret. It is possible that the palace which was the only (serviceable) stone built residence in the Crater, is the one on the left of Prinsep's picture. Regrettably there must be some doubt however because Haines locates the Sultan's house to the north-east of the minaret which would place it approximately on the site of the old Aden Municipality building.

We do not know whether Prinsep had time to look around Crater; probably not. Most likely he had to rush back through Main Pass, Ma'allā and Hujayf to rejoin his ship, bound for al-Quṣayr. There on the Egyptian Red Sea coast he disembarked on the 19th January 1842. It took him and his fellow passengers five days to reach the Nile at Luxor, far too long under normal circumstances.

4. Bellairs

Lieutenant Walford Thomas Bellairs, Royal Navy

Four years after Prinsep left Aden, another prolific amateur artist, Lieutenant Walford Thomas Bellairs, RN, born *c.*1794, was among the transient passengers from England visiting the port. That was in 1845. He returned there in 1847 on his way to England. It was a fateful voyage, the beginning of the end of his forty one year career spent since the age of fifteen in the Royal Navy. An accomplished painter, he was the son of an infantry captain, John Bellairs (1757–1843) and the grandson of an Uffington man, James Bellars [*sic*] who died in 1799 aged seventy nine. His brothers. John, Harry and Abel Walford, he rarely saw. Bellairs, although married, seems to have been a lonely and inconsequential person, having received no promotion during the whole of his commission in the Royal Navy. The shipping company to which he was attached for a time found him complaining and boorish. Happily he drew much pleasure from painting, excelling as a much respected artist.

After serving as a Cadet and a Midshipman, Bellairs was commissioned as a Lieutenant in 1819 and was posted to a ship in the West Indies, afterwards seeing service in the Coastguard. Later he was transferred to the Indian Ocean and China Station and by 25th June 1845 was in Lisbon en route to Penang. Calling at Malta, Cairo and Suez, still a passenger, he arrived at Aden on 14th July. Here he painted three coastal views of the peninsula with which we are not concerned as they are not of topographical interest. On arrival in Ceylon he joined the P&O steamer *Lady Mary Wood*[22] as Admiralty Packet Agent, being transferred two years later to the *Pekin* for similar duties. Aboard this ship, in July 1847 he was on his way to Suez and went ashore at Aden for a time on 1st October. One of the pictures which he painted on that day has survived. It is a watercolour on buff paper, about nine by six inches in size and portrays, to use his own title, 'The Great Pass at Aden'. The *Pekin* took him up the Red Sea to Suez and soon he was in England. It had not been a sentimental journey.[23]

'The Great Pass at Aden' (Plate 37)

Of all the sights at Aden, the Main Pass, as it came to be called, was at once the most disenchanting object to behold and the most important landward access point to the Crater. The roads from Tawwāhi and from Barrier Gate converge just to the north-west. The road then turns through a great cleft in the natural outside wall of the Crater. It always has been strongly defended from the hills on either side. A stone and brick built bridge spanned the gap to provide easy access between the defence works to the west and east of the pass.

The main interest of the picture is that we can now see some detail of the original brick and stonework of the bridge as built by the early British military engineers. Aden historians are accustomed to seeing representations of the pass from the south; this one is from the north, that is to say from outside the Crater. The painting is probably the first document to show a flexible footbridge, with rope handrails, slung across the gap. This must have performed three functions. It enabled the military guards to obtain a more extensive view to the north than that which they would otherwise have obtained from the ground. It allowed them to take up a safer position than that on top of the brick and stone built arch. Thirdly, the flexible bridge would provide easier and faster access to the ground than would the permanent bridge, the purpose of which was to connect the hill fortifications of the Crater's exterior rim. The presence and location of three soldiers in the picture infers that there was always at least one Sepoy on the flexible bridge, and that a stone staircase (left of the picture) gave access to it from the roadway. There was also at least one Sepoy outside the Crater guarding the road leading south through the pass. The stone staircase remained long into the twentieth century, having eventually acquired a handrail.

Alas, camels no longer pass through the eye of this needle. The narrow pass has long since been violated. The brick and stone bridge (and for that matter its small companion) is no longer there. A dual carriageway passes through the once historic access, widened considerably to suit the luxuries of modern civilization. Early artists, and indeed the map makers, have shown how nature fashioned the original, and now considerably altered, northern coastline of the Aden peninsula.[24] An artist has here shown us how a piece of the Aden natural landscape has been considerably changed.

The hapless Bellairs may, after all, be the hero of the piece. He is perhaps unique in that he was the first to demonstrate how a piece of Aden mountain was changed in shape. He showed what it looked like in his day. He chose a mundane subject and turned it into an interesting picture. His painting must become the standard document showing how the bridge over Main Pass was designed. Even the blocks of stone and/or bricks can be counted; the numbers of stone stairs and of rifle loopholes across the parapet are easy to discern.

Three years later Bellairs was dead. At least he died in the land of his fathers and in the arms of his long-suffering wife. It was a year full of sound and fury.

5. The Way Home

Prinsep's return home. Two routes through Egypt

Regrettably both Prinsep and Bellairs can only be followed homeward for a comparatively short distance after they left Aden. Both left scant evidence by dating very few of their paintings—some purposely only with the month and/or year. We bid them *au revoir* on their departure from Egypt for Europe. Fortunately each followed a separate route to Cairo enabling us to share the experiences of each of them. The routes on which they travelled (albeit six years apart) would finally converge at Cairo. Prinsep had travelled down the Nile from Karnak, seeing the sights on the way. Bellairs had no option other than to go to Suez, since the *Pekin* was taking him part way home from Ceylon and he was not a fare-paying passenger.

Initially the Bombay–Egypt steamers called at two ports in the Red Sea. Passengers could book their voyage to disembark at either al-Quṣayr (Egypt) or at Suez. The Prinseps chose to go to al-Quṣayr, the trip normally taking seven to ten days and disembarked there on 18th January 1842. As this date is one which has been confirmed it enabled a reasonable conjecture to be made that they had arrived in Aden on 7th January 1842. The call at al-Quṣayr was later discontinued and the steamers sailed direct from Aden to Suez and of course vice-versa. In spite of this decision, the era of calling at both ports had long been popular with passengers. It meant that those who wished to see some of the sights of the Upper Nile and had disembarked at Suez, needed, after reaching Cairo, to travel up-stream for a few days so that they could see those wonders of Egypt. On the other hand those who came from al-Quṣayr still had to drop down the Nile for some days to reach Cairo whilst their fellow passengers from Suez were safely relaxing in Shepheard's, the British, Raven's or one of the other, less expensive, hotels.

The al-Quṣayr to Qina route

The journey across the desert to Qina, Thebes or Karnak on the Nile took five or six days. Travellers rode mules or camels or were seated individually in what appeared to be a carriage body with a covered roof and without wheels. There was a seat inside and a door at each or one side. This box shaped 'cabin' was flanked by two long balks of timber secured firmly to each side. They were approximately fifteen feet long and served as shafts for the transporting animals or men. The whole, including the passenger, was powered by two camels, two mules or four men.

The Prinseps reach the Nile

Prinsep would have seen the local shaykh at al-Quṣayr (I would describe it as a miserable, run-down seaside village) and arranged the hire of camels, mules, guards and guides for the eighty-five mile ride to the Nile. The journey during that period was very primitive. The general direction is due west and the track meanders through a wadi mostly walled-in on either side by high cliffs or individual outcrops. High on some of the cliffs were old watch towers and there were a number of unidentifiable ruins of buildings along the way. Five different contemporary travellers each found the same five but differently named, 'settlements' along the route and at some of them water could be bought as the caravan progressed. When I trekked inland on this track in 1943 en route to Kharga Oasis I found little evidence of habitation, water for animals was hard to find and expensive to buy.

And so to Cairo

Prinseps sighted the Nile on 24th January and proceeded initially to Luxor. It was some time near mid-February before they reached the pyramids of Geeza just south of Cairo, he having painted at least thirty-five pictures on the way. If the couple had followed the normal procedure they would have stayed in Cairo for perhaps a week or ten days. Eventually they would have made their way from Cairo to Alexandria by river and canal. There was plenty of interest and hotel accommodation there. Ships from most of the north Mediterranean ports, particularly from France, took English passengers to the start of their journey north across France or Austria and Germany to one of the Channel or Baltic harbours. They had missed the interesting desert journey from Suez to Cairo. It is not difficult to reconstruct that journey between Suez, Cairo and Alexandria. Bellairs made this interesting trip across Egypt from the Red Sea to Alexandria six years later.

Bellairs; Homeward in 1847

Although it is unnecessary to follow Bellairs' return to England, it is certain that he sailed up the Red Sea from Aden in October 1847, landing at Suez possibly just over half way through that month. Ships from Aden were scheduled to arrive on the 12th and 17th of each month and to sail on the 4th, 19th and 28th. Suez (population about 7000) was a miserable collection of buildings, mostly hovels, and had no docking facilities. On its seaward side was a small artillery battery. Nearby were the customs house, a bazaar, a mosque and some coffee shops, whilst the desert gate—a kind of local showpiece of the town—stood on the landward side of the port. Suez was also honoured with the presence of an American consul and Her Britannic Majesty's vice-consul, Mr G. West. There was the inevitable coal dump by the shore and two hotels existed, one of which went under the name of Wood's.

Bellairs was soon to travel 84 miles west to Cairo and the journey would normally be accomplished in 24 hours. In 1841 his fare from Suez to Alexandria would have been £12.15*s*. By good fortune it had now been reduced to £8 per head. Prinsep had missed the bargain but it did not matter as he had taken a different and much more expensive route.

The first thing to do on landing was to make some arrangements to stay the night. Early the next morning Bellairs had to organize his transportation to Cairo. His choice was difficult as all methods were uncomfortable. Originally passengers had to travel on camels assisted and supervised by a posse of camel-drivers. Now horse-drawn vans were used, relays of horses being arranged along the route. A four wheeled van drawn by four horses took eight passengers. There were also four wheelers drawn by four horses which carried four passengers. In addition there were two-horse, two-wheeled vans which took four passengers. Women could at one time hire a sedan chair powered by two donkeys. Luggage went by camel and the mail by donkey. If Bellairs was wise he would have chosen a single animal, horse, camel or donkey. The vans were unbearably hot, passengers sat bolt upright and cheek by jowl, and the desert surface was *very* bumpy.

At least there was some relief at each of the seven halts provided on the journey to Cairo. At each of these a brick or stone building had been erected with money provided by the Bengal Steam Committee. They were ten miles apart and each had a primitive mechanical semaphore system so that one could keep in touch with the other. Soon after the official inauguration of the 'halts' they were re-named 'stations' and numbered 1 to 7 from west to east. The central halt was No. 4 station. Facilities at each station varied. Generally speaking, stations 1–3 and 5–7 had a rest room and some stabling whilst the central station, No. 4, had two public and two private rest rooms, a large saloon, a ladies' 'lounge', a servants' room, a water tank, a kitchen and some bedrooms. Water was brought forty-five miles to station 4 from the Nile and filtered through porous jars. Station 4 was the place normally used for a three or four hour halt or an overnight stop. Meals could be bought here; breakfast was 2/-, dinner 4/- and port was 5/- per bottle. Stout, ale and porter were about 1/10 per bottle. The food available was generally mutton, chicken, pigeon, vegetables and fruit. Water was four pence per bottle. A few years after the construction of the stations, tents were pitched permanently mid way between each of them. Passengers were able to use these for rest or shelter.

There seem to have been few complaints. Passengers were only too glad to get to the comfort of their Cairo hotels. From there they could prepare for the journey north west down the east branch of the Nile aboard one of the minute steamers the *Lotus, Delta* or *Cairo* from Būlāq, the port of Cairo, to Atfe. Here Bellairs might have had a choice. He could either board a barge or track boat on the Maḥmūdīyyah Canal and be towed forty eight miles east to Alexandria by a steamer the *Atfe*. Otherwise he may have caught a minute steamer, called the *Jack O'Lantern* going in the same direction. Either vessel would dock at the southern boundary of the large estate of Muḥarram Bey, constituting, in those days, what was virtually an exotic and private southern suburb of Alexandria. For those going to England the choice of route was large. Bellairs was probably anxious to get home and so chose to travel across France to the Channel.

6. Conclusion

Purchase, pleasure, criticism, education; these are probably the main reasons why people look at pictures. Here we are not concerned with purchase or pleasure and only a little with criticism. Criticism in the present context can only be negative, in that no purchase is in prospect. That function can only be of use if it affects our credibility of what the artist has produced. If we can substantiate a statement that, for example he has painted that mountain the wrong shape or that he has put those islands in the wrong place or half of the picture is out of perspective, then it is reasonable to question whether the artist has given a completely true record of the history which we are looking for. We are not concerned with technical criticism. In other words we ask if his evidence can be a trustworthy contribution to our historical investigation. Has he perhaps, although taking his licence to make the mountain more beautiful than it is, done a good job in spite of it and produced for us an adequate answer to our question? Here our judgement must play an important part. The enquirer who has sat on the spots where the artist set up his easel a century and a half ago is at an advantage. He can say that this or that is wrong or he can say that something is important because it was not known until now that a particular feature of the natural or man-made landscape existed at that time.

It is perhaps fitting that the staid and unemotional Bellairs should reveal in detail the technicalities of an unloveable subject, the Main Pass. It is difficult to imagine that there are any photographs of this subject taken by generations of British soldiers, sailors, airmen, politicals and tourists, or even by the local professional, Coutino, which have surpassed Bellairs' painting.

The vast majority of the one hundred or so pictures which he painted are romantic views of South Asian ports or other exotic coastal scenes ranging from Point de Galle to Hong Kong.

Prinsep's first two pictures are of different bays adjacent to each other on the north west coast of the Aden Peninsula. They both show us virgin land, hills and beaches and a coastline which has long since disappeared. The low land, seen in both bays, has, for a century, been completely built over and considerable coastal infilling carried out. The painting at Jabal Ḥadīd is probably the only one existing of that view which was executed during that general period. In spite of the inaccuracy of the shoreline and the alignment of the islands that picture must give a good idea of the primitive military arrangements at Barrier Gate. It contains a further confirmation that, even three years after the occupation, there were very few European troops forming part of the garrison. Although the view of Crater gives the impression that Aden had grown at a more rapid rate than it actually did, it is of interest because it shows that the 'valley' between Main Pass and the end of the Manṣūrī range was still not built over except at its extremity where there already existed a number of indigenous buildings three years before Prinsep's visit. There were however (as shown by Prinsep) a few buildings in the foreground at the mouth of the Kushāf wadi. The painting of the 'Bazaar' has value because it shows that the minaret has not changed in appearance except that it has long since been renovated without altering its design or decoration. Nonetheless the picture confirms what an insanitary settlement existed in Crater even after three years of British occupation. It is of course only fair to say that Haines had no European municipal staff to attend to such problems and was completely occupied with military business locally and political matters with Bombay and the local Sultan.

As for the artists, we know little about them after they left Aden. Prinsep was in no hurry to leave Egypt and to cross Europe and there are indications from one of his paintings that he returned to Egypt in 1870, four years before he died. Bellairs never returned. When he landed in England he was fifty three, a sick and unhappy man, and died three years later. All artists made a significant contribution to the illustration of the Aden of the 1840s then on the threshold of prosperity lasting a century and a half. They furthered our knowledge of a then defunct community soon to flourish again and to acquire an international importance such as it had never before experienced.

To study these old paintings is not so much to appreciate technique or to admire scenery for its own sake, but to walk again in the steps of the artist. Here we are led beside still waters in the tropical heat of summer; here no palm trees wave in the breeze and no birds sing. In Aden, men and mountains meet to share their experiences of history. Here we may indulge our enduring quest for the past and, it must be reluctantly admitted, more than a little nostalgia.

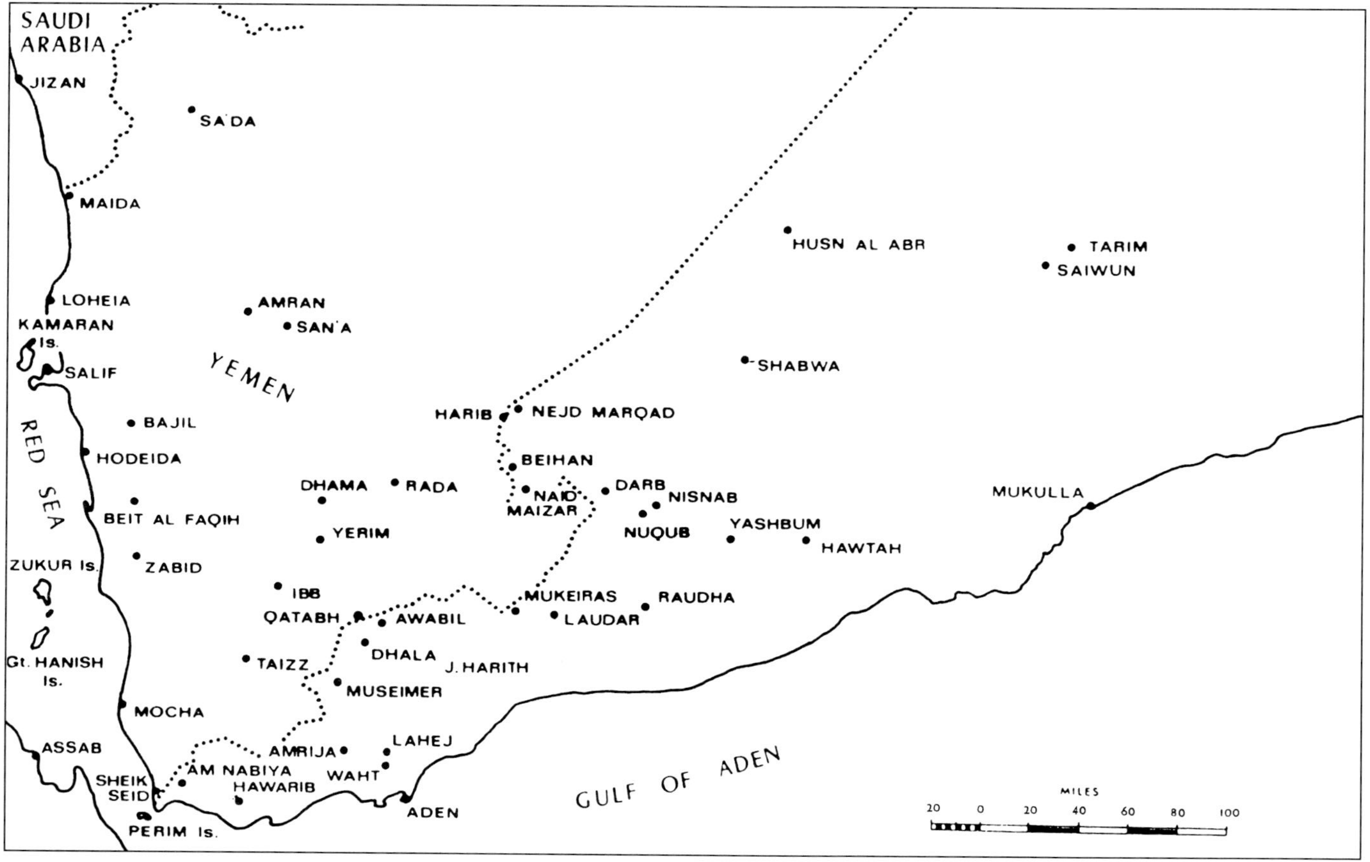

Plate 1: South-West Arabia.

Plate 2: Aden *c.*1800 by Captain Hanchett (showing Ṣīrah).

Plate 3: Aden 1800 by Captain Hanchett 1800.

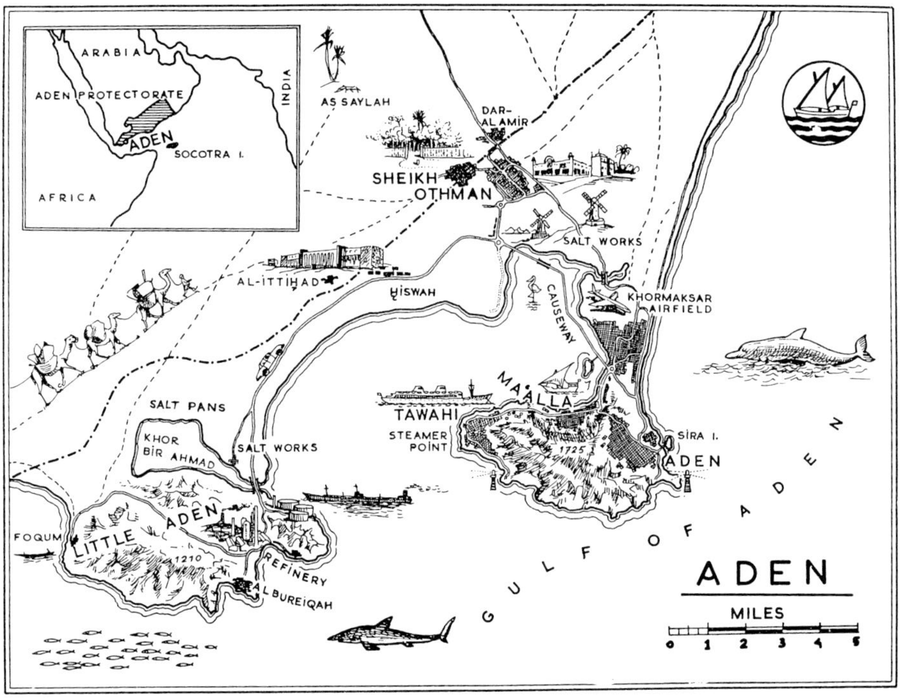

Plate 4: Aden general plan, 1962.

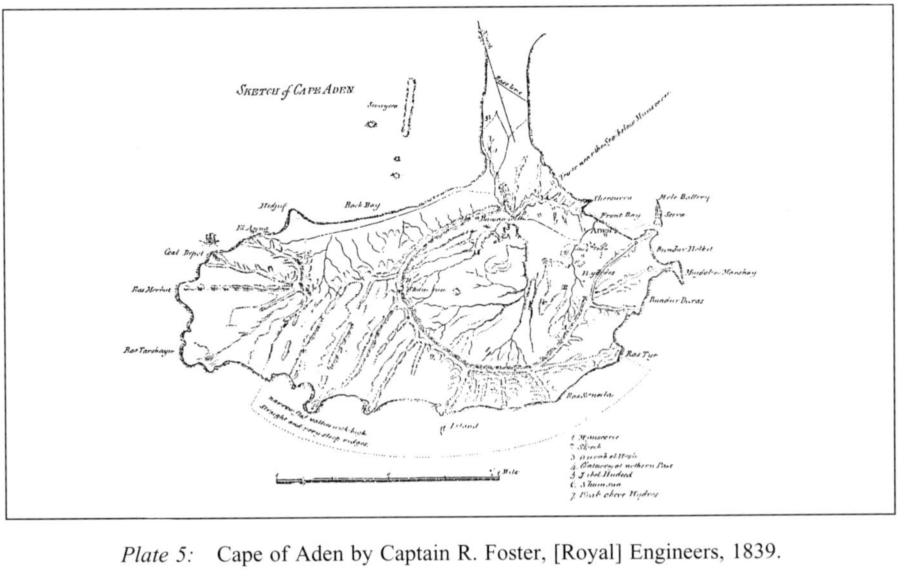

Plate 5: Cape of Aden by Captain R. Foster, [Royal] Engineers, 1839.

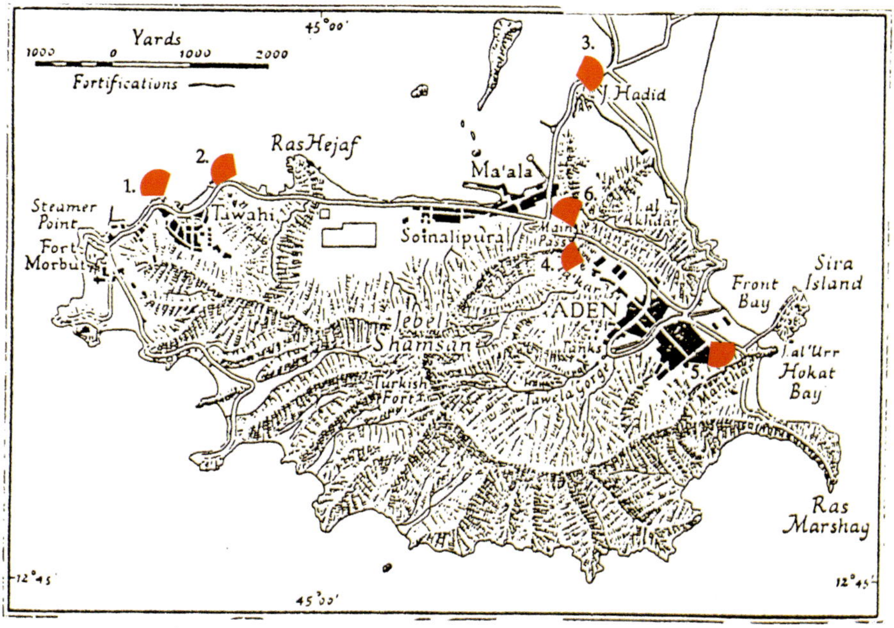

Plate 6: Aden. Location of Prinsep's and Bellairs' easels; Prinsep 1–5, Bellairs 6.

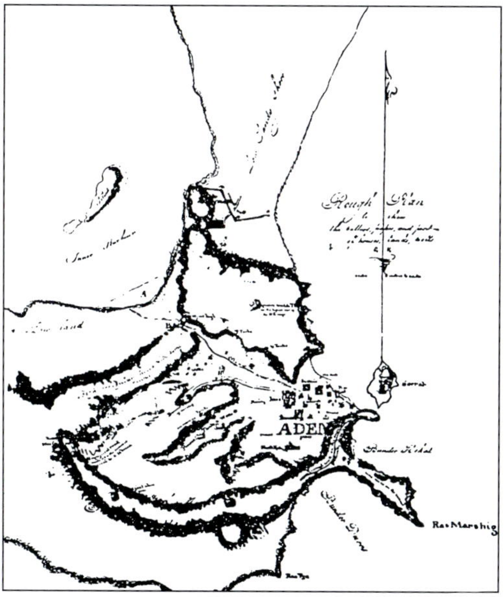

Plate 7: Aden 1839 by Commander S.B. Haines.

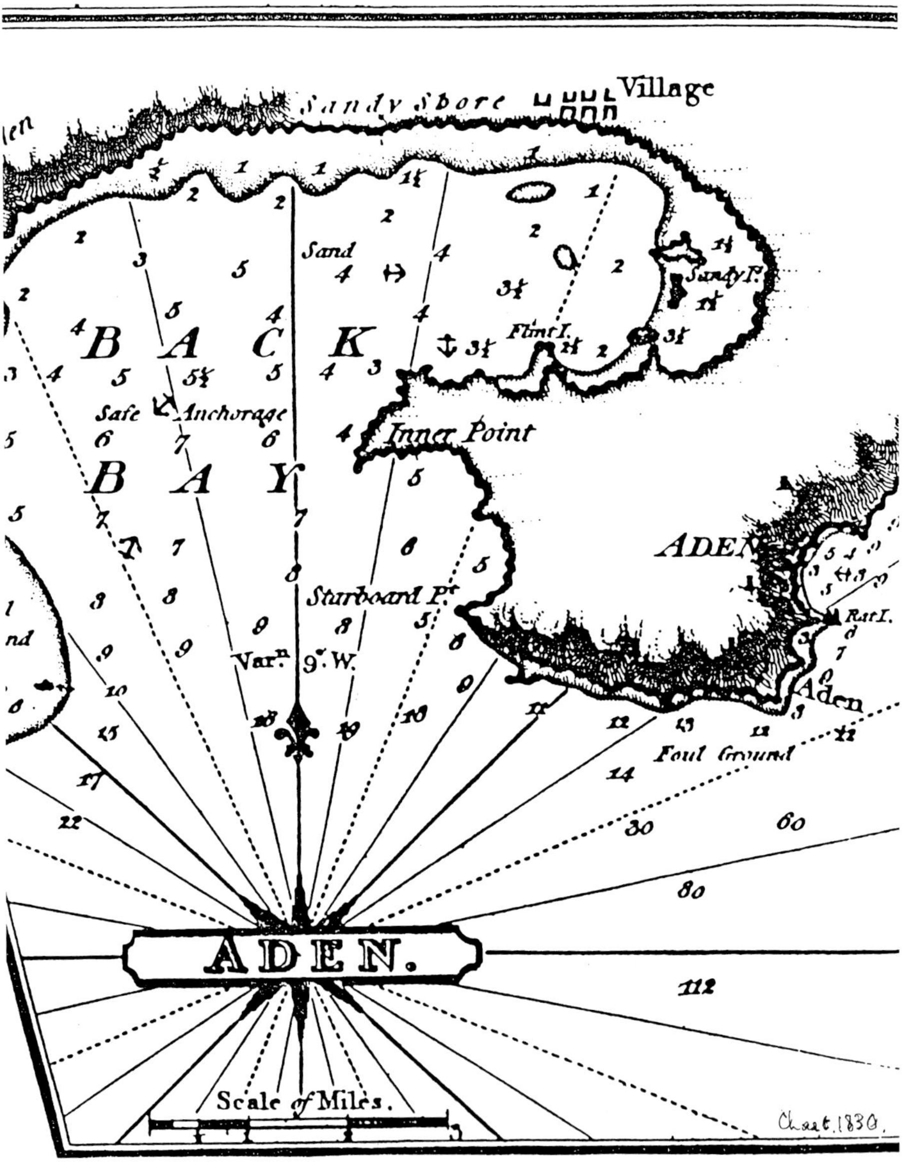

Plate 8: Aden Back Bay 1830.

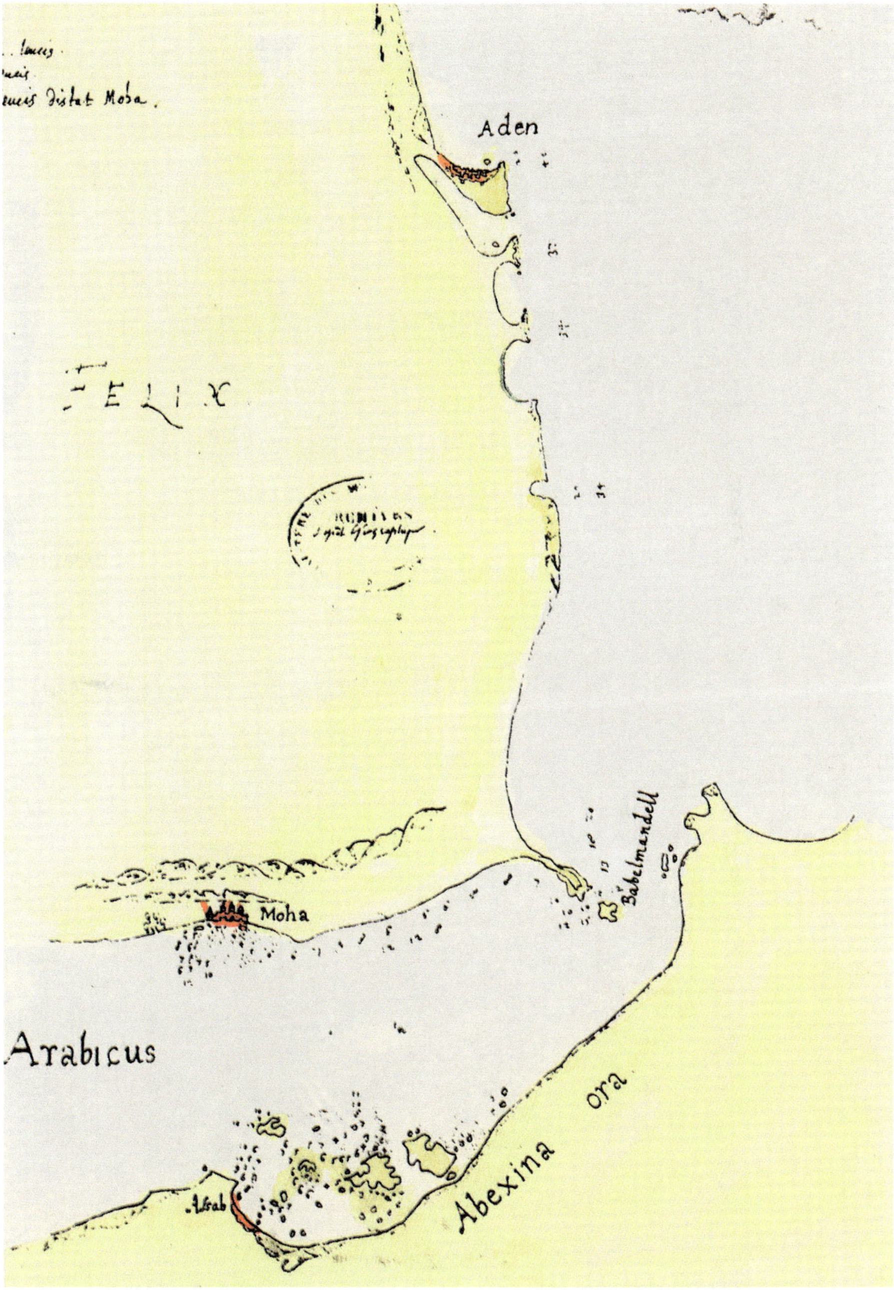

Plate 9: Straits of Bab el-Mandeb and Aden, shown on Dom Joaõ de Castro's manuscript chart which was made at sea during January 1541, and now in Paris.

Plate 10: Ḥuqqāt Bay by W. Delamotte 1841.

Plate 11: South-west corner of Ṣīrah Island, Aden. The coal dump juts out towards the reader.

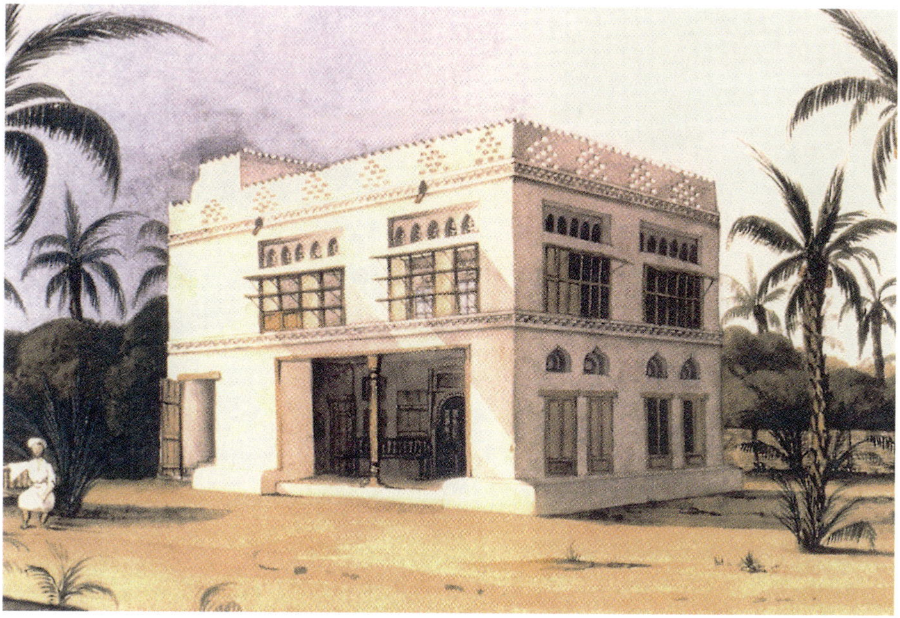

Plate 12: Sheikh's house at al-Mukhā, 1832, by Richard Kirk.

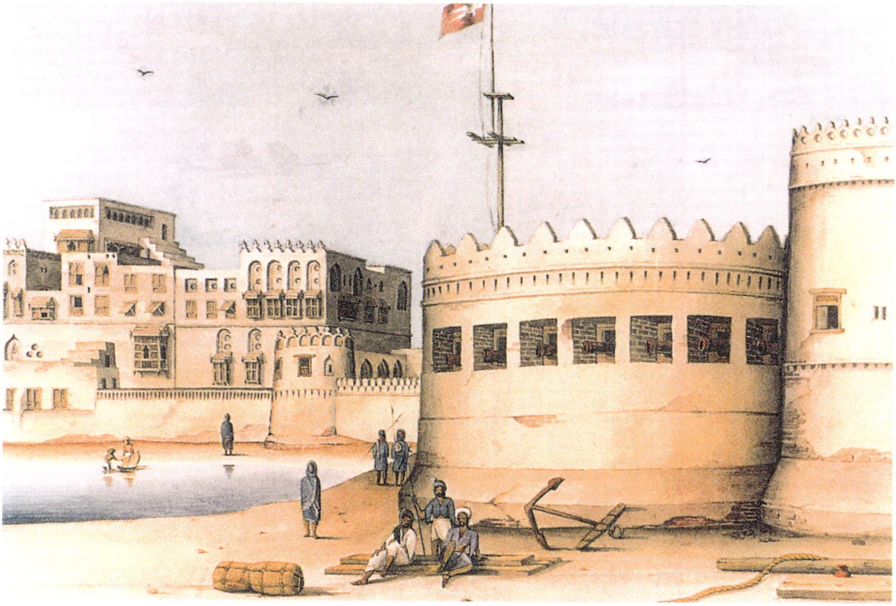

Plate 13: Bastion facing jetty at al-Mukhā, 1832, by Richard Kirk.

Plate 14: Prinsep: 'Landing Place at Aden'.

Plate 15: Tawwāhi from the air (shows most of the area covered by Prinsep's 'Landing place at Aden').

Plate 16: Tawwāhi from the east *c*.1890.

Plate 17: Prinsep: 'View of Aden with Jebel Shamsan'.

Plate 18: Prinsep: 'Aden Harbour'.

Plate 19: Prinsep: 'Aden, the Plain and Town'.

Plate 20: Prinsep: 'The Bazaar at Aden'.

Plate 21: The Salāmah Minaret today. Other buildings replaced.

Plate 22: Prinsep: 'Koseir' (*sic*).

Plate 23: ‘Cosere on the Coast of Egypt’ by Captain Robert Morsesby *c*.1840.

Plate 24: Prinsep: 'In the Desert near Koseir'.

Plate 25: 'Luxor'.

Plate 26: Prinsep: 'The Nile at Qena'.

Plate 27: Prinsep: 'Water Fountain, Cairo'.

Plate 28: 'Somali Boys at Aden' *c*.1870.

Plate 29: 'Landing the Shore End of the Bombay Cable at Aden' *c*.1870.

Plate 30: Aden (Lopo Sõares' Fleet) 1521.

Plate 31: An Army Officer: 'Steamer Point, Aden'.

Plate 32: An Army Officer: 'Views of the Island of Seerah and Camp Aden'.

Plate 33: An Army Officer: 'View of Aden'.

Plate 34: J.R. Rundle: 'Sailors and Troops Landing'.

Plate 35: J.R. Rundle: 'Storming of Aden'.

Plate 36: J.R. Rundle: 'The Sultan's Palace'.

Plate 37: W.S. Bellairs: 'The Great Pass at Aden'.

Plate 38: The Main Pass, 1930.

Plate 39: W.H. Bartlett: 'Suez'.

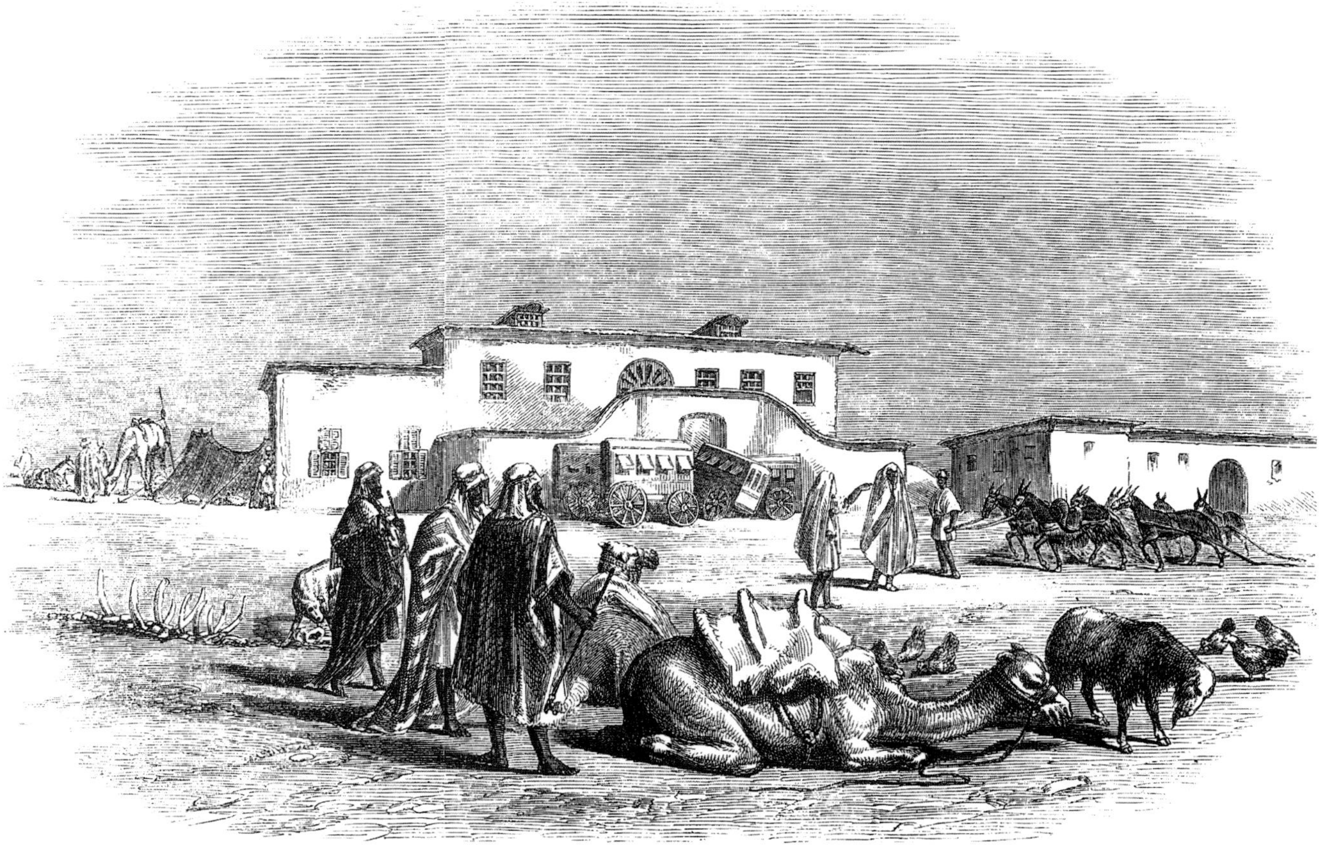

Plate 40: Central Station. Suez–Cairo overland route, *c*.1840.

Plate 41: No. 2 Station, Suez–Cairo overland route, *c*.1840.

Appendix 1*

People and places on the route to India

This annexure deals with the Red Sea and the Indian Ocean at the beginning of the last century. It discusses briefly, how the Bombay–Suez steamship route was planned and how the Arabian Peninsula was affected. In order to do so we shall initially be concerned with Egypt. There follows an outline of the various port facilities in the Red Sea and the Indian Ocean which the British and Indian Governments considered. Finally a tentative appraisal is submitted on the extent to which the inauguration of the Bombay–Suez steamship route affected the course of events in South West Arabia. The era is 1830, a mere century and a half ago; and I have tried to be as brief as possible there is inevitably some repetition.

Europeans had been travelling across the Nile delta since the seventeenth century—mostly up into the Levant—but it was not until the evacuation of the French from Egypt and the subsequent rise of Muḥammad ʿAlī as Viceroy of Egypt at the beginning of the nineteenth century that an organized England–Egypt–India overland journey became a reality.

Business and political interests of Great Britain, France and Egypt were foremost in furthering the project of rapid transit between Alexandria and Suez. The advent of steam navigation at the beginning of the nineteenth century gave impetus to the idea as did the Indian Government, who wanted to short circuit the Cape route to England in order to speed up mail, and, to a lesser extent, passenger communications.

Waghorn, a pioneer

Thomas Fletcher Waghorn, eulogized by Charles Dickens after his death, is popularly credited with the establishment of the overland route. He appeared on the scene when much of the spade work had been done. Today he might be described as an entrepreneur and a whiz-kid. He was certainly a thorn in the

* This is a summary of a lecture given by the author in 1982 at the University of London, under the auspices of the Seminar for Arabian Studies.

flesh of the Post Office for many years. Nevertheless he deserved much credit. He spent all his own capital on his overland projects and was obviously no business man; he died a pauper at Snodland in Kent, being followed shortly by his widow in the same unhappy circumstances.

The overland route was an bold venture, the greater part being the sea journeys between Europe and Africa and the long haul of 1600 miles between Suez and Bombay.

The route from England varied considerably but a normal one would be Dover–Boulogne–Marseilles. From Alexandria passengers and couriers took a boat on the Maḥmūdiyyah Canal to Atfe on the Nile. They then changed vessels and sailed up river to Cairo via Būlāq. Cairo had five hotels, even in those days, including the Oriental and Hills' (later run, then owned by Samuel Shepheard). The eighty four mile Cairo–Suez journey, by camel-litter or later by horse-drawn van, took passengers through six desert way-stations where food and drink would be available at some of them and where a change of horses and/or a night's sleep might be obtained. At Suez, passengers embarked on board a steamship for the journey down the Red Sea and across the Indian Ocean.

Official problems

People and steamships need food, water and coal, and pick-up points are required. Food and water were not too difficult to obtain and sailing ships with almost unlimited and free power had been a flexible means of sea transportation. Now power was no longer to be as free as the wind, coal was not indigenous to most of the area and Indian coal was not of a quality high enough for the new steamships. Ports of call, therefore, had to be firmly established, coaling stations organized and administered and coal brought from England round the Cape to Bombay where it was transhipped for further distribution—a veritable exercise in logistics which taxed the minds of the authorities.

The British and Indian governments, in selecting suitable coaling stations, had to take account of a number of factors, not the least of which was political expediency. Navigational and meteorological requirements were important as was the availability of labour, food and water. Overnight accommodation for passengers was probably thought of as an added bonus. Last but not least was the requirement for facilities for the storage, transportation and loading of coal.

By virtue of its geographical position the South and West of the Arabian Peninsula, including its off-lying islands, was destined to play a large part in the selection of coaling stations by the British and Indian Governments. Disregarding Bombay and Suez, seven out of the nine locations taken into account were Arabian. One territory, the Maldives, was considered because of traffic coming from Calcutta. Many were called but few were chosen.

Al-Quṣayr

Al-Quṣayr was stocked with coal in 1829 as were certain other ports in preparation for the voyage of the *Hugh Lindsay*, the first steamship to ply between Suez and Bombay (1830). It was soon abandoned because the Suez–Cairo route was quicker and safer than travelling from al-Quṣayr to Qina on the Nile and then downstream to Cairo.

Jeddah

Although used fairly regularly by European sailing ships, Jeddah rapidly fell into disuse by steamers. It was one of the places where coal had been positioned in 1829 but its use was rarely necessary even in the early steamship days.

Kamarān

Kamarān Island had been proposed by Captain Francis Head, a steamship lobbyist of the time, before 1833 and Thomas Love Peacock, an East India Company servant and the author of *Headlong Hall* told a House of Commons Committee in 1834 that Kamarān would make a better port than al-Mukhā. Both Thomas Waghorn and Lt Wellsted were opposed to Peacock's views. To some extent Peacock was an armchair traveller and Wellsted and Waghorn, in that order, had far more experience of the Red Sea than he had. Both the latter—and they were seafaring men—told a House of Commons Committee in 1837 that Kamarān would be quite useless as a coaling station. It was considered seriously but never used.

Perim

The isle of Perim was occupied by the British in 1799. It was soon abandoned in August of that year because of the lack of sufficient water and for certain tactical reasons.

Peacock had recommended Perim to the House of Commons in 1834 as the best location between Suez and India. He was obviously lacking in adequate expertise. It was considered by Parliament in 1834 but rejected. The island was occupied again, permanently this time, by the British in 1857 in order to thwart French ambitions in that direction. A lighthouse was built there in 1861 and Perim again sank into obscurity until early this century when it became the scene of a long wrangle between rival coal and shipping merchants in both London and Aden.

Socotra

Coal was put into the island of Socotra in 1829 in preparation for the *Hugh Lindsay*'s voyage in the following year and again in 1833. It was occupied by the British in 1835 for six months and had been considered seriously by

Parliament as a coaling station. However, the reasons for its rejection for that purpose were similar to those which caused the evacuation of British troops—disease, water shortage and poor anchorages.

al-Mukallā

As a possible substitute for Aden or al-Mukhā, al-Mukallā was well placed geographically. It was the only port of any consequence, with the possible exception of Bīr ʻAlī, on the Ḥaḍramawt coast. Coal had been placed at al-Mukallā for the *Hugh Lindsay* in 1829. There were however, some difficulties. It could not be approached during the south-west monsoon and its use was soon abandoned as the range of steamships increased and it became possible to complete the Bombay-Aden voyage without refuelling.

The Maldives

Coal was first placed on the Maldives in 1833 but there were political problems and the islands were too reef-bound for the navigators of the period. They were considered but never used, although a great amount of survey work was carried out in the group by the Indian Navy.

Al-Mukhā

There remained, therefore, Aden and al-Mukhā as the final contenders. It was really the rapidly increasing range of steamships which finally necessitated only one port of call between Bombay and Suez. Aden and al-Mukhā both seemed well qualified.

At al-Mukhā the limited facilities were more suitable—more so certainly than at any of its eight competitors, including Aden.

Disregarding the Portuguese in the sixteenth century, Europeans had been regular visitors to, and often resident in al-Mukhā from the beginning of the seventeenth century and during the next three hundred years or more British and other European representatives lived there intermittently. There were four 'factories' (French: *comptoir*) in the town: the Dutch and English in the north west and the French and Americans in the south west. There was a good jetty built about 1758 by British engineers and coal was first dumped there late in 1828. Although the town was large it had been declining rapidly since 1720 and in 1830 the mud-brick walls and buildings had been neglected for a century or more. There was no suitable shore accommodation for passengers although occasionally a passenger and certainly a ship's captain might be lucky enough to sleep in the English factory for a night or two. Of all the ports in the Red Sea, al-Mukhā had been the most used by British ships, both sailing and steam, up to the time of the British possession of Aden in 1839. The reasons for al-Mukhā's decline have been related elsewhere, but from both the navigational and commercial points of view was fast becoming unsatisfactory, trade was declining and the roads were rapidly silting up, necessitating the anchoring of steamships further and further out into the bay. This in itself gave rise to the lengthening of the lighterage time, with the consequent increase in delays in taking on coal.

Al-Mukhā was used little after 1839 for overland passengers and it finally fell from grace for this purpose in favour of Aden. Nevertheless ships of the Indian Navy called there frequently during the following decades.

Aden

Aden was, of course, a very different matter and it finally won the prize having, in retrospect been the only contender of any consequence. Its great assets were its geographical location and its adequate natural harbour and roadsteads. The original town, Crater, faced eastward into Front Bay which had, for centuries been Aden's traditional anchorage, although Mu'allā and Slave Island had always used their beaches for dhow building. In its heyday the town covered about three square miles and one source quotes Aden, before the sixteenth century, to have had a population of some sixteen thousand—a highly suspect figure. It was however, at that time a flourishing fortified town. In the first quarter of the eighteenth century there is documentary evidence of there being a jetty running a short distance into the sea.

British troops moved to Aden from Perim in August 1799 and stayed many weeks, having been welcomed there by the Sultan. Forty years later when the British occupied Aden their reception was less than friendly and the invading force had to fight its way up the beach. It found a population of about six hundred living in a hundred dilapidated buildings made of mud or straw or, exceptionally, of stone. One of the few stone buildings, the Sultan's house was located to the south of Inscription Hill. The jetty was still there and the remains of a dock were found about a third of the way down the shore from the north. The sea wall had all but disappeared but Rundle's drawing made on the day of the invasion shows that there were still some traces of it. Regrettably they have long since disappeared. Crater at that time was little more than a vast ruin field.

England's reason for capturing Aden in 1839 was not merely to acquire a coaling station. It is not necessary to conquer a piece of territory merely to use it as a port of call and a re-victualling depot. There were other reasons—political, military and commercial. Other European powers, especially France, had been taking an unhealthy interest in the area. Muḥammad 'Alī, Viceroy of Egypt, had been advancing south through Asīr and the Yemen, the Americans had cornered the al-Mukhā coffee trade and possession of Aden by the British would go a long way towards retrieving it.

Coal at Aden Coal from Bombay was first dumped at Maqilein on the south west shore of Ṣīrah Island (it is now a peninsula) by the Thetis over ten years before Aden's conquest by the British and the dump was replenished the following year by the Owen Glendower. At the time of the occupation in 1839 the Anne Chrichton also brought further supplies. The British government had been happy to rely on the good graces of the local Sultan for the coaling of its ships over a period of ten years and when a British officer who has left his permanent memorial on the west coast of Australia, Captain R.H. Fremantle R.N., went ashore from H.M.S. Challenger in 1830, no objections were raised by the Sultan to the existence of coaling facilities for British ships.

Up to October 1839 it was normal for steamships to anchor in Ḥuqqāt Bay, just to the south of the coal dump. It soon became obvious that a better anchorage existed in Back Bay—Banda Tawwāhi—and between 1842 and 1850 coal hulks were anchored at the entrance to Back Bay also serving intentionally as blockships. In 1842 the old *Semiramis* had been converted to a coal hulk and was stationed at Tawwāhi the following year. She was soon supplemented by the *Charger*. The *Charger* lasted until 1847 before being broken up and the *Semiramis* followed shortly to the breaker's yard.

Very soon a large area at what was later called Steamer Point was made into a coal dump. This dump was on the sea shore, it can be located exactly, about 30 yards north of the site later occupied by the Luke Thomas building in the Crescent. This area has long since been dry land due to reclamation schemes and the shore line is now some quarter of a mile away. Archaeologists of the future will find Welsh fossilized carboniferous deposits under what two generations of Adenis knew as Hubaishi Street, Gas Street and Larcombe Road—all no doubt long since re-named. The P&O Company later occupied this site and an additional one was created at the same time on the coast a few hundred yards to the west and to be known as the Government Coaling Ground.

Although Crater had been the traditional site of Aden's town, from 1840 Tawwāhi began to grow into a settlement not only as an airy site for the bungalows of the military and the administrators but as a commercial centre for the servicing of visiting shipping and passengers. The ruinfield of Crater was slowly cleared and a busy town grew up to fill the area alongside the military installations. Late in the last century the grounds occupied by the coal dumps at Steamer Point—by then known as 'the coaling grounds' were required for development and stocks were run down. But new 'grounds' were already being created at Ras Hujayf and these finally replaced those at Steamer Point.

On Ras Hujayf the Aden Coal Company was located on the east of this peninsula and Luke Thomas-Cowasjee Dinshaw on the west. To the west, across French Bay, where the Messageries Maritimes landing pier and boat shipway existed, a coal depot administered by the firm of Eduljee Manackjee was located.

At that time the bay in front of the Crescent was named Ordnance Bay and on the west side of the eastern headland of Ordnance Bay were located the British India (steamship company) coal grounds. To the south west of this ground, a dump called the Australian coal ground was situated. The Ras Hujayf and other grounds grew larger and larger until oil fuel eventually became the standard bunkering requirements for shipping.

Between 1855 and 1865 coal consumption in Aden doubled but the death knell of the overland route had been sounded in 1856 by the building of the Alexandria–Cairo railway, the Cairo to Suez extension being finished three years later. The completion of the Suez Canal in 1869 accelerated the further development both of Tawwāhi and Crater.

Passengers at Aden Most passengers calling at Aden in steamships were able and anxious to get ashore for as long as possible. The early steamships were dirty and a layer of coal dust lay everywhere and permeated into every cabin. During the coaling operation conditions on board were much worse. Passengers were brought ashore in lighters or rowing boats. The shingle beach where they landed was next to and east of the first coal dump at the west end of the Crescent. Like most of the original northern coastline of Aden it has long since ceased to exist. Men were carried ashore through the sea on the backs of Arabs or Somalis and later the women walked along planks from lighter to dry land, resplendent with hats, veils, crinolines and parasols. A night or two's sleep ashore was always welcome.

There was a hotel at Tawwāhi as early as 1843, indicating that hotels were some of the first buildings in the Crescent. It is not certain but this first hotel of the early 1840s, (its name is not known) was almost certainly owned by a Parsee, Sorabjee Cowasjee. Records exist of his being lent money by the Aden administration for improvements to his then rather primitive establishment. There were others in the Crescent of which early photographs exist and which continued well into the twentieth century. One was run by a Frenchman: the Grand Hotel de l'Europe in no. 7 block facing the circle later made for the erection of Queen Victoria's statue.

Another hotel was the Continental owned by Prestonjee and Sons who later became ships chandlers. Basing themselves in a hotel in the Crescent most transit passengers of the period, to relieve boredom, made the journey through Maʻallā and the Main Pass to Crater, as generations of short stay visitors have done since, certainly up to 1967.

Conclusion

The transit passenger trade and the supply and servicing of ships was the basis upon which Aden grew from 1839 onwards. Alongside this was all the business arising from the accommodation and maintenance of the military, which, after 1946 had increased from a few hundred men in the 1840s to many thousands.

The existence of the overland route to India was an interim measure, lasting barely a third of a century at the end of a long era of 370 years between Vasco da Gama and Ferdinand de Lesseps. It played a small but essential role in thc development of East–West communications. It was an inevitable historical development as inevitable as the building of the Panama Canal or the Trans-Siberian railway. Most of all it was the major factor in the regeneration of Aden's prosperity in modern times, a prosperity increasing over a period of 130 years, the like of which it had never seen and will probably never see again. As a remote Indian Ocean haven, Aden was lucky in that it had thirty years to develop its expertise in preparation for the opening of the Suez Canal thus having the foundations laid during that period for the increase in trade which was to follow.

The overland route, like all such projects, could not have been initiated and developed without the minds of the businessmen like Waghorn and Shepheard in Egypt and the Parsees in Aden. The Indian Navy surveyed, and fought alongside the soldiers; the politicians and the functionnaires planned and the engineers build and maintained. In this tiny facet of South Arabian history they were largely unsung but if there were heroes, perhaps the bravest of them were the early passengers. They had to put up with it all.

Appendix 2

Some selected extracts from ***Sketches of Aden***

BY AN OFFICER IN THE QUEEN'S ARMY, 1848*

Name—Boundary—Extent—Soil—Climate—Divisions—Bays and Islands Steamer Point—The Town and its Inhabitants—Miscellaneous Information The Turkish Wall.

The Peninsula of Aden, or *Arabiae Emporium* as it was termed by the Romans, is situated in the Province of Yemen or Yaman in Arabia Felix; the latter appellation implying in Arabic, the right hand, or south of the temple of Mecca. It is difficult to account for its present name with any degree of certainty. Probably it was called after Ad, the son of Aws, who was the great grandson of Noah, but this must rest chiefly on conjecture. It is bounded on the North by Arabia Felix, whilst its remaining sides, viz South, East, and West are washed by the Sea of Bab el Mandeb, which signifies the Gate of Tears; and was thus named on account of the many disasters that formerly befell ships endeavouring to enter those Straits.

Its latitude North is 12° 45' 10", and its longitude East 45° 9'. The Isthmus connecting it with the main land is at high water 1320 yards in breadth. Indeed there seems to be but little doubt that Aden was formerly an island. The gradual increase of the Isthmus within the last few years, the appearance of the bases of the rocks themselves, which in many places bear evidence of having been washed by the sea, as well as the numerous shells which are everywhere to be found on the sands, but from which the ocean has long since receded, serve to confirm this opinion. In point of convenience, and to expedite our overland communication, a better place could hardly have been selected for a coal depot. It is equidistant between Bombay and Suez, whilst by water it is 100 miles from the entrance of the Red Sea, and about 145 miles from al-Muchā.

---

* The full title is *Historical and Statistical Studies of Aden in Arabia Felix during a two year Residence in that Colony*, Madras, 1848. The officer does not divulge his name.

The greatest length of Aden is about 5½ miles, its breadth varying from 2 to 3 miles and upwards. Its soil is of igneous origin, but although there are no records that I am aware of in existence to prove that volcanic eruptions have ever taken place in Aden, yet its general appearance, in the opinion of various geologists, is sufficiently confirmatory of the fact.

"Along the entire coast of South Arabia," says Harris, "there is not a more remarkable feature, than the lofty promontory of Aden, which has been flung up from the bed of the ocean, and its formation is altogether Volcanic. The Arab Historian Masudi of the tenth century, after speaking of the Volcanos of Sicily, and in the kingdom of Maha Rah, alludes to it as existing in the desert of Barhat, adjacent to the province of Nasafan, and Hadramaut in the country of Shahar." "Its sound like the rumbling of thunder might then be heard many miles, and from its entrails were vomited forth red hot stones with a flood of liquid fire."

"An amphitheatre of dimensions sufficient for the Devil's punch-bowl is formed by two Volcanic ranges, once in connection, but obviously rent asunder, heaved outwards, and canted in opposite directions by some violent eruption that has forced an opening to the ocean."

All those ingredients which indicate volcanic matter are here to be met with such as compact basalt, pumice stone, obsidian, quartz, chrystal, and specular iron ore. Large masses too of trachyte composed of considerable quantities of alkali are frequently to be found. These rocks it is affirmed, when exposed to atmospheric influence, peel off in laminae, beneath which is found a saline efflorescence. Many of the rocks present a lurid appearance, whilst in other places they assume a green, and sometimes a purple hue. It would far exceed, however, the limits of this work to enter into detail regarding the geological structure of this wonderful place, I must now bring the reader acquainted with its general features—and endeavour to convey some idea of the desolate spot in which an European has to serve.

Here no trees afford shelter from the piercing rays of a tropical sun—no songs of birds, no murmuring of chrystal rills are ever heard, not a blade of grass, not a weed can be seen—the scene around is one of barrenness and utter desolation. The parched steeps and the thirsting sands below seem vainly to implore the sky for rain. It is withal the most dreary, and monotonous of places that the imagination can conceive. The few quadrupeds that dwell there, are in accordance with the savage nature of the soil—the wildest animals such as the hyena, the fox, and the wild cat, are almost the sole denizens of the sterile rocks around, and often make "night hideous" with their cries; whilst loathsome reptiles, such as the snake, scorpion, tarantula, and centipede infest the rude dwellings of their hapless owners.

Disagreeable, however, as such a locality must naturally be for the residence of an European, from the absence of amusements and useful employment; from the want of variety, and deprivation of the ordinary comforts of life, still, it must be admitted, that Aden possesses great mercantile as well as military advantages. Indeed so early as in the reign of Constantine the Great, it was celebrated for its fortifications and its traffic, and was for many years the principal entrepot of Eastern Commerce. Although the natural productions of this Colony are few as it yields little besides water (itself a treasure to the Arabs), Coral from which lime is made, and basaltic stones admirably adapted for building; yet, even these contribute to make it a valuable acquisition. But its admirable position, commanding the entrance into the Red Sea—the commodiousness and security of its harbours,—together with its lofty hills naturally strong, and which might by the aid of art be rendered impregnable, entitle the possession of Aden to be considered of the greatest value and importance to the British Government.

With respect to the climate of Aden, I cannot pronounce it unhealthy, although fever and scurvy have hitherto thinned the ranks of the Military, Native as well as European. In the progress of these "Sketches" ample information will be given under this head.

There are only two seasons in Aden, the hot and the cold. The former commences in April and lasts till the end of September; the latter begins in October and continues to the end of March. So cold indeed is it in the month of January, that warm clothing is indispensable, nay—at night a blanket is a perfect luxury. Indeed in some parts of Yemen, if we may credit Bruce, the water freezes on the mountains.

People during this season, hitherto confined to their houses, feel their frames till now relaxed invigorated, and the sallow cheek of yesterday assumes the ruddy hue of health. In the hot season, on the contrary, the intense heat, the scorching, suffocating winds—the terrible shimals, or dust storms, form so disagreeable a variety, to say nothing of the consequent misery and discomfort which have to be endured, that men's minds sicken beneath their baneful influence, nay even life itself becomes well nigh insupportable.

Let those whose sad destinies compel them to reside at Aden during this season, repair if possible to Steamer Point, there they will be at least secure from the clouds of dust and the suffocating heat, and discover that the Thermometer stands some 10° lower than it does in the camp.

September is the most trying month in the year. During this month in addition to shimals, another wind termed *Simoom* blows from the North and comes direct from Arabia. Its approach may generally be detected by the dark and lurid appearance of the sky, and although it seldom lasts longer than an hour, (during which time the air is every where impregnated with particles of sand) it is found to be exceedingly relaxing and oppressive—, men pant for breath, the face receives a complete coating of dust, the skin feels parched and fevered, and should one venture out, the eyes cannot see, and the ears are soon filled with gritty sand.

There appears to be no regular rainy season in Aden, indeed for years together this sterile Cape has been without a drop of rain! Sometimes, however, the dark clouds in their course, as though ashamed to withhold the precious drops so bountifully bestowed on happier lands, appear to compassionate nature's desolate child and shed them like the pitying tears of a mother, upon its parched brow!

That Aden has been denied rain for many years together, is a fact; to which the oldest inhabitants bear testimony.

The Adites were afflicted with a four years drought for their impiety, and numbers of them who resided in Aden at the time must have suffered in like manner.

When Bruce visited the Emir Ferhan, Governor of Konfodah, which means the town of the Hedgehog, he was much amused in learning from that personage, that abundance of rain fell in Arabia, and, when the Emir demanded the cause of his merriment he replied: "that the reason was, he had travelled 4,000 miles in twelve months, and had neither seen, nor heard of a shower of rain till then. He further remarked that though he might perceive he understood his language well, for a stranger, yet had he asked him what was the Arabic for a shower of rain, he could not have told him."

At different periods the wells have dried up from want of rain, and Arabia has been subject to all the horrors of famine. Hence doubtless the reason for the many tanks that have been built near the rocks about Aden; and here I cannot but suggest the necessity of erecting cisterns for the use of the troops, similar to those at Gibraltar, in order to guard against the possibility of drought.

Arid as the soil of Aden generally is, it has nevertheless been occasionally visited by heavy rains at different periods.

Sale mentions the inundation of Aram, which calamity befell the tribes settled in Yemen, soon after the time of Alexander the Great. This flood carried away the whole city of Saba and the neighbouring towns, and broke down the mound which the inhabitants had built.

In the year 1842, it fell five inches in about as many hours. The last violent shower took place on the second of May, 1846; it began in the morning and lasted without intermission for the space of six hours. Many of the houses suffered considerably; some were completely destroyed. I saw my own apartment nearly inundated by the rain—a terrible torrent descending from the hills around, rushed into my verandah, and destroying both furniture and wearing apparel, rendered my dwelling for many days uninhabitable.

In one part of Aden, near the town, the furious waters uniting, speedily formed a deep river, bearing away everything in its progress into the Sea, in trying to cross which some soldiers of the gallant corps then stationed at Aden, well nigh lost their lives.

On the road leading to the Main Pass, (of which I shall shortly have occasion to speak,) the carcases of various animals lay scattered on the ground, and fragments of rock fell with a fearful crash from the heights above. The scene was melancholy to behold; yet, what was far worse, the damp and unwholesome exhalations that followed when the rain subsided and the sun again shone forth, were the forerunners of that dreadful malady the Cholera which soon afterwards visited Aden and swept away so many of its inhabitants.

The dews at night are frequently very heavy and render sleeping in the open air, (a common occurrence in Aden,) though agreeable for the time, dangerous and unwholesome as they generally produce colds and rheumatism.

The Bays about Aden are exceedingly picturesque, but with the exception of Back Bay, at Steamer Point, are inconsiderable in extent. The anchorage in the latter is excellent and certainly the best and safest in Aden, being capable of admitting the largest ships at all seasons of the year. The average number of vessels in harbour daily are from ten to eighteen—and these usually lie in five or six fathoms water. The total number of ships that arrived during the year 1845 could not have been less than forty-seven, for the most part laden with coals from England.

The other Bays which are situated near the Camp. viz., Front Bay and Holkot Bay are chiefly remarkable for their excellent fish of which numbers are daily caught by the Arabs, and sold in the market at a reasonable price.

The former is fordable at low water, and, when the tide is ebbing, the beach is literally covered with curlew and terne in quest of prey.

The beach at Holkot Bay has of late become a sort of Sanatorium for invalids, and might prove an agreeable promenade, were it not for sundry revolting spectacles which the eye has occasionally to encounter; such as fragments of human bones that have been burnt by the Hindoos, and the carcases of camels and other animals that lay scattered upon the sands.

The Aden Bays are interspersed with numerous small islands, viz. Little Aden situated near Steamer Point, which is inhabited, and contains a number of dark, gigantic rocks—Seera island near the Camp, which is an immense rock from whose summit bristling with cannon—signals are made to ships on their approach, and several others which though very diminutive, contain abundance of delicious oysters, and shells of exquisite beauty.

The Peninsula of Aden consists of three stations, viz. Steamer Point, the Town of Aden in the vicinity of which is the Camp, and the Durab el Arabi, or the Turkish Wall.

These are all commanded by a succession of lofty ridges of spiral and multifarious forms, extending nearly from East to West in an irregular direction, of which the highest is Gebel Shumshan, 1800 feet above the level of the sea. The others which are remarkable for their Military strength, rather than their elevation, seldom rising above 800 feet, are Durab el Hosh, near the Main Pass or entrance into the town, and Gebel Hadid, or the Iron mountain, the fortification of which is rapidly progressing, and Seera which has been already mentioned.

Upon landing at Steamer Point,* a stranger cannot fail to be struck with the sterility of the soil, around the amphitheatre of bold and naked rocks, and its comfortless and dreary aspect compared with our noble sea-ports at home. But the inconvenience felt by the overland passenger on landing is soon forgotten by the novelty of the spectacle before him.

The uncouth, but slender figures of the Simoilies (who come from the opposite coast,) rendered doubly forbidding by wearing huge red wigs upon their heads, and dirty pieces of cloth round their bodies.

The Seedies, black as the coals they carry, with their broad shoulders, expansive chests, and muscular limbs, and countenances expressive of good nature and content—the cringing and effeminate Jew, who may easily be known by his gabardine and his skull cap, from which ringlets descent on either side of his swarthy face; or the naked and hardy Arab, who chanting some rude song, urges forward his weary Camel.

The usual mode of conveyance for passengers arriving at Steamer Point is on donkeys, for neither palanquins, nor vehicles of any description are to be obtained; yet even these useful quadrupeds are often with difficulty procured.

The houses of which numbers have been erected by the Military, though built of slender and rude materials are cool enough to reside in. They consist for the most part of little more than wooden uprights, common mats made of the leaves of the date tree, and reeds of which a kind of ornamental trellis work is made.

The great drawback to people residing at Steamer Point, and which I fear it will take some time to remedy, is the difficulty and expense of procuring water and provisions there. Families have been known to pay for the former from 50 to 60 Rupees (£6) per month, a sum sufficient for the same period to supply a person with wine. To remedy the evil various schemes have been agitated; boring has been attempted, but after much labour and expenditure of Government money this has proved unsuccessful and been finally abandoned. Private individuals with a praiseworthy providence worthy of imitation, following the example set them by the Turks, have erected tanks near Steamer Point, from some of which after the heavy rains many thousand gallons of water have been procured. At Bir Omheit, however, on the opposite coast situated a short distance on the other side of the Bay, there is a well from which, sometimes,

* There is a good Hotel at Steamer Point kept by a Parsee for the accommodation of passengers.

the ships in harbour obtain sweet water; but this is the property of the Arabs. With respect to provisions, no bazaar or market has yet been established at Steamer point, consequently all supplies have to be procured from the Camp, a distance of at least five miles. Great therefore is the inconvenience to which sojourners at the Point and the Masters of shipping are subjected.

The Town of Aden is the next place to which I would direct the reader's attention. After traversing a long and dreary road extending to a distance of about four miles, the first object that engages the attention of the traveller is the Bab el Yemen or Main Pass, through which the Town is entered. This pass has been cut through the solid rock, and has recently been completed by the British Government after much expense and labour.

It is strengthened on either side by walls of solid masonry of considerable extent, height, and thickness. These are loopholed, and in the bastion near the gate some guns have been judiciously planted. The heights immediately above also present a formidable line of defence. Across the pass a stone bridge has been erected, but its utility in a military point of view has been questioned. Near this, two isolated trees may be viewed which are reared with considerable trouble, and present to the spectator a pleasing contrast to the sterility of the soil around. After passing these on the left a good road leads to the heights above, which separate the Town and Camp from the Turkish Wall. On the other side rises the cloud capped summit of Gebel Shumshan the height commanding Aden, which lies some distance apart.

On a place comprising an area of about three square miles, surrounded by an amphitheatre of naked rocks the town is built on the ruins of the old one, of which little remains but a heap of loose stones. From the Main Pass its appearance is striking and novel, so much so, as to leave at first on the mind of the beholder a somewhat favourable impression. But the delusion soon vanishes, for, on a closer inspection it is found to contain a number of hovels of the most wretched and abject description, but little superior to which (I think I may assert without fear of contradiction,) are the dwellings of the Military in the Camp hard by. The Minaret of Menalah, however, the Mosque of Seik Hydroos and the Masonic Lodge are goodly edifices in their way and are certainly ornaments to the place, yet there are hardly more than a dozen good substantial buildings in Aden, for the most part built since its occupation by the British. The Lodge was erected in 1846 at an expense of 3,000 Rupees (300£) and to the praiseworthy exertions of one of the Queen's Regiments, stationed there at that time, the public have mainly to be indebted. At that period there were upwards of 40 Freemasons belonging to the Lodge. The Custom House, the Native Hospital, and the Parsee Shops are the only other buildings worthy of notice.

The charges for European articles purchased in the shops are very exorbitant, they being often sold for more than three times their actual value.

In a recent number of the U.S. *Journal* it is stated regarding the mosques at Aden, "that though small they are very numerous; and one is shown where the Caliph Ali, the son-in-law of the Prophet, read prayers." I have never, however, been able to discover this sacred edifice. Two paltry looking buildings, which stand completely in the back ground, are used for the performance of the Protestant and Catholic worship. These have been raised by private subscription, the former has not been consecrated.

Built in the same unpretending style of architecture are the Post Office, the Treasury, the Commissariat Stores, while the residence of the Military are mean and uncomfortable in the extreme; yet the outlay for erecting one of these buildings, may be estimated at from 500 to 1,000 Rupees. These frail dwellings are not infrequently unroofed by the violence of the periodical winds, and afford but indifferent protection to Europeans from the burning sun. The inflammable materials too of which they are built render the greatest precautions necessary to prevent them catching fire. The fact of the whole of the Lines of the 10th Regiment N.I. having been burnt down in the short space of two hours is a melancholy proof of the precarious tenure of household property in Aden. There is little doubt, however, that as soon as the fortifications which are progressing are completed, that good, substantial barracks will be built. A few years ago barracks had actually been commenced on an extensive scale, but the situation selected was found to be so bad that after considerable labour and expense they were abandoned. It is stated though just commenced that they have already cost one Lac and a half of Rupees. There are two exceedingly good sites which have been considered eligible for barracks, one close to the Camp, the other near the Turkish Wall, but the latter I should pronounce to be the best, being more spacious, convenient, as well as healthy. The estimated sum to build barracks for the accommodation of 2,000 men would be no less that 45,000£.

The native prison in Aden contains about 100 convicts, their crimes for the most part being murder, or robbery. These unfortunate criminals have been sentenced to various periods of hard labour on the public roads, and may be daily seen working in chains surrounded by a strong guard of Sepoys. It is worthy of remark, however, that crime has been gradually on the decrease, since the British occupation of Aden.

The Police force in Aden is insufficient for the effectual maintenance of order, their number not exceeding 35 men altogether; it is therefore found necessary to employ the military to assist them, a measure fraught with inconvenience to the service as they have other duties of a more responsible and urgent nature to perform.

The civil jurisdiction in Aden is vested in the Political Agent and his assistant, and there is also a Superintendent of Police. Minor punishments, such as corporal punishment, imprisonment, or fine, are occasionally inflicted in the bazaar for petty offenses, yet these are comparatively few, when the number of inhabitants in the town is considered.

The Aden market is generally well supplied with fish, meat. provender, and other articles of the best quality, most of which are brought in by the Arabs from Lahidge, and other villages adjacent to Aden; and every morning at daybreak a long string of Camels may be seen moving in file from the Turkish Wall laden chiefly with firewood, grass, kirby, and jowlies. The average number of Camels that arrive daily may be computed at about 250.

In the year 1845 no less that 86,000 Camels entered Aden with stock of every description, being considerably in excess of what they amounted to in 1846; the cause may be attributed to the supplies having been so frequently stopped during that year; in consequence of the advance of Syed Ishmael against Aden, of whom I shall hereafter have occasion to speak.

The curious observer can hardly fail to be struck with the strange appearance of the bazaar and its frequenters as he proceeds along the crowded streets indeed, I have often wondered how accommodation could be found for so many thousand souls in so limited a space, and why plague, pestilence, and famine visit not their abodes.

The truth is, however, with regard to the first, the hovels if you may so term them, in which the squalid tenants are huddled together, like pigs, seem adapted to their simple but sordid natures. Others it is true deprived even of these possess no other roof but the canopy of heaven and lie at night on the ground exposed to the heavy dews with nothing save a dirty covering thrown over their bodies, wallowing in filth, yet apparently contented.

The inhabitants seem to trouble themselves little about either sickness or privations, and their ordinary wants which are few are easily supplied; if ill, nature is their only doctor, if poor, poverty causes them but little uneasiness.

A native of Aden is generally speaking a niggard in his habits, and to save a few pence, he will deny himself his proper allowance of food, nay even the actual necessaries of life.

Others again with equal self denial have been known to amass sums, which though little in an Englishman's opinion would be wealth to them.

Of this description I may include most of the money lenders about Aden, who having at length obtained sufficient capital lend money at a most usurious interest. It is worthy of remark, however, that penurious as the habits of the Natives may be in general, all contribute liberally towards their respective religious festivals, whether they me Musselmen, Hindoos, or Jews.

I have more than once strolled through the Town of Aden, partly to obtain some insight into the character of its heterogeneous population, and partly with a view of becoming acquainted with their habits. Their simple and primitive manners, their different avocations, and their various costumes, present a striking and interesting picture. In one place might be naked Arab of slender but muscular proportions feeding his weary camel that lies beside him with morsels of green kirby, and tending him with the greatest care. In another place the way-worn pilgrim who has journeyed far over the trackless desert, with scarce a covering on his thin, emancipated form, destined perhaps to encounter still more hardships and still more privations. Now, an Arab female, or a Jewess with unaffected modesty suddenly disappears and conceals herself behind the rude lattice of her humble dwelling. Next, your attention is directed to a stall where a warm dispute has commenced between its sable occupants and two youthful and effeminate Hindoos, whose erect port, snow white turbans, slippered feet, and scarfs thrown carelessly over the shoulder, proclaim them to be the very beau ideal of Native dandies. The storm of words increases, and continuing for full twenty minutes proves at length to be about an anna or a pice, being a debt of long standing for value received in rice! near all this busy scene is a venerable Musselman at his devotions, who raising his meagre arms prays aloud and prostrates himself on the earth. On the other side of the way two Arabs are enjoying the soothing influence of their bookahs, or some Native barber sitting crosslegged is shaving with extraordinary care, the head of some worshippers of Vishnu. But the most singular spectacle presented is that of various Arab ladies, whose faces are shrouded from the prying gaze of man, by means of a veil made of coarse blue cloth which is fastened closely round their heads, thereby giving them "a resemblance to the horned owl."

Yet should the spectator chance to see their faces uncovered, he will find no display of personal charms but on the contrary view the features in all probability of some withered hag, from whose nose a golden ring dangles some ten or twelve inches in circumference, whilst round her arms and legs a profusion of bangles are displayed.

The tanks and Parsee garden situated at the further extremity of the town, are not altogether unworthy of notice. The former were erected by the Turks soon after their occupation of Aden in 1538, and were all lined with jasper or marble and covered with handsome domes; yet however great their splendour then, there are but few traces of it remaining now. These tanks are of various dimensions, their form being semi-elliptical, some of them are 68 feet in length and 20 feet in depth.

The Parsee garden which is a short distance from the tanks is the only spot in Aden where horticulture on a small scale has been pursued with any degree of success. Constant irrigation, however, as well as care are required to preserve theses few, unwilling representatives of Flora from decay. In this garden is a Parsee Chapel the neatest and best built in Aden, close to which is a walled building, without a roof, in which the Parsees exposed their dead uncoffined and unburied, a prey to kites and vultures.

The town of Aden is well supplied with water and contains about 300 wells of which only four contain sweet water, all the rest being more or less brackish, and even the best that can be procured is considered unwholesome, being impregnated with deleterious mixtures.

The best wells have been cut through the solid rock and are surrounded by good rubble walls from 3 to 4 feet in diameter, and from 100 to 150 feet in depth. A medical gentleman of my acquaintance residing in Aden, and whose opinion regarding these wells is entitled to consideration, asserts, that the water in them never rises above twenty feet when it remains stationary during the hot and cold weather, decreasing a few feet at night and rising to the same level in the morning. He accounts for the brackish taste of some that are lower than the valley by their flowing or filtering through soil containing saline ingredients. This may certainly be the case, yet on the other hand, water which is brackish has been found to improve in quality by the process of filtration through an argillaceous soil. The celebrated traveller Bruce states, when at Corseir, he used for experiment's sake to filter the brackish water, through sand and thus made it drinkable.

> "The source," says Dr. Malcolmson, "from whence the wells are supplied, has been and still is, an interesting subject of speculation. Some say that it is merely the rain which falls on the hills filtering through the crevices of the rock, as in other places; this argument, however, is not tenable, as the rain that falls on the hills is almost entirely carried off to the sea, and even after the heaviest fall that we have witnessed here, the wells have not been affected in the slightest degree, thereby plainly showing we must look elsewhere for an explanation. A second party again assert that it is produced by exhalation supplied by subterranean heat; this is far fetched theory not requiring notice. My opinion is and I believe the principle of artesian wells will bear me out, that the wells are supplied by subterranean and submarine currants, which flow from the high hills in the interior and that its channel of conveyance being between two beds of lava, the wells of Aden perforating the upper bed; the height which the water attains in the wells being the same as at its source in the high land. This is substantial in my opinion in a most decided manner, by the surface always resting at the same height, the surplus water escaping to the sea, which it enters either in a submarine sheet of water or spring, as at Perim, and other places on the other side of the persian Gulf where it is not unusual for divers to go down in four and a half fathom and bring up fresh water. This is an established and well known fact to all who have visited that shore."

It is a singular circumstance that however objectionable the brackish water may be, many prefer it as a beverage to the sweet, and such is the force of habit that a remarkable instance is stated of a Soldier who was supplied with the latter having mixed a little salt with it to make it palatable. It is acknowledged that the brackish water contains great medicinal properties, and people on their first arrival at Aden would do well to abstain from it as a beverage. About one quart of this water was sent to England some time ago to be analyzed and was found to be composed as follows; viz:—

Chloride of Sodium
Chloride of Magnesium
Chloride of Calcium
Sulphate of Magnesia
Carbonate of Potash.

It has been affirmed and I believe with some truth that when used too frequently to wash the hair it is apt to become prematurely grey.

It is hard to say to whom the inhabitants of Aden are indebted for the discovery of the first well of sweet water. Ibn Battuta of Tangiers informs us that Aden in his time was "a large city but without either seed, *water*, or tree;" and a period of about 500 years is stated to have elapsed since then. Probably, therefore, it was not until after the Turks took possession of Aden in 1538, that the best wells were dug. Be that as it may the possession of them has been the cause of many bloody feuds, for they have been as they are at present a source of wealth to hundreds.

According to a moderate calculation The Arab water carriers in Aden realize on an average from 2,600 to 3,000 Rupees a month by the sale of water.

The boring of Artesian wells still continues to be prosecuted in Aden with indefatigable industry, yet it is to be feared they will terminate in failure like other previous attempts of the kind.

Situated about 2 miles from the Camp is the Outpost of the Turkish Wall, in which 350 men are constantly kept on duty, and is the key indeed of the position. Immediately in rear is a range of almost inaccessible heights which are always well guarded, and reinforced in the event of attack.

The present wall was built by the English soon after their occupation of Aden, and is in fact hardly more than a heap of loose stones, about four feet high and three feet broad, and extending to a distance of a mile across the sandy Isthmus which divides Aden from Arabia.

It, however, offers an obstacle to the Arabs and prevents the possibility of our Troops being taken by surprise. Why it should be called the Turkish Wall seems an anomaly not easily to be accounted for, considering that the original Durab el Arabi, or Turkish Wall, is no longer in existence. Its chief strength consists in three field works and redans built of sandbags placed at judicious distances from each other, upon which are mounted about twenty guns, the curtain on each side of them being protected by ditches and *chevaux de frise*. Each extremity of it is washed by the sea and flanked by strong redoubts. The bay on the left of this position is fordable at low water, by which the Main Pass or entrance into the town may be approached, whilst that on the right is so shallow, that an enemy by moving along the foot of the heights near Orrock Point might gain access into the town itself. Yet in either case according to the most approved mode of defence, he would have to sustain a murderous fire not only from the redoubts but from the Troops stationed above. The guns at the wall are kept constantly loaded with grape and canister, a linstock being always lighted and at hand. During the night a long chain of sentries are posted along the wall with loaded muskets, with orders to preserve the strictest vigilance, and to retire to the field works in case of attack. In the event of alarm a rocket is sent up from the left redoubt which is immediately responded to by a gun from the heights, so that in half an hour afterwards every man may be on his allotted post.

The heights when properly manned present a most formidable line of defence; thick walls of solid masonry are built along the entire ridge, whilst at almost every point guns of various calibre are planted with great judgement. This ridge which divides the Turkish Wall from the town runs almost parallel with another of much greater extent and elevation, these gradually receeding, now jutting forward, assume an irregular, curvilinear appearance, and surrounding the town, are almost united at the Main Pass. The strongest and most secure position on the heights will be the Durab el Hosh near the Main Pass, to which the Commandant and his staff repair when threatened with an attack. The advantages of this post are obvious, for not only can the movements of the Arabs at an immense distance off, be discerned with accuracy from its summit, but the communication with the troops and inhabitants which remain unbroken. At the further extremity of the heights near the camp is Orrock Point, a small rocky eminence on which are mounted two guns and to which about 100 men are generally detached, for the double purpose of guarding the approach to the heights as well as to prevent the town from being entered by the enemy in that quarter. If the Arabs were to succeed in passing Orrock Point, they would have to sustain a murderous fire from the guns in Camp and from those on Seerah Island.

Besides Durab el Hosh and Orrock Point are give other posts which are numbered from right to left, and which are almost inaccessible to an enemy in front, whilst in rear the troops are protected by impregnable heights which have already been mentioned.

The Aden Field force in 1846 barely amounted to 1,800 men, a number insufficient for the proper defence of the heights, but which has since, however, been increased. The following was the manner in which the troops were distributed in the event of an attack:

Height and Main Pass about	700 Men
Turkish Wall	500 do.
Reserve	421 do.
Garrison and Regimental Guards	176 do.

It is affirmed that the Arabs can at any time raise upwards of 100,000 fighting men in the province of Yemen alone to bring against Aden. The British it is true possess over the Arabs the advantages of military knowledge, discipline, and resources, and are protected by a position rendered strong by art as well as nature, whilst armed at every point upwards of forty guns are ready at a moment's notice to pour forth their iron storm. On the other hand the Arabs can at all times stop their supplies, hover about the neighbourhood, and prudently avoiding an attack, harass the troops and keep them in a constant state of vigilance and preparation, as was the case in August, 1846, when they advanced in great force towards the Turkish Wall, and prevented the usual supplies from being brought for nearly three weeks.

The Turkish Wall is perhaps as dreary a spot as the mind can well conceive. Reader, picture to yourself a desert in your front, high and barren rocks behind you, with scarce a sound to interrupt the death like stillness around, save the distant murmuring of the sea, or the shrill cry of the culture in quest of prey, or betimes the rude song of an Arab urging forth his Camel as he hurried along matchlock in hand, to his desert home. Yet the solitude of the place is favourable to reflection and study. I have often on a cool evening strolled, quietly by myself, along the numerous crags by the sea side, or watched, seated on a rock, as the golden sun was setting, in a pleasing state of reverie the sportive splashing of the waves, as the tide flowed swiftly on, the hermit crabs clinging the while like mariners in distress to the sea girt cliffs.

There is something irresistibly soothing, alone and unobserved in listening to the hoarse and hollow music of the turbulent ocean. Then it is the mind for a time disregarding all meaner things, and shaking off the fetters of worldly restraint, can learn to appreciate the boundless and sublime works of nature, than whom no better preceptor can be found.

**Historical Summary of Aden—Capture of Aden by the British in 1839—
The Arabs attack the Turkish Wall—Advance of Syed Ishmael.**

There are few places in the world of which the geographical position and history are so little known, and with whose value and importance we are so little acquainted as Aden; indeed until of late years its very existence to most ordinary people amongst us was unheard of. Like other cities it has flourished, and has fallen, and now lies, alas! at the foot of dreary rocks, a heap of stones and rubbish, prostrate in the dust. It is true other edifices have sprung up from the ruins of this once celebrated emporium, built centuries ago by the Turks—yet even these are fast sinking to decay beneath the ruthless hand of time and tottering seem about to mingle in one common grave.

The town of Aden built on the extinguished crater of a volcano, is said to have been originally founded by Ad, and completed by King Shedad his son, of whom says Sale:

> "The Eastern writers deliver many fabulous things, particularly that he built a fine palace, adorned with delicious gardens, to embellish which he spared neither cost nor labour, proposing thereby to create in his subjects a superstitious veneration of himself as a God. This garden or paradise was called the garden of Irem, and is mentioned in the Koran, and often alluded to by Oriental Writers. The city they tell us is still standing in the deserts of Aden, being preserved by Providence as a monument of divine wrath, though it be invisible, unless very rarely when God permits it to be seen, a favour once Kolabah pretended to have received in the reign of the Khalif Moāwyah, who sending for him to know the truth of the matter; Kolabah related his whole adventure:
>
> that as he was seeking a Camel he had lost, he found himself on a sudden at the gates of this city, and entering it saw not one inhabitant, at which being terrified, he stayed no longer than to take with him some fine stones which he showed to the Khalif."

Sale then alluded to the sins of the Adites proceeds as follows:

> "The descendants of Ad in process of time falling from the worship of the true God into idolatry, God sent the Prophet Hûd, (who is generally agreed to be Herbert) to preach and reclaim them, but they refusing to acknowledge his mission, or to obey him. God sent a hot and suffocating wind, which blew seven nights and eight days together, and entering their nostrils, passed through their bodies and destroyed them all, a very few only excepted, who had believed in Hûd and retired with him to another place. That prophet afterwards returned into Hadramut, and was buried near Hasec, where there is a small town now standing called Kebr Hud, or the sepulchre of Hud."
>
> "Before the Adites were thus severely punished, God to bumble them, and incline them to harken to the preaching of his prophet, afflicted them with a drought for four years, so that all their cattle perished, and themselves were very near it; upon which they sent Lokmān, (different from one of the same name who lived in David's time,) with sixty other to Mecca to beg rain, which they not obtaining, Lokmān with some of his company stayed at Mecca and thereby escaped destruction, giving rise to a tribe called the latter Ad, who were afterwards changed into monkeys."

The historian Crichton in quoting from the Koran in his "History of Arabia," is hardly correct. Talking of the above Tribes, he says, "they had been chastized with a three years' drought;" now, I do not find it stated in Sale's that it was a "three years' drought," but that it afflicted them with a drought for *four years*. Nor does that writer mention one word about "all their cattle that perished." Far be it from me to cope with so learned an authority as Crichton, but it must at the same time be acknowledged that unless an historian quote with accuracy, he will often lead his readers into a labyrinth of error.

There appears to be strong presumptive proof of the correctness of the Koran, regarding this destruction of cattle; for in some antique poems found written on marbles, midst the ruins of a fortress, on the coast of Hadramaut, near the emporium of Aden, we find in the last three lines of poem 2d "and neither foot nor *hoof* remained."

From the period when Shedad built Aden until A.D. 50, little that can be relied upon is known relative to its history, when the Romans after the direct passage of the Indus had been secured by Hippalus, (the first who sailed in open sea from Arabia to India), caused Aden to be destroyed, the better to secure the monopoly of the Indian trade.

Towards the close of the fifth century, or according to some writers A.D. 529, Dhu Nowas a bloodthirsty Jew, surnamed the Lord of the burning pit, caused 20,000 Christians to be thrown into a pit filled with combustibles, to which burning faggots were applied, where after enduring the most acute torture, death terminated their sufferings. This inhuman act soon met the punishment it deserved. A Christian who escaped the general massacre, thirsting for revenge, applied to the Nayash, or king of Abyssinia, who was also a Christian to undertake the invasion of Yemen. That monarch immediately dispatched an army of 70,000 men under the command of Aryat, his son, with injunctions to kill every Jew, to pillage a third part of the country, and to take captive a third of the women and children.

On landing at Aden, Aryat burnt his ships determined to conquer or to perish. The Arabs weakened by dissensions and taken by surprise were routed with great slaughter. Dhu Nowas, it is stated, "fled, and finding himself pursued, he spurred his horse to a rocky precipice, and threw himself into the sea." Aryat succeeded to the Government of Yemen, but his reign was of short duration. A traitor, named Abraha, who landed with the expedition, and who had been slave to a Roman merchant, revolted, and having by various arts and machinations succeeded in gaining a number of adherents, determined to offer battle. Eventually, however, to avoid the risk of a civil war, it was agreed to decide the contest by single combat in which the Abyssinian hero was treacherously stabbed by a slave, not however, before he had wounded his antagonist in the face.

The first act of Abraha upon assuming the reins of Government was to endeavour to convert his new subjects to the Christian faith. He also, we are informed, built a church of unparalleled magnificence "on the altar of which, says Nuvairi, a huge pearl was placed, of such brilliancy that on the darkest night it served the purpose of a lamp." It is said that he had determined upon making Sanaa, the Jerusalem of Arabia, whence pilgrims should in future repair instead of to Mecca—nor was an opportunity wanting to carry his designs into execution. At night, during a solemn festival, the church was indecently profaned by two of the Koreish. Nothing could appease his wrath upon this being brought to his knowledge, he hastily assembled an army of 40,000 men and placing himself at their head, marched against Tuhama, the inhabitants of which he routed, upon the plea of their having refused to transfer their religious allegiance to Sanaa. Proceeding towards Mecca, which he determined to attack, he and his army were completely overthrown, a miracle it is said relieved the city, and innumerable flock of birds having cast pellets of baked clay down upon the besiegers. Abraha alone reached Sanaa where he died of a loathsome disease.

Upon the death of Abraha, his two sons, Yascum and Masruk, succeeded to the throne. Their tyrannical and licentious conduct soon spread the flames of disaffection amongst the Arabs.

Nor were other competitors wanting; Seip a descendant of the last of the Hamyarite princes profiting by the popular discontent, applied for military aid to Khoosroo, king of Persia, a powerful prince possessing enormous wealth. He at first received an unfavourable answer. "Thy land," said the king, "is distant and barren. Its only productions are ship and camels; these we want not; nor can they tempt the Persians to so fruitless an enterprise."

Eventually, however, his request was acceded to, and having obtained auxiliaries amounting to 3,600 men composed of malefactors and condemned criminals. Seip returned to Arabia; a battle was fought near Aden, where Masruk was slain by an arrow from the hand of Wehraz, a Persian nobleman who commanded the expedition.

Seip was soon afterwards appointed Viceroy, in the name of the Persian king. His cruelties to the Abyssinians led to a conspiracy, and after a reign of four years he was assassinated by a slave while hunting near his own capital.

From this period until the conquest of Yemen by Mohammed, the Persians appointed the succeeding princes under the title of Emirs, the last of whom Badhan embraced the new religion.

In the 10th year of the Hejira or A.D. 631, Ali bin Abon Talib was sent into Yemen to propagate the Mohammedan faith, and it is said, converted the whole Tribe of Hamdan in one day. Their example was speedily followed by all the inhabitants of that province, and the tribes at Aden and its neighbourhood soon became proselytes to the new creed.

From the time of Mohammed and until many centuries afterwards Aden appears to have been governed by tributary Chiefs or Governors, to follow whom in succession, with the recital of their bloody feuds, conquests, and oppressions, revolting atrocities and wanton licentiousness would not only be superfluous, but far beyond the limits of these sketches, I shall therefore proceed to the statement of matters which more immediately relate to the condition and resources of Aden.

From the 11th to the 16th century most writers agree in stating that Aden was the greatest entrepôt of Eastern Commerce, and in A.D. 1487 was in the zenith of its prosperity.

According to Marco Polo who visited Aden in the year 1298 or at the close of the 13th century, "the Port of Aden was a great market whence horses were exported to India, and to which was brought the greater part of the spices and other Indian produce destined for the ports of Europe. From Aden these goods were sent in small vessels to Suez, whence they were transported Overland to Alexandria. To the north of Aden, on the western side of the Persian Gulf, was Escier, at present Adsgar, the neighbourhood of which produced a great quantity of frankincense."

Cavilham, a young nobleman of Castile, to whom we are indebted for the discovery of the passage to India by the Cape of Good Hope in the year 1487, separated from his friend Alphonso de Payva, who was appointed to accompany him "at the Arabian Sea Port of Aden." The discovery of the Cape, which soon after followed, was the first great blow to its maritime importance, and from this period Aden gradually declined in its Commerce.

In the 16th century the Portuguese General Albuquerque set sail for Aden with a powerful fleet, but on reaching that port which he attempted to take he was repulsed with the loss it is stated of 2,000 men.

In A.D. 1538 it fell into the hands of the Turks under Solyman the magnificent, who committed great excesses and in whose possession it remained until 1603 when it was taken by the Persians.

Crichton, however, states that in the year 1609 it was still in possession of the Turks when Sharpey visited it, and was the key that led him into all the treasures and sweetness of happy Arabia. About a hundred years afterwards when the French put into a harbour, they described the town of Aden as of considerable extent, and containing several elegant buildings. Of these the finest were the public baths, they were all lined with marble or jasper, covered with a handsome dome, open at the top for the admission of light and adorned inside with galleries supported by magnificent pillars. The markets were stored with meat, fish, and other provisions of excellent quality as they are indeed to this day. Many of the houses were handsome, but the heaps of rubbish and ruins testified that its ancient splendour was gone.

In the wars between the Turks and Portuguese Aden suffered repeated devastations, and the Commerce for which this port was once so celebrated was at length transferred to Mocha.

After the expulsion of the Turks, Aden until the year 1730 belonged to the Imām, the inhabitants however groaning under his oppression, at length threw off the yoke, elected a Sheik, and declared themselves independent.

It was in the year 1800 that the English appear to have first turned their thoughts towards Aden. During the administration of the Marquis of Wellesley in India when the French determined to cripple the British power in that country, by sending and expedition to Egypt, he conceived the bold project of attacking the French in the rear, by the march of an Indian Army to Egypt to co-operate with an Army from home. The question of occupying Aden was then discussed, but objected to by his Excellency on the several grounds of its unfitness for a Naval station, and for maintaining an influence on the coast. The design was ultimately abandoned.

Captain Haines of the I.N. at present Political Agent at Aden, was sent to investigate the circumstance and to request that the property and stores belonging to the "*Deriah Dowlut*" should be taken care of for the British Government; but the Sultan denied all knowledge of this infamous transaction, although the greater part of the cargo had been offered for sale in the bazaar. That functionary finding his efforts to reason with him disregarded, and that he had little to expect from His Highness but duplicity and subterfuge; after warning him of his conduct, and recommending him as he valued the friendship of the British, to preserve the property of the rightful owners, departed from Aden.

Doubtless the British Government were delighted at the opportunity which now presented itself of converting the nefarious proceedings of the Arabs to their own advantage—they never otherwise could have had an excuse for occupying Aden; for an appeal to arms on their part without some shadow of reason would be contrary to the established principles of international policy, and would have justly raised a general outcry from all quarters.

We accordingly find agreeably to instructions received by the Bombay Government from Calcutta, after reparation had been demanded for the insult offered to the British flag, and promised and refused by the Arabs, and that they still persisted in retaining the cargo, that even further persuasion was recommended, and the Bombay Government were informed, that in the event of matters being satisfactorily adjusted with the Sultan, that an amicable arrangement might be made with him *for the occupation of his port as a depot* for coals and harbour shelter.

The determined attitude of the English, at length induced the Sultan of Lahidge to give a Bond, payable a year after date, for 4.191 Crowns and to restore property to the value of 7,809 German Crowns. Thus much having been reluctantly obtained from the Sultan, the cession of Aden was the next thing to be accomplished, by no means so easy a matter as had at first been anticipated. For the furtherance of this measure handsome presents were made to the Sultan, and the question was finally demanded as to what sum he considered adequate for the cession of Aden. But it was long before his decided answer could be procured. Indeed his conduct throughout appears to have been exceedingly vacillating as well as dilatory, whilst ignorance and want of judgement pervaded his counsels.

On the 16th of January, 1839, the force destined to occupy Aden arrived in three transports, under the Command of Major T.M. Baillie of the 24th N.I., an Officer whose subsequent conduct proved himself to be well worthy of the confidence reposed in him. Tow Ships, H.M. "*Volage*" 28, and "*Cruizer*" (Brig) 16, also accompanied the expedition. The Troops consisting of detachments from the 1st Bombay European Regiment, the 24th N.I., and about 40 European Artillerymen, Sappers, hardly exceeded 750 men. The dispositions for the attack were well arranged, and on the 18th January about 600 men were landed under the command of Major Baillie, in two divisions. The right commanded by Major Osborne was directed to push on and occupy the Sultan's palace, whilst Major Baillie took charge of the left, with which he determined to communicate and advance with the right as soon as possible.

Captain Willoughby of the Artillery was directed to proceed on board the "*Terror*" (bomb) and superintend the working of an 8 inch mortar and 12 pounder carronade, and Lieutenant Western of the Engineers to assist him in the bombardment of the Port in the Island of Seera and the lower battery.

The former Officer was further instructed to land as soon as possible with the storming party, from the "*Mahe,*" with a 12 pounder howitzer, leaving a small detachment on board to act as marines if required whilst the remainder of the troops on board the "*Coote*" left as a reserve, were ordered to disembark in the morning and form on the beach. A detachment of about 70 men and 2 guns under the command of a Subaltern was sent to take up a position in the Island opposite and adjacent to the Pass.

These dispositions having been completed the attack was commenced by the British on the morning of 19th January, under cover of a tremendous fire kept up by the little squadron in the Bay. The enemy who amounted to upwards of 1,000 men, commanded by the Sultan's nephew, defended themselves in the island of Seera with great bravery, but were compelled, after a few hours desultory fighting to yield to British discipline and valour.

Aden was left in quiet possession of its new masters until the 11th November 1839, when the Arabs doubtless thinking to take the British troops by surprise, advanced at daybreak to the number of 5,000 strong, and attacked the out-post which had been formed at the Turkish Wall, where a few temporary field works had been erected. The Arabs, however, were completely routed and lost nearly

100 men, not a single casualty occurring on the side of the British. This affair was thus handsomely alluded to by Colonel Capon, an officer of great merit who commanded the garrison: "the promptitude of the troops in manning the works, with the excellent practice of the guns completely defeated an attempt which appears to have been conducted on their part (the Arabs) with much secrecy and suddenness." The defence of the upper works was pronounced to be *excellent*, and it is stated that the "*Euphrates*" (launch) under Lieut. Hamilton, contributed in a great measure to the success of the troops. The judicious arrangements of the Political Agent (Captain Haines) and of Colonel Capon were highly extolled both by the Governor in Council at Bombay, and Major General Sir J. F. Fitz-gerald, then Commander of the forces at Bombay. Their conduct was even brought to the favourable notice of the Court of Directors.

From this period until 1841 the Arabs appear to have been comparatively peaceful, when it was again found necessary to resort to coercive measures, the Arabs refusing or neglecting to furnish those supplies for which the inhabitants and military mainly depended on them. We accordingly find that on the 5th of October, 1841, Colonel Pennycuick of the 17th Regiment (Queen's) an Officer of great promise, marched into Arabia at the head of about 500 men, and destroyed the Arab posts of Sheik Medi and Sheik Othman, and skirmished between those places until the 6th instant—a decided measure which appears to have produced the desired effect. At another period, a small body of Arabs, probably with no other intentions but those of plunder, succeeded in making good their way by the left of the Turkish Wall, (at that time its weakest point of defence,) and even entered some of the Officers' dwellings—they paid dearly, however, for this wanton act of aggression, several of them having been slain and the rest routed in the attempt.

In the year 1846 hostilities were again commenced on the part of the Arabs, against the British force at Aden, headed by a religious fanatic of the name of Syed Ishmael, who was said to be a native of Tunis. This imposter, partly by working on the credulity of the Arabs, and partly by intimidation, succeeded in collecting together a considerable force, which the fears of the timid inhabit-ants speedily exaggerated to 10,000 men, though it is doubtful whether half that number ever advanced towards Aden. To prepare for such an adversary, prompted by religious enthusiasm and the hopes of gain; followed by men of known daring, who expected splendid rewards in this world and eternal felicity in the next, required a person of no ordinary foresight, energy, and ability—such a man however, was found in the person of Colonel Milner, an Officer of great merit.

On the 12th of August, 1846, information having been received of the approach of Syed Ishmael, orders were immediately issued by that Officer for a body of 200 men to reinforce the out-post at the Turkish Wall, completing its strength to about 500 bayonets. About 700 men were directed to occupy the heights as well as the Main Pass, 176 more were allotted for the garrison and regimental guards, and the remainder amounting to about 400 men were ordered to be kept as a reserve. About sunset the whole of the Queen's Troops were formed into column by sound of bugle in double time, and shortly afterwards moved with great steadiness, and in the best of spirits to their various posts on the heights—the sepoys and artillery also repaired to their prescribed stations.

A detachment of irregular cavalry (Suwars) acted as police in the town. An attack from the enemy that night was considered certain, but they did not appear until several days afterwards, and the troops were a good deal exposed to the sun, as well as wearied by the harassing nature of their duties; but there was not a murmur, not even a whisper of discontent; unremitting zeal and prompt obedience were conspicuous throughout. On the 16th instant at about 1:00 a.m. the loud booming of guns from Durab el hosh and the Turkish Wall, told that the enemy were night.

These in the stillness of midnight together with the clashing of arms, and men "hurrying to and fro," had an imposing as well as a pleasing effect on the imagination—I thought at the time of the exquisite lines of Byron.

> "But hark!—that heavy sound breaks in once more
> As if the clouds its echo would repeat;
> And nearer, clearer, deadlier than before!
> Arm, arm! it is—the cannons opening roar."

For a full quarter of an hour the firing continued, when all again was hushed. The enemy it appears had approached with a view of reconnoitring the British position, little dreaming, no doubt, of their proximity to their guns, and that they were about to be so roughly and so unceremoniously handled.

In a moment, the signal being given, a destructive fire of grape and shrapnel was opened upon the Arabs who alarmed and discomfited, fled in great confusion, leaving some of their wounded, a number of creases, matchlocks, behind them in their flight. The loss of the Arabs has never been correctly ascertained, from the practice which they invariably adopt in all their encounters of carrying off their killed and wounded; for they ever regard it as a national slur to let them fall into the hands of infidels! Their loss, if the intelligence of the scouts may be credited was about 25 killed and wounded. Two of the latter whom the Arabs were precluded from bearing away, on account of the darkness of the night, were discovered next morning, weltering in blood, their bodies frightfully mangled, and were immediately conducted to the General Hospital, in which they were treated with the greatest care by an experienced Surgeon. They died a few days afterwards of their wounds.

It is worthy of remark that these infatuated men appeared quite insensible to pain—nay even smiled during the operation of extracting the bullets from their wounds. Our notions of humanity towards our enemies, appeared to them to be very inconsistent.

"You make war," they said, "against us, you slaughter us without remorse, and yet when you take us prisoners, you treat your enemies like friends."

Nor must I omit to mention the following occurrence though trifling in itself. The Surgeon upon opening his case of medical instruments, which he exhibited to their astonished gaze, was immediately asked by one of the wounded Arabs, for what purpose they were intended, and whether he was going to put them to the torture. Upon his replying in the negative and informing them that his intention was to prolong their lives if possible by amputation their limbs, provided they themselves did not object; both of them expressed considerable surprise, declaring it was the custom in their own country to put the prisoners taken in battle to the torture, or at all events to death.

They objected, however, to undergo a surgical operation, feeling convinced that their lives could not be prolonged by any human means beyond the period that God decreed.

For several days after the petty demonstration of Syed Ishmael nothing could be seen of the enemy—their efforts were considered paralysed, and it was thought that being in all probability disheartened by failure, and weakened by dissensions among themselves, as well as deprived of the necessary means of carrying on the siege; the cause of Syed Ishmael had been forsaken, and that the various Arab Tribes learning discretion from dear bought experience would immediately disperse and return to their homes.

On the morning, however, of the 9th August, at about 8 o'clock they were again descried advancing to the number of 1,200 towards the Turkish Wall. Some might be perceived mounted on their war-camels, others on horseback, galloping at full speed, and not a few on foot, moving to almost certain destruction; without order and regularity, and evidently without any prearranged plan of attack. As might be expected, this unorganized rabble were soon dispersed by the fire of the British guns, to which some shots from the gunboats in the bay under Lieutenant Hamilton, materially contributed.

Syed Ishmael thus baffled in his futile demonstration upon Aden, endeavoured to stop the British supplies from Arabia, in which for a time, he was successful, for during a period of nearly three weeks none could be obtained. The tribes friendly to the British, in endeavouring to furnish these, were frequently engaged in deadly conflict with our adversaries. In these engagements, the former overpowered by numbers, would occasionally seek the Turkish Wall as a protection. The consequence was that the Troops stationed there on duty, (to whom the safe guard of the Camp was intrusted,) unable to distinguish friend from foe, were compelled to disperse them with showers of grape and canister; and on one of these occasions two Arabs were severely though unavoidably wounded.

These men having been conducted to the British outpost, were attended upon by two Native Doctors, whose method of treatment was as barbarous as it was unskilful. Probing the wounds of their unfortunate patients, and pouring into them a composition of boiling oil, herbs were amongst the least violent remedies applied.

We cannot but lament the blind fanaticism, the total want of military skill displayed, in these last as well as previous attacks, of our brave but too credulous adversaries—whilst all good men must deplore the wanton effusion of blood, which might have been avoided had they shown but ordinary foresight and judgement. Their leader, Syed Ishmael, in whom it would appear they placed implicit confidence, though not wholly destitute of talent as well as education, rendered himself despicable, as his letters will show, by threats never to be realized, and pomp of tone as vapid as it was absurd.

The following may be considered as a fair specimen of his epistolary correspondence to the Political Agent at Aden, about the time of the expected attack.

TRANSLATION.

"*Letter from Syed Ishmael to Captain Haines, Political Agent at Aden.*"

"Praise to God and peace to my Lord Mohammed."

"Draw near oh ye people of the *Book* for there is a subject of discourse between us regarding the Almighty alone with whom I place no partner, and besides whom I allow no God, to which I testify as a Moslim saying Bismillā rahman el raheem.

From Abdullah from the slave of God, the upholder of the Law, named Ishmael ibn ul Hassan el Hessanie, the pardoned of God, to the Great Commander of the Feringhies.

Peace be to those who go in the right path, who fear wickedness and succumb to the Almighty.

Further it is said by the glorious and Most High God, my mercy is all abundant and right, therefore that every people give alms, and that they who fear me keep in the paths of rectitude—that they follow the paths of *the Prophet*, the founder of Prophets as is directed them in the Books of the Zarah and Evangelists, that they rule with equity and that they cast out abominations, and that they avoid evil things.

The Prophet has also said that the glorious God sent the Angel Gabriel that those who are converted to Islam by *the Book* are doubly blessed. You have heard that

I have come down upon you with an overwhelming force of just and holy men, on account of this Divine Mission, and that you have no power of withstanding my large army. I am unwilling to use harsh means, until I have politely written to you. If you agree to listen to my advice and submit yourselves humbly to me, you will be doubly blessed by God at once, and you and I at once become of the same creed—having been so long of different persuasions—what is mine will become yours, and what is yours mine. But if you will not take this advice, I am blameless for what will happen—God will be on my side, and my strength from him against you—Him who is my God and yours—you know all, I have not come from a distant land to amass money and wealth, I seek but the glory of the Almighty and my trust is in Him, in all I say or do He is my Vakeel.

3RD RAMAZAN, A.H. 1262."

Notes and References

1. Possibly 1986.
2. I am immensely grateful to Patrick Conner, that distinguished gentleman of the art world who, while I was engaged on this research, so kindly guided me through the intricacies of his profession.
3. *Report on Operations against the Zeidi Imam 25 June–25th August 1928*, Air Ministry London, November 1928, Ref. A 81606 pp. 65, *Military Report on Arabia,* War Office Sub Division C2, London, 1904.
4. Coal was dumped at Ṣīrah Island in 1829 in preparation for the first India–Egypt voyage of the new steamship *Hugh Lindsay*. This paddle steamer, 411 tons, was built in Bombay dockyard and launched in 1829 not, as described in Gordon Waterfield's *Sultans of Aden*, 'brought out from England'. I picked up minute pieces of coal from a wide area of the original dump, located on the south-east shore of Ṣīrah in 1948. No coal was put there after 1830. The beach is still tinged black in colour.
5. The coaling function at Aden had been re-established in Back Bay before the British occupation in 1839. Up to this time Haines had spent much of his Indian Navy service afloat, mostly on survey work in the Persian Gulf, the Red Sea and on the south coast of Arabia. His fifteen years in Aden enabled him to live for some of that time with his wife, a rare happening for a naval officer of his rank and circumstances. He has often been considered a martinet. In fact the opposite seems to have been the case. Junior officers, midshipmen and volunteers had a high regard for him and he publicly and officially referred to them as his friends. He was aboard H.M.S *Volage* at the capture of Aden in January 1839 but was not in command of the operation as has been erroneously recorded by several writers. Haines was first to describe Aden in any detail as late as 1839 although Captain Charles Howe Fremantle, Royal Navy, had briefly reported on his visit in 1830. See Eric Macro, Fremantle at Aden in H.M.S *Challenger* 1830, *Arabian Studies* 6: 211–12.
6. For example, Emma Roberts, *The East India Voyager* (1839) and her *Notes of An Overland Journey through France and Egypt to Bombay* (1841). The latter was published posthumously.

7. The standard works on the Overland Route are Halford Hoskins, *British Routes to India* (London 1928) and John K. Sidebottom, *The Overland Mail* (London 1948). A modern consideration of the subject with particular reference to Aden and South Arabia is the subject of the present writer's 'South Arabia and the Overland Route to India', *Proceedings of the Seminar for Arabian Studies* 12: 49–60, London, 1982.
8. *Historical and Statistical Sketches of Aden, in Arabia Felix, During a Two Years' Residence in that Colony*, printed in Vepery, Madras, 1848.
9. This comment does not apply to some work done by Professor R.B. Serjeant and H.T. Norris with F.W. Penhey. See R.B. Serjeant, *The Portuguese off the South Arabian Coast*, Oxford 1953: 47 and 169; and H.T. Norris and F.W. Penhey The Historical Development of Aden's Defences, *Geographical Journal*, London 1955, 121.1: 11–20.
10. For example 'Aden' by Landells *c.*1840. See also Eric Macro, 'Arabia Before Photography', *Proceedings of the Seminar for Arabian Studies*, 17: 7–126, London 1987.
11. It is no longer original to observe that this overland route, as opposed to that through the Euphrates valley, was overland in name only. The London–Alexandria and Suez–Bombay sea voyages covered 6700 miles. The Suez–Alexandria journey was one of 170 miles, a fortieth of the whole. Some passengers travelled from Marseilles or Leghorn to the English Channel. These figures cannot of course apply to them.
12. (a) *The Overland Route of William Prinsep (1794–1874)* London 1984: 5–6
    (b) Some biographical details of the Prinseps in India are given in an unpublished document in the India Office Library, London, written by Sir Henry Thoby Prinsep and titled: *Three Generations in India* [undated].
    (c) John Prinsep flourished in India during the latter half of the eighteenth century, he pioneered the Indian indigo trade and the printing of cotton fabrics in Bengal. An East India Company servant and friend of Warren Hastings he, together with Alexander Cunningham, discovered the copper mines at Rotasgarh. They were however of limited value, the details being recorded by Prinsep on 30th March and 1st September 1780 in two memoranda sent to Hastings (India Office Library and Records, Home Miscellaneous No. 62). John Prinsep had seven sons and a daughter (born in India?) Little is known of the second and third sons other than their names, Charles and Thomas. Charles appears to have been an East India Company servant, distinguishing himself by compiling a *Record of Services of the Honourable East India Company's Servants in the Madras Presidency from 1741 to 1858.* Madras 1885 and an undated pamphlet *An Account of Steam Navigation ... in British India* [*c.*1850]. The fourth son, Captain Henry Thoby Prinsep, (1792–1878), was Secretary of the Bengal Government for sixteen years and was a member of the Council of India. He eventually returned to England and settled at Little Holland House, London, which became a popular resort for the artistic fraternity. Valentine Cameron Prinsep (1838–1904), his son, was to become the artist of the family.

    Born in Calcutta he studied under a friend of his parents, G.F. Watts, and worked at the studio of Gleyre in Paris. Valentine Prinsep was well connected; a friend of Burne-Jones, with whom he went to Italy in 1969 and of Millais, he joined the Hogarth Club, founded in 1858 by Rosetti and his friends.

With Rosetti and others he decorated the hall of the Oxford Union. A triumph came to him when he became R A at the age of fifty-six although he had first exhibited at the Academy when he was twenty four, his work being later influenced by Frederic Leighton (1830–1896). He was the painter of the famous picture of General Gordon in Chinese costume and was himself a model for one of du Mauriers' characters in *Trilby*. Valentine was an unlikely but enthusiastic amateur soldier and became on of the founders of the famous Territorial Army regiment, The Artist's Rifles, which still flourishes. A playwright also and a novelist, he left a biographical fragment published in London in 1879 and titled: *Imperial India. An Artist's Journals*. This he illustrated with his own portraits of Indian rulers.

Another distinguished Prinsep was a younger brother of William. He was James R. Prinsep, born in India 1799. He soon became an accomplished lithographer. In 1828 he was appointed to lithograph maps of the Ganges and Hughli from the old surveys of Colebrooke. He was also a contributor to the *Journal of the Asiatic Society of Bengal*, e.g: vol. 4 et seq. He studied architecture under Pugin and later undertook some architectural work in Benares. He was the first to interpret certain inscriptions at Askoka and he ran the Calcutta mint in 1819 becoming assay master. A noted scholar and archaeologist, he became secretary of the Asiatic Society but his health failed in India and he travelled to England in the hope of recovery. He died there two years later on 28th April 1840. On a bank of the Hughli near Calcutta stands an archway erected to his memory by local citizens. His two volumes of *Essay on Indian Antiquities* were edited by Edward Thomas and published posthumously in London in 1858.

(d) *Eastern Encounters. Orientalist Painters of the Nineteenth Century.* London 1978.
(e) Wilfred Meynell. *Valentine Prinsep, Painter and Dramatist*. London 1893.
(f) Valentine Prinsep. *Art Journal* London 1905: 33–34.
(g) H.T. Prinsep. *History of the Political and Military Transactions in India during the Administration of the Marquis of Hastings*. 2 vols. London 1803.
(h) Patrick Conner (ed.) *The Inspiration of Egypt*. Brighton 1983.
(i) Edward A. Prinsep was another, lesser known, member of the family who was said to be the oldest of the nine brothers.

13. C.R. Low, *History of the Indian Navy*, London 1877, 2: 139–40.
14. The P&O's aspect of this and other of their early transactions with the British Government are discussed in Boyd Cable, *A Hundred Years History of the P&O 1837 to 1937*, London 1937; David Divine, *These Splendid Ships. The Story of the P&O*, London 1960; David Howarth and Stephen Howarth, *The Story of the P&O*, London 1986.
15. The operation culminating in the conquest of Aden under the command of Captain H. Smith RN (not Commander S.B. Haines as is often assumed) took place on 19th January 1839. Prinsep was in Aden almost three years later.
16. Centenary of Cowasjee Dinshaw, *Port of Aden Annual*, Aden 1954–1955: 30–32.
17. Named after Major General T.E. Scott who was Political Resident, Aden, from 1920 to 1925.

18. Luke Thomas and Company Limited. *Port of Aden Annual.* Aden, 1950: 44–46. The Compagnie Messageries Maritimes in Aden. *Port of Aden Annual.* Aden. 1964–1965: 58.
19. The spur is Jabal Manthar. It finishes at Jabal al Urr, the northern arm of Ḥuqqāt Bay.
20. Xavier Richer, *Au Yémen du Sud*, Boulogne 1976: 118.
21. James Sparkhall Rundle was Mate aboard H.M.S. *Volage* (captain: H. Smith) at the capture of Aden in 1839. He led the first landing party and himself planted the Union Jack in Aden territory. He was, later the same day, sent to occupy Ṣīrah and to silence the guns there, forcing the defenders to surrender. Sixty eight years later Rundle's granddaughter married General Reginald Wingate, then a Lieutenant, and later, in Aden put in charge of the Ṣīrah defences. Placed in the archives of the National Maritime Museum at Greenwich, the collection of Rundle's Aden drawings could not be found although the Museum's records showed that they were in its custody. The explanation (in 1970) was that they had disappeared.
22. *The Lady Mary Wood* (533 tons) was built at Liverpool in 1841 as a paddle ship and initially ran between the Iberian peninsula and England. From 1845 she saw service in the Far East and was sold by the P&O in 1859 to the Indo-Netherlands Company in Hong Kong.
23. *Lt Walford Thomas Bellairs R.N.* (*c.*1794–1850) London 1982: 3–5. Bellairs also contributed to *The Route of the Overland Mail to India*, London 1850.
24. Port Development at Aden. *Near East and India*, London, vol. 37: 465. 24th April 1930 and Port Development at Aden. [*sic*] *Port of Aden Annual*, Aden 1956: 29–32.

The Canon and Proportion of Pre-Islamic Arabian Sculptures

Hamid I. Al-Mazrou

The primary purpose of the present paper is to throw some light upon the main stylistic principles of South Arabian human statuary and their origin. An attempt is also made to determine the main factor influencing the traditional South Arabian statuary.

The Main Stylistic Principles

When the sculptor produces any carved work, he usually attempts to show his personal concept through the theme of his work.[1] The criterion of his success depends not only on the technical proficiency of the sculptor, but also upon many vital components: the purpose of the work; whether it was intended to represent the secular or cultic; and the controlling forces of the sculptor's environment. Each of these purposes has an inherent character; thus, the sculptor logically endeavours to crystallise the form of his theme to correspond with the prime purpose of the occasion. Such being the case, it is essential to start our investigation with the circumstances in which the statuary art was produced. To approach our objective, certain aspects of South Arabian culture need to be considered.

Burial customs are probably the ideal sarting point. As with other Semitic races, the South Arabians strongly believed in the concept of after-life.[2] Consequently, very complicated ritual and magical practices were performed during the burial ceremony. The deceased were not only buried with items they had used in their lifetime but, more important, with votive or memorial representations bearing their names.[3] Indeed, there is no exaggeration in assuming that the belief in after-life not only instituted a permanent motive to produce a new flourishing stylist tradition, but also laid down the fundamental principles of early statuary art. In all probability, this was crystallized by the funerary stelae which were basically erected to commemorate the deceased and not as things of beauty.

We shall try to establish how the human form of the free-standing sculptures derived from the votive stelae. Let us examine two traditional South Arabian types, the first one (Plate 1) showing a rectangular slab.[4] The upper part is occupied by a stylized human face in low relief, the eyebrows and nose are formed by a T shape in low relief, while the eyes have an almond shape. The second type (Plate 2) also exhibits a rectangular slab,[5] but here the face stands out more from the slab, permitting a new transitional stage in which we see not only the evolution of a sculptured face, but also the initial stage of forming a complete statue. It is necessary to reconsider the rectangular shape of the stelae on which only the top parts were worked, whereas the lower halves are left plain.

Perhaps the unfinished image published by C. Rathjens[6] represents the second stage of fashioning a statue (Plate 3). The image in question obviously adopted

Plate 1.

Plate 2.

Plate 3.

its stylistic lines from the conventional funerary stele mentioned above. In this image, the sculptor raises the head from the stele, and, furthermore, the hands are suggested by two small protruding squares. Also, a medial line was chiselled out, probably to mark off the bust from the lower part of the body.

The next illustration[7] (Plate 4, Fig. 1) reflects, in our opinion, the third stage of development of the South Arabian human figure. Here, the sculptor works the lower part of the slab by chiselling out the middle section and the features of the knees are revealed. Similarly, the protruding squares of the previous representation (Plate 3) are fashioned here to indicate the hands stretched out. Clearly the anatomy of the body of such a form of human representation is inaccurate, as the sculptor has isolated the parts of the body from its natural

Plate 4.

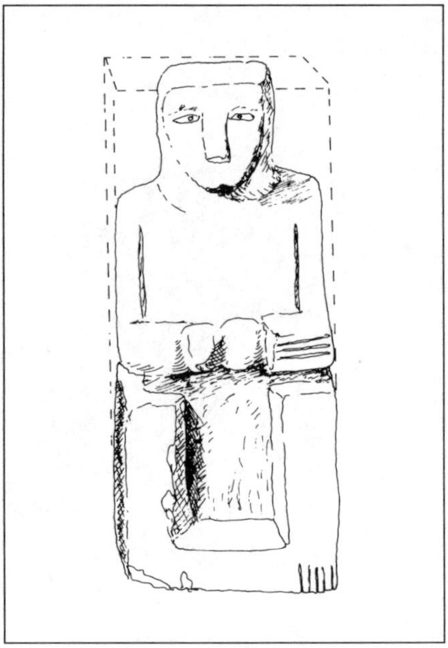

Figure 1.

shape, this due possibly to the dependence of the sculptor on a linear design which results in the appearance of angulation. Such a stylistic aspect, however, became a common feature in traditional South Arabian statuary and it continued until the decline of the South Arabian kingdoms.

From the foregoing comparison, what are the conclusions that can be drawn about the original principles of free-standing sculpture? As regards the origins of style, I am firmly convinced that it evolved from the memorial funerary stelae as the photographs (Plates 1 & 2) show. Thus we are dealing with a prototype style which in all likelihood derives its main stylistic structure from a religious background. Consequently, this form of art continued to retain its rigid character in order to accord with its cultic function.

The main stylistic principles of the memorial statuettes scarcely changed, especially in the seated examples. In fact they became standard features. What happened to the design of the later statuettes was that the sculptors began gradually to get rid of the schematic design and angulation, so that the carved figures started to take a further step towards the natural human shape.

Thus, one can explain why most of the human statuary of South Arabia was produced in small size, and has a diminutive appearance. Furthermore, we can see why the tops of heads were cut flat as in the traditional memorial stelae.

Notes and References

1. Gardner, H. 1960. *Art through the Ages*. London (3rd edit.), 4.
2. Kensdale, W. 1955. *The Religious Beliefs and Practices of Ancient South Arabia*. Ibadan (Nigeria), 1–5.
3. Kensdale, W. 1955, 4.
4. British Museum Object no. 122010.
5. Pirenne, J. 1977. *Corpus des inscriptions et antiquités sud-arabes*. I/2, Louvain, 553.
6. Rathjens, C. 1953. *Sabeica*. Hamburg. II, Photo no. 137–138. See also Object no. 190034 in the British Museum.
7. British Museum Object no. 190032.

Notes on Contributors

Hussein Abdullah al-Amri is Professor of Modern History in the University of Ṣan'ā' and at present serving as Ambassador of the Republic of Yemen to the Court of St James in London. He is author of numerous publications on the 19th–20th century political and intellectual history of the Yemen.

W.J. Donaldson is the author of articles on Arabian fisheries development and on Islamic metrology, and his forthcoming book *Sharecropping in the Yemen: a Study in Islamic Theory, Custom and Pragmatism* is to be published by E.J. Brill. He holds degrees in geography and Arabic, including two doctorates.

Ali Tigani ElMahi is a member of the Department of Archaeology, Sultan Qaboos University. Apart from teaching, he is currently engaged in archaeological excavations in the Sultanate of Oman. He is carrying out field studies and documentation of traditional practices related to environment, adaptive socio-economic structures and their success, resource exploitation and subsistence strategies. His research interest also extends to African archaeology.

Caesar E. Farah is Professor of History in the Department of Afro-American and African Studies in the University of Minnesota.

Ulrike Freitag and *Hanne Schönig*: *Freitag* is a lecturer in Middle Eastern History at the School of Oriental and African Studies, University of London. She has written on modern Syrian and Arab historiography and edited a book on *Hadhrami Traders, Scholars and Statesmen* (with W.G. Clarence-Smith). She is now working on a book on the reform movements in the Hadhramawt in the 19th and 20th centuries.

Schönig studied Islamic languages and sciences at Mainz University, where she also taught for a number of years. Since 1995 she has been publications manager and researcher at the Orient-Institut of the Deutsche Morgenländische Gesellschaft in Beirut (Lebanon). She is currently working on a book on customs and traditions in the Yemen, with special reference to traditional cosmetics.

David Insall is an ex RAF officer who has lived many years in Oman. He has published on Oman dialects and other Omani cultural subjects.

Eric Macro has travelled extensively in Africa, Asia, North America and Europe over an extended period, being particularly concerned with the Middle East and Central Asia. Since 1945 he has researched many Middle Eastern subjects and lectured in England for five or six years on the Arabian Peninsula. His two bibliographical studies, *Arabian Peninsula* (i) and *Yemen with Notes on Mocha* (ii) were published by Miami University in 1958 and 1960 respectively. He has recently completed a three hundred thousand word biography on George Wyman Bury, the South West Arabian explorer who died in Cairo in 1920. He was awarded the OBE in 1967.

Hamid I. Al-Mazrou teaches in the Department of Archaeology and Museology at the College of Arts, King Saud University, Riyadh.